The Institution of
Intellectual Values

ST ANDREWS STUDIES IN
PHILOSOPHY AND PUBLIC AFFAIRS

Founding and General Editor:
John Haldane
University of St Andrews

Volume 1:
Values, Education and the Human World
edited by John Haldane

Volume 2:
Philosophy and its Public Role
edited by William Aiken and John Haldane

Volume 3:
Relativism and the Foundations of Liberalism
by Graham Long

Volume 4:
Human Life, Action and Ethics:
Essays by G.E.M. Anscombe
edited by Mary Geach and Luke Gormally

Volume 5:
The Institution of Intellectual Values:
Realism and Idealism in Higher Education
by Gordon Graham

Nigel Paterson —
April 2006

The Institution of Intellectual Values

Realism and Idealism in Higher Education

Gordon Graham

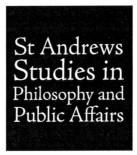

IMPRINT ACADEMIC

Published in the UK by Imprint Academic
PO Box 200, Exeter EX5 5YX, UK

Published in the USA by Imprint Academic
Philosophy Documentation Center
PO Box 7147, Charlottesville, VA 22906-7147, USA

ISBN 1 84540 002 X

A CIP catalogue record for this book is available from the
British Library and US Library of Congress

Cover Photograph:
St Salvator's Quadrangle, St Andrews by Peter Adamson
from the University of St Andrews collection

Contents

Introduction

The opening and longest essay in this collection is a revised version of a short book published in 2002. Its title is a deliberate allusion to John Henry Newman's *The Idea of a University*. Newman's essay, originally a series of lectures (or 'Discourses') delivered in Dublin in advance of the establishment of the Catholic University of Ireland in 1854, which first appeared as a set of pamphlets, and soon after bound together, is still in print.

The context for these lectures was a dispute that has no interest for most people today. Newman was providing a theoretical defence of the Irish Catholic hierarchy's objection to the secular university colleges established in Ireland by the British Government in 1845 (though ironically this Catholic alternative eventually formed the basis of the National University of Ireland which united most of these same colleges). He mounts his defence on the strength of a thesis that is unlikely to meet with much support in contemporary universities, namely the impossibility of a secular, non-religious university education. As a consequence of this context, a central part of his argument has to do with the role and teaching of theology, a subject absent from the curricula of most modern British universities, and a minority subject where it is still taught. A further, substantial part of the lectures is devoted to reconciling the authority of the church with the investigations of modern science, another topic likely to be of limited interest today.

Yet despite these important differences between Newman's time and ours, *The Idea of a University* (especially Discourses V, VI and VII) still has things to say that are relevant to thinking about contemporary universities.

More surprising than this continuing relevance, however, is the fact that in the one hundred and forty years since Newman wrote, his book has had no significant successor, even though monumental changes have taken place in universities during this same period. More striking still is the fact that Newman's is one of very few attempts *ever* made to think directly about the nature and purpose of a university. Given the age of the institution, and its importance to the intellectual and cultural life of this country over many centuries, this is a remarkable fact.

There are a few exceptions to this generalization. Ronald Barnett is an educational theorist who has made 'higher' education his special subject and written several books about it, but they differ from Newman's in being intended for a largely 'professional' readership of educationalists and hence written in professionalized style. A volume with aspirations to a wider audience is *The New Idea of a University* by Duke Maskell and Ian Robinson (London, 2001) where Newman is expressly discussed. Maskell and Robinson explore what they see as a radical departure among contemporary universities from the 'old' idea and they claim that in recent times '[t]he university has been remade not in defiance of Newman but in indifference to him. But he says things that, if anybody paid attention to them, could not fail to kill instantly our new orthodoxy about the universities making us rich' (Maskell and Robinson 2001: 25). Now whatever the justice of their complaint, the fact is as I have just suggested, that the context of Newman's lectures was inevitably quite different to that of the present day. His *Discourses* undertake to characterize and defend what has come to be known as a liberal education. Though often cited in defence of more arcane subjects by university teachers, the actual influence that is to be attributed to his book has probably been overestimated. It is the traditional American liberal arts college that has come closest to Newman's ideal, not the universities of Britain from whose experience his reflections arose. There is to my mind a dangerous romanticism in thinking that, once upon a time British universities were suitably Newmanesque until the arrival of utilitarian Philistines, and Maskell and Robinson constantly run the risk of falling into this trap. In several places Newman's 'arguments' are weak, as it seems to me, and to call upon them is unlikely 'to kill instantly' the ideas that have won favour in the minds of many modern academics. Nevertheless, there is something important to emulate in Newman's enterprise — the spirit of inquiring clearly and critically into the very idea of a university and its value.

The purpose of the first essay, then, is not to review or revitalize Newman's arguments, though, since a number of the themes he addresses are still topical, I shall refer to some of his claims from time to time in the chapters that follow. Nor is it my aim to deplore the present and lament the past, a charge that might be brought against Maskell and Robinson with some justice. Rather, my purpose is to draw attention to a number of interrelated issues that are of considerable contemporary significance, to examine them in a sustained way, and in this way, it is to be hoped, begin a discussion that is long overdue — namely some inquiry into how we should regard universities and what it is reasonable to expect from them.

The publication of the original version led to a number of invitations from academic institutions in Britain and Europe to lecture on some of its themes. In every case, the invitation arose from the belief that traditional academic values and institutions have come under close scrutiny, and sometimes attack, in the light of changing circumstances. Some of these are quite extraneous changes — the explosion in information technology for instance — and others are more endogenous — the pressure to engage in research across disciplines, or to 'skew' scientific inquiry in the pursuit of funding. Rather than simply re-iterate topics discussed in the original short book, I took these opportunities to extend the discussion into broader areas. There are clear points of contact, though I have not expressly identified them, and the additional essays are free standing.

The discussion of all these topics faces a special difficulty, the risk of being pigeon-holed, that is, of being automatically bracketed with one of two opposed positions. On the one side there is the modernizer who believes that old ideas must be abandoned in the face of the necessity to deal with 'reality', and on the other there is the 'traditionalist' who believes that every such move sells the pass on values and institutions that are vital to civilization as we know it, and to which we should fight to return. Yet these two views are caricatures of each other. 'Realism' in this context tends to mean pragmatism — accepting imposed solutions so that universities survive, not so much to fight another day, as just to see it dawn. 'Idealism' means taking a principled stand even in circumstances that virtually guarantee its futility. If serious thinking about universities and the policies that should govern them is to take place, it is essential that the straight-jacketed thinking this sort of dichotomy inevitably induces be abandoned. Yet in a simplistic way it does reflect, dimly, an important distinction between, on the one hand, the pursuit of objectives that stand some chance of being realized and on the other the rejection of goals entirely dictated by political fashion or public purse strings. The truth is that in this context, as in nearly every other, practical rationality requires us to engage in a dialectical relationship between realism and idealism. Ideals that have no realistic prospect of coming about are practically worthless; survival, even prosperity, that is not in any way determined by critically chosen goals cannot count as success. In all the topics I discuss my aim has been to steer an intelligent course between this particular version of Scylla and Charybdis.

These remarks explain the title of the collection. *The Institution of Intellectual Values* is deliberately ambiguous since it might be taken to refer to the university as just such an institution, or to the business of finding ways in which intellectual values can be given institutional expression. My concern is with both these questions, which are evidently interrelated, and my subtitle indicates that it is in the dialectical exchange between realism and idealism that I think the most illuminating sort of answers are to be found.

This very complexity, however, gives rise to the second difficulty. The variety of topics that need to be considered if we are to introduce any measure of coherence into thinking about the modern university is very considerable. It is necessary to sketch the history of the institution, to consider the ideas of higher education and academic research, to record recent social trends, to look at a spectrum of social policies, to explore cultural images, to examine educational methods, and to review the economics of public finance. This range of tasks is somewhat daunting. Yet it is at heart, in my view, philosophical, and it is questions in the philosophy of education which must make the running.

My approach to them is that of a professional philosopher, largely because that is my discipline. Yet I hope that readers from all disciplines and none will find the treatment both interesting and novel. There are topics which are not properly speaking those of philosophy, yet there are things about them that only a philosopher would, or could, say. The nature of a university and its activities are among these. If my professional mode of thinking and writing has enabled me to preserve in their exploration philosophy's intellectual virtues — chiefly clarity and rigour — then these essays will have the merit of setting out certain questions, and some answers to them, in a manner which makes their debate more precise, and hence more profitable. At any rate, this is my aim, and, given the breadth of the subject, to have realised it is as much as could be reasonably wished for.

Universities: The Recovery of an Idea

1. A very short history of universities in Britain and abroad

The mediaeval university

No one can say precisely when university education began in Britain. Although we know that Oxford was Britain's first university, and was founded after Paris, Bologna and several others on the continent of Europe, we do not know exactly when 'the clerks of Oxenford' first started to study and teach. The early part of the twelfth century seems likely, perhaps because from 1167 English students were barred from attending the University of Paris. Certainly, by the end of the twelfth century, Oxford was established to a degree sufficient for it to be regarded as a distinct place of learning. Then in 1207, or thereabouts, some of the Oxford clerks migrated to Cambridge, and England's second university began. Amazingly enough, it was over six hundred years before a third was founded. The two universities added very many constituent colleges over this long period, of course, but while in these colleges fellows taught and students learned, it was the universities that had the right to confer degrees. And of these, for the greater part of English educational history, there were only two.

But the third university in the British Isles came into existence not so very long after, at St Andrews in Scotland. Started somewhere between 1411 and 1413, permission to found Scotland's first university was given initially by the renegade Pope in Avignon, though readily confirmed by Rome when the schism which had resulted in the existence of two rival popes ended. In the course of the same century further universities were established at Glasgow (1451) and Aberdeen (1495) also by the express authority of the Pope. Both drew their inspiration from Europe, the first Principal of Aberdeen coming from the University of Paris. In 1582 the University of Edinburgh was founded. Edinburgh was different to all the rest, both North and South of the border, in that, though it was inspired by Presbyterianism, it was a civic not a religious foundation (and to this day has no college chapel). It was the City Fathers, not the Church Fathers who called it into existence and the Crown which gave it the authority to confer degrees. But before the end of the century there was one further religious foundation in Scotland. The Reformation brought about the establishment in Aberdeen in 1593 of a Protestant rival to King's College, named Marischal College after the Protestant Earl Marischal of Scotland who was its creator, and for over two hundred and fifty years (until 1860) they remained separate universities, allowing Aberdonians to boast that their city had as many universities as the whole of England.

A little earlier (1591) Dublin University, with just one college — Trinity — had come into existence, modelled closely on the Oxbridge pattern. As Ireland's first and oldest university, it became a place of some distinction in its own right, being the Alma Mater of Oliver Goldsmith and Edmund Burke amongst others, though it never quite emerged from the shadow of Oxford. The fact that for the first three hundred years of its existence only Anglicans were allowed to attend it, gave it the image and reputation of both a representative and a bastion of the Protestant Ascendancy, which it retained until well after the Republic of Ireland had been established. As a consequence, though it was Ireland's only university for 250 years, until very recently it was never really an Irish one.

By the end of the sixteenth century, then, Britain had eight universities, five in Scotland, two in England, one in Ireland. It was over a hundred years before there were any more. With the exception of Edinburgh, they were all religious foundations, of greatly differing sizes. As in their continental counterparts, their founding subjects were Theology, Law and Arts and a large part of their purpose was to provide education originally designed for the professional classes of the middle ages. This was less true of Edinburgh and Dublin, and in all of them other interests and subjects developed of course, medicine having been on the curriculum since early times in Scotland as it was in other parts of Europe. But up to this point British universities were inheritors of, and for the most part formed by, the mediaeval conception of a university — a place of learning and training, commonly (though not always) made up of four 'Faculties' of which Arts was foundational. When the next wave of universities came, they arose from a rather different spirit and took a different form.

The modern university

In this respect, however, in comparison with other European countries Britain was slow to develop the modern university, if we characterise the modern university as a non-denominational institution in which natural science played a significant part and where theology and history were subject to critical intellectual scrutiny. This was less true in Scotland. There, university professors such Francis Hutcheson and Adam Smith played an important part in the Scottish Enlightenment, and the University of Edinburgh established itself at the forefront of medical science. But it was Germany that led the way in the transformation of the medieval university, the first stirrings of this new conception usually being associated with the establishment of the University of Halle, by Lutherans, as early as 1694. And it was in Germany too that it developed most rapidly, so that by 1809 the University of Berlin was offering laboratory based courses in experimental sciences, a sharp contrast with the educational goals still being pursued in Oxford, which, according to Newman 'after a century of inactivity ... was giving no education at all to the youth committed to its keeping'.

It was another twenty years, and 133 years after the foundation of Halle, before Britain showed signs of following suit. London University (later University College London), opened its doors in 1827, called into being by the desire to provide mechanics and other relatively lowly occupations with education, quite irrespective of religion. Because it admitted Jews, Roman Catholics and Non-conformists, London University was denied a charter, and so was unable to award degrees. But its creation still had its effect. Within four years, it prompted the establishment in London of another new university college – King's – which, being an Anglican foundation, was able to obtain a charter. (In 1843 King's London was replicated in the Queen's College, Birmingham. Queen's also received a royal charter, but ironically it was its being an Anglican foundation, in the strongly non-conformist Midlands which, in the end, prevented it from becoming a fully fledged university.) In 1836, King's was followed by the creation of the University of London, organized on a federal pattern. Over the next few decades other colleges opened, existing colleges became affiliated, and the result was that England finally had in its capital city a third, large university, one with a quite different character to the two ancient universities which had existed for so long before.

A notable feature of the new university was the provision in 1849 for 'external' as well as 'internal' students, that is to say, students who could study for London degrees at home and at a distance, rather than being required to be resident in a constituent college. The creation and relatively rapid growth of London University had several important effects. First, the much looser federal structure than had existed in Oxford and Cambridge was quickly copied in other parts of the British Isles. The 1840s saw the creation of university colleges in Belfast, Dublin, Cork and Galway, later united into the National University of Ireland. Not long after, the University of Wales began, also a federal structure. Second, the fact that it was possible to study for a degree at London university while continuing to live elsewhere broke the traditional residential pattern of the ancient universities of England and thus extended higher education to a far wider section of the population. This was a more notable change in England than in Scotland. Existing as they did in what was generally a poorer country, the Scottish universities did not attract large endowments, and tended to serve a much less affluent class of student. Nor were they confined by the same religious restrictions. Indeed, for quite a time, the only access poor students from England and Ireland had to higher education was by attending Scottish universities where it was possible to pay relatively small fees for tuition and examination and make one's own arrangements for board and lodging.

Developments abroad

The 'external' examination system developed in London made it possible for people in relatively far flung parts of the empire to take degrees, and thus it was that the London pattern and character of university education came to be a major influence on the development of higher education in other parts of the world. Its influence was not exclusive, however. First, events in Europe steered the ancient universities there (or some of them) in quite different directions. Perhaps the most radical change was the impact of the French Revolution on universities in France. Like so much else identified with the *ancien regime* the universities suffered from a combination of hostility and neglect, to the point where they almost ceased to exist. Under Napoleon the term 'university' virtually fell out of use, and by the time it was current again a completely different kind of institution had emerged. The Napoleonic university is a department of State, and the professors who staff it are civil servants. Its remit is highly functional — to school citizens in the knowledge they require to promote the country's social and economic well being. The central idea overturned by Napoleonic reforms was that of the university as a self-governing community of scholars, and with it went the autonomy of the institution to set its own academic agenda. This is not quite the same as confining its curriculum to technology or sciences with practical value, though the emphasis was indeed on useful knowledge. It may serve the prestige, and hence the interests, of the country to be at the forefront of purely theoretical inquiry, but even so, such inquiry is not undertaken for its own sake but for the sake of the benefits the officers of the State perceive it to have.

Almost diametrically opposed to this conception was the vision of the university famously expounded by Karl Wilhelm von Humboldt (1767–1835), Prussia's first Minister of Education and brother of the famous German naturalist and explorer Alexander von Humboldt. Von Humboldt's conception of the university was that of a community of scholars devoted to intellectual inquiry entirely for its own sake, without any requirement that their studies be practical or profitable. This was more than an idea, in fact, since he had the opportunity to found just such an institution in the Friedrich Wilhelm University of Berlin, subsequently renamed the Humboldt University of Berlin in his honour.

For present purposes it is important to see that the Humboldtian conception of the community of scholars engaged in pure inquiry for its own sake was a novelty. Though the two are often conflated it is not to be confused with the mediaeval university model that preceded it. Whereas Humboldt's university takes no interest in practical subjects, the mediaeval universities had a concern with professional education from their inception. Even the seven 'liberal arts' which formed the foundational curriculum in the lower Faculty of Arts, were thought to take a large part of their value from their role as the springboard for professional studies.

Interestingly, this conception was more lastingly perpetuated in North America, thanks to the powerful influence of the Scottish tradition on the establishment of colleges and universities in the United States and Canada. The American 'liberal arts college' is in fact a replica of the 'Faculty of Arts' in the reformed Scottish universities of the eighteenth century, from which graduating students went on to divinity school, law school and medical school. This pattern remains, but only in a small way, having been overshadowed by the Land Grant and State universities of the nineteenth century, but it embodies the mediaeval pattern in a modern form and is to be contrasted with the Humboldtian intellectual haven no less than the Napoleonic Department of State, elements of which will both be found in the huge American universities of today.

The start of expansion

At the time that London was founded, the emergence of new universities seems, somehow, to have been in the air, perhaps because the British became aware of an unflattering contrast with continental Europe where the 'modern' university, the Napoleonic polytechnic and Humboldt's ideal in their different ways all suggested a vitality that Oxbridge lacked. It is sometimes disputed whether the claim of being England's third university does not belong to Durham rather than London, because there was an abortive attempt to establish a university there in the 1650s during the period of Cromwell. But it was not until much later — 1832 — that a further attempt was successful. In any case, though Durham eventually spawned the University of Newcastle, it was the existence of London University which was chiefly responsible for the next phase of university expansion in Britain. Colleges that initially prepared students for London degrees fairly quickly became universities in their own right. This was true in several major cities, notably, Bristol, Birmingham and Manchester, the Victoria University College in Manchester being founded in 1851, Mason's College Birmingham in 1875 and University College Bristol in 1876. Several of these in turn gave birth to other colleges which then became autonomous — Liverpool and Hull are instances — all of them coming to be known collectively as the 'red brick' universities.

Given the federal structure of London and Wales and the creation of the Irish Free State which removed most of the National University of Ireland colleges from the British system (Queen's, Belfast was the exception), the precise number of universities in Britain by 1950 is not in itself altogether significant for purposes of comparison. But whatever way they are counted, the preceding hundred years had witnessed a dramatic expansion of institutions, academics, subjects and students, with a very much wider spectrum of people having access to higher education, greatly enhanced by the admission of women from the 1880s onwards. Even so, the participation rate was still relatively small, not much more than 2% or 3% of the school population probably, though higher in Scotland than in the rest of the United Kingdom. Notably it was lower than in several European countries, and dramatically less than in the United States or Canada. It was concern about this poor participation rate that led to the next expansive phase, a consequence of deliberate Government policy.

The Robbins Report of 1960 recommended the creation of a large number of wholly new universities. The motivation behind it was partly economic and partly egalitarian — to provide Britain with a population sufficiently highly educated to capitalise upon rapidly changing economic and technological conditions, and to ensure that anyone who had the ability to benefit from tertiary education could do so irrespective of their financial circumstances. The result was the formation over the next few years of the so-called 'plate glass' universities. These had several distinguishing features. First, they were purpose built on green field 'campus' sites. Second, it was not just the buildings that were planned *de novo*. Most of the new institutions made special attempts to depart from traditional forms of degree course and academic organization. Thus the University of Stirling adopted a continental two 'semester' system rather than the normal pattern of three terms, the Universities of Sussex and East Anglia taught in interdisciplinary 'schools' rather than the customary 'departments', and several others founded new and interdisciplinary degrees in, for example, American Studies or Comparative Literature.

Polytechnics

Dramatic though these developments in universities were, they do not tell the whole story of the expansion of higher education in Britain. The nineteenth-century faith in self-improvement, and education as a means to it, had thrown up very many 'mechanics institutes' whose purpose was to provide the artisan classes with the means of acquiring more directly 'useful' skills than were available in the traditional university, or even in the new universities of London and Durham. It was not long, however, before many of these began to interest themselves in the more theoretical sides of 'the mechanical arts', and subjects such as engineering and pharmacology made an appearance in their curriculum. Some of these became universities after a time — the Universities of Strathclyde and Loughborough are notable examples, as is the Royal Technological Institute in Manchester which became the University of Salford. That is to say, they became autonomous institutions entitled to set their own standards and award their own degrees. But others became Colleges of Technology, governed, like schools, by local authorities and subject, also like schools, to external scrutiny.

In the later 1960s it became government policy to expand this sector of education also. And so the polytechnics came into existence, though the name was not adopted in Scotland where they continued to be known as Colleges of Technology. As inheritors of the mantle of the old mechanics' institutes, the principal purpose of the polytechnics was to provide a practical, technological education. However, before long, the range of subjects taught in polytechnics expanded to include social studies and some of the arts and humanities. Degree courses in all these disciplines were subject to the scrutiny and approval of the Council for National Academic Awards, and the polytechnics remained under the financial control of local authorities. It was inevitable, as the range of subjects grew, that 'the Polys' would come to regard with envy the academic autonomy and relative financial independence of the universities. A factor, too, was their status. By and large, universities were regarded, by those within and without them, as having a 'superior' educational status, and this comparison was exacerbated as the Polys offered more subjects which had been the traditional prerogative of the universities.

All this was altered by the Education Reform Act of 1988. Among other important changes this granted polytechnics degree awarding autonomy, and financial independence from local authorities. It also allowed them to apply for university status, and in the first few years of the 1990s, almost all of them of them were granted it, virtually doubling the number of universities in Britain, roughly from fifty to a hundred. One dramatic effect of this was to increase the proportion of the population enrolled in university study to unprecedented heights – about 20% in England and Wales, and higher still in Scotland. It also changed the status of a large number of educational institutions. Now the former Polys had the right to award degrees according to standards set by themselves, they could appoint professors (which they did in large numbers), and could join the Committee of Vice-Chancellors and Principals. Even more importantly, they entered into direct competition for financial support from the University Funding Councils.

Universities and the state

These funding councils, also set up by the Education Reform Act of 1988, were themselves the outcome of an important part of the history of universities in Britain. Whatever university autonomy may mean, it does not mean, and never meant, freedom from state interference. Almost from the beginning, governments interested themselves in the universities. Early on Oxford and Cambridge colleges were patronized by kings and barons, and the University of Aberdeen, founded more than 500 years ago, was the protégé of James IV, King of Scots, who saw it as a small but important element in the establishment of political independence from the Holy Roman Empire. Edinburgh, whose founders were Presbyterians and consequently lent no credence to the authority of the Pope, turned to James VI of Scotland (later James I of England), for their official sanction.

The role of the state in the provision of higher education, in fact, has been continuous. All the ancient universities — Oxford, Cambridge, Dublin, St Andrews, Glasgow and Aberdeen, were beneficiaries of grants of money and the bestowing of privileges on the part of the Crown, including in several cases the award of 'copyright library' status, which entitled the holder to receive free a copy of every book published in Britain. Nor was this all. From time to time they were also subject to regulation and direct control. Many Regius Chairs — professorial appointments made by (or at least subject to the approval of) the monarch, which still exist — came into being in an attempt by government to counteract academic nepotism. In the middle of the nineteenth century, the state of the universities in Scotland was believed to have sunk so low that a Royal Commission of inquiry was established. As a consequence of its deliberations, Parliament passed the Universities of Scotland Act of 1858, determining from outside just how they would be organized and run. The Act (with amendments) continues to govern their powers and structure to this day.

These are salutary facts for anyone inclined to think that the thraldom of academia to government is of recent date, and that university autonomy requires a completely 'stand-off' approach on the part of the state. In Britain there is only one wholly independent university, the University of Buckingham. Buckingham deliberately eschews all forms of dependence on state finance. This has secured it a certain sort of freedom. On the other hand, it has made little impression on British university life as a whole, and it should be noted that it too was dependent upon the government to grant it a charter for the awarding of degrees.

The truth is, history shows that the state will interest itself in anything that is of social and cultural importance. This observation is two sided. If universities are institutions of consequence, they must expect government interference; freedom from such interference means that they are of no consequence.

A more accurate assessment is that the singular, almost exclusive dependence of universities upon the Exchequer is of relatively recent date. It is not as relative as many think, however. The University Grants Commission (UGC) was set up in 1921, before the establishment of several red brick universities, and well in advance of the plate glass and the former polytechnics. At first the amount of money distributed was small in relation to the other funds universities had at their disposal, and the UGC was so constituted that it would provide a buffer between government and higher education, a way of protecting the independence of the latter from the purse-strings of the former. Though the UGC's total budget was set by the Treasury, the distribution between individual universities was not. Moreover, the Committee's being composed in large part of academics was meant to ensure that distribution was based on academic merit, not political favouritism. For quite a time it appeared to work well, though the proportion of university income that came from government grew steadily. After Robbins this steady growth became a flood. Established as well as new universities gratefully received a huge increase in resources. It flowed from other sources also, namely the increasingly important Research Councils who provided financial support for both postgraduate students and for academic research programmes in medicine, engineering, science and social studies. It would not be inaccurate to say that during this period, with a few exceptions (the wealthy Oxbridge colleges), for the first time British universities became completely dependent on the state's largesse — through student fees (paid by local government but reclaimed from central government), statutory grant from central government *via* the UGC, and research money, again from central government, *via* the Research Councils.

All these sources of support diminished somewhat in the 1970s. Then serious reductions came, in the 1980s, when the government of Margaret Thatcher resolved that state spending had reached unmanageable proportions, and that every sector would have to bear its share of reducing public expenditure. Moreover, all beneficiaries should be held to account for the effective use of the funds they received.

There followed a period of retrenchment. The UGC made suggestions to individual universities for closure and contraction and many of these were put into effect. Though in theory independent of government policy, the UGC capped student numbers and recommended management reform and other initiatives very much in keeping with the political current of the times. The universities responded with a striking degree of compliance. Believing their survival to depend on the restoration of government support, over the next decade they made immense and important changes, many of which will be considered in more detail in later sections. Their compliant attitude did not win them political favour, however. Arguably the important Education Reform Act of 1988 took little account of what had happened, or of the views and wishes of university teachers. However this may be, by licensing the conversion of polytechnics to universities it hugely expanded the numbers attending universities, while at the same time setting up a new system of finance — separate Funding Councils for England and Wales, Scotland, and Northern Ireland. These Councils had not much more money to distribute but many more claimants. They also had significantly greater powers of initiative and review than the old UGC had had.

There were three ways in which the new Higher Education Funding Councils came to exercise central control on universities as a whole. The first was through funding initiatives, in which sums of money were set aside for specific areas of student recruitment, teaching or research, and awarded largely by competition, the terms of which were set by the Councils. In this a pattern was being followed which had been set by the Research Councils. More recently this aspect of control has been extended through 'conditions of grant'. These are general criteria upon which the whole of State money paid to a university through the funding council depends. Initially their formulation has fairly unspecific, but greater specificity can be expected, and in any case the Napoleonic principle has been established. Though legally autonomous, British universities must perform functions set for them. The second form of control extended an innovation of the UGCs, namely periodic Research Assessment Exercises, exercises unique to the British university system, though other countries have been looking at the introduction of something similar. Subject panels were established whose task was to judge which universities were producing the best research and scholarship so that they could be rewarded accordingly. The third was the introduction of Teaching Quality Assessment. Here too subject panels were established which, unlike the Research Assessment panels, included external representatives of commerce and industry as well as academic members, and their task was to determine how well institutions were providing for the teaching of the subjects they professed.

Thus in a very short time, though there had emerged no formal equivalent for universities of Her Majesty's Inspectorate of Schools, and despite the fact that universities remained in theory autonomous bodies, they had been forged into a state 'system' largely paid for by the state and subject to extensive central control.

It is important to observe that within fifteen years or so, British universities had been changed very significantly, and though the attitude of the universities themselves was largely one of passive compliance, very many of those who had served university education and research diligently and well objected profoundly to the changes that had come about and believed them to be largely detrimental and possibly irreversible. It was common to hear the complaint that from being the best in the world, the British University was now at most second rate. We are not for the moment directly concerned with the justice of this complaint, but only with observing that it was widely made, and in part confirmed by the so-called 'brain drain' in which leading academics, and especially scientists, took other posts abroad, notably in the United States. The size of this 'brain drain' tended to be exaggerated, but there is little doubt that many first rate academics, either by emigration or through extensive early retirement schemes, left a system which had ceased to command their respect, still less enthusiasm. Furthermore, the changes that had taken place must have been evident to generations of graduates who had benefited from a collection of universities which, unlike those in most other countries, offered a fairly uniform, and high, standard of education to everyone who gained entry to them. Why then did the changes take place without significant public or political complaint, and why did the radical 1988 Act meet with only minimal resistance from the official Opposition? The answer lies in the fact that the autonomy, reform and financing of universities were not issues of any electoral significance. And the reason for this lay not so much in the actual character of British universities as in their public image.

The public image of the university

In democratic politics, there is reason to think, it is how things are widely perceived, not how they are, which is of crucial importance. Few people have the time, interest or ability to look into the complex matters of historical and social fact which rational decision making requires. In a representative democracy, accordingly, for the most part these things are left to elected legislators and professional civil servants. But at regular intervals, as a check upon authoritarian excess, governments are subject to the popular vote. No doubt this is a bad system — but perhaps, as Winston Churchill famously remarked, all others are worse. At any rate it is how things are. When elections come, parties prepare manifestos, but very few read them. Nor do many voters take the trouble to inform themselves about the issues. Rather, they cast their votes on the basis of a mixture of traditional loyalties and popular images, impressions and ideas formed from what they see and read in a wide range of media.

It is a serious mistake to think that these media are all in the business of informing. It is probably true that nowadays people take their ideas of the political issues confronting them almost exclusively from television, radio, newspapers, books, magazines and to a lesser extent the Internet. Certainly attendance at lectures, talks and political meetings is very low. But all these media contain far more than the relatively dispassionate recounting of pertinent facts. This is not a claim about secret conspiracies, wilful distortion or hidden agendas. It is just true that modern media contain a great deal by way of visual images, story telling and dramatic representation. It seems likely to me that such things have always played an important part in social and political life. Certainly they have done so for a very long time; the political cartoon has a venerable history. In any event, their role in contemporary opinion forming is considerable. Accordingly (though this is an hypothesis), it is plausible to think that if we want to find the principal influences on most people's understanding of universities in the last few decades we should look to works of fiction rather than recitations of fact. It is not the reports of select committees, royal commissions or statistical investigations, which few read or have access to, but popular images which have had most influence, reinforced by news reporting whose wholly understandable concern is not merely to inform, but to attract and hold an audience.

There is reason, I think, to believe that five highly successful novels contributed enormously to the public perception of British universities. These were Kingsley Amis's *Lucky Jim*, Tom Sharpe's *Porterhouse Blue*, Malcolm Bradbury's *The History Man* and David Lodge's *Changing Places*, followed by *Small World*. The impact of *Porterhouse Blue* and *The History Man* was specially marked since these were adapted with great success for television. What is striking about this collection is that it is, so to speak, comprehensive; it covers the full range of institutions which comprised the British universities of the early 1970s. *Porterhouse Blue* is set in an Oxbridge college, *Lucky Jim* in a red brick, and *The History Man* teaches sociology in a new university of the 'sixties. Lodge's two novels have an international setting. *Changing Places* contrasts British and American universities, not, in the end, to the advantage of the former, and *Small World* is an amusing mockery of the pretensions of the career intellectual on the international conference circuit.

These are all satires. The successful satirist, it has been said, must be in love with his victim. This is probably true of each of these writers (if Amis could ever have been said to be in love with anything), and it explains why they found some of their most enthusiastic readers amongst academics themselves. But the effect of the satire is likely to be different upon those less well acquainted with and hence less attached to the object of scorn. Taken together, in fact, they presented an attitude of relentless ridicule towards the diverse range of British universities, and limitless ammunition for their enemies, further compounded by the popular, and repeated, television series *A Very Peculiar Practice*. Like all good caricatures these imaginative works bore a striking if highly exaggerated relation to the reality they pilloried, but those who knew little of and had no reason to value the real work and purposes of universities, were not in a position to assess the degree of exaggeration.

The result, in my view, was the creation of an image which could only attract antipathy on the part of politicians and the voting public. This attitude was strengthened by news reports throughout the 1960s of student protest and rebellion, culminating at one point in an attack upon the Queen at the University of Stirling. Any reasonable person, faced with heavy taxation and cuts in public expenditure, and at the same time unfamiliar with universities and the values they embodied, would be driven to question their claims on the public purse, or at least support demands for greater accountability.

So it was that the protests of academics in the 1980s, which were in any case both mixed and muted, fell upon deaf ears. The mixed nature of their message, as it seems to me, arose from two sources. First, there was serious anxiety, one might almost say panic, about how to cope with the end of a regime in which their jobs were secure and the flow of resources to support them seemingly unlimited. Second, there was deep uncertainty about what exactly it was that they could say in their own defence. What *were* universities for? Why *should* society at large value them? Was there not *something* to be said for radical revision and review?

These are all good, if unsettling questions. The fact is, however, that in what a well-known prayer from the office of Compline calls the 'changes and chances of this fleeting world' they have as yet been unanswered. The universities of Britain have been blown hither and thither by modularization, semesterization, academic audit, quality assurance, staff appraisal, resource allocation modeling, on-line management, student evaluation, research assessment and countless other 'initiatives'. What they have not done is to deploy their own intellectual resources to take critical stock of these changes. Consequently, they have not exhibited that very critical independence which must lie at the heart of their rationale. The point of subsequent sections is to try to repair this deficiency, to ask what it is that makes a university education worthwhile, what the value of academic research is, and what light the values both of these central functions embody might throw upon the changes that have been imposed upon universities. The hope is that arriving at answers to these questions might contribute something to the crucial task of restoring to institutions of higher education a formative role in their own future.

To address these topics properly it is necessary to step back from the immediacy of contemporary concern and ask some rather more fundamental questions.

2. Explaining the value of university education

Training versus education

What is a university for? When Pope Alexander IV granted a Bull for the establishment of a university in Old Aberdeen, he set out the hopes that James IV of Scotland (or more probably his adviser Bishop Elphinstone) had for such a place.

> Now, a petition lately presented to us on the part of our dearest son in Christ, James, illustrious king of Scots, desiring that the condition of his people be improved, and considering that in the north-eastern parts of the said

kingdom there are some places, separated from the rest of his kingdom by arms of the sea and very high mountains, in which dwell men who are rude, ignorant of letters and almost barbarous and who, on account of the over great distance from the places in which universities flourish and the dangerous passage to such places, cannot have leisure for the study of letters, nay, are so ignorant of these letters that suitable men cannot be found not only for the preaching of the Word of God to the people of those places, but even for the administering of the sacraments; and that if in the famous city of Old Aberdeen, which is near enough to the places foresaid, there should flourish a university in every lawful faculty, very many men of the said kingdom, and especially those parts, would apply themselves to such study of letters and acquire that most precious pearl of knowledge, the ignorant would be informed, and the rude become learned.

The rather splendid wording of this, and the faith it expresses in the sheer power of education, may serve to disguise the striking similarity it bears to what might be said in favour of starting a university nowadays. It cannot be disputed that the modern university is a very different place to the mediaeval one. No modern British university any longer offers courses in canon law, theology is a minor not a major subject, and the medicine taught today has been transformed from the sort of study with which it began almost out of all recognition, thanks to relatively recent advances in the biological and chemical sciences. Nevertheless, the Papal Bull conveys a twofold aim — the training of professionals and the advancement of learning. In other words, from the start Aberdeen, in common with all other universities of similar age, had a dual purpose — vocational training, and education for its own sake. It provided doctors, lawyers and priests, and it gave the populace the opportunity to obtain 'the most precious pearl of knowledge' in the form of an education in the liberal arts. Its service to the locality therefore (and this relation is also an important part of the rationale of its foundation) was

both to provide for what we now call manpower needs
and to civilize.

What this fact reveals, I think, is that a certain sort of
purism about universities is not only out of place, but was
never in place. It has sometimes been suggested that the
distinguishing mark of universities, as opposed to other
institutions of further and higher education, is their concern with knowledge and the pursuit of learning for their
own sake, not for the sake of some external practical end.
This is the Humboldtian conception of a university, and it
is in fact Newman's claim in *The Idea of a University*. But
Humboldt's conception has rarely if ever been realized,
and in my view Newman has not infrequently been misunderstood on this point. The contrast he draws between
'education' and what he calls 'instruction' is a subject that
will be examined in greater detail in the next section. However, it must be admitted that there is an interpretation of
what he says plausible enough for some people to have
claimed his support for the contention that the distinction
between study in and for itself and study for the purpose
of acquiring a skill or a training is what originally marked
the difference between universities and polytechnics, a
distinction which, the same way of thinking maintains,
has been catastrophically blurred by the merger of the two
sectors.

But Aberdeen's Papal Bull, which is wholly representative of its period, shows that even the most ancient universities were centrally engaged in practical training and only
partly concerned with the pursuit of learning for its own
sake. The training they offered, it is true, was for the professions, not for practitioners of what later became known
as 'the mechanical arts'. The significance of this point is
one to which we will return. For the moment, it is important to note that at least one familiar contrast — between
practical and non-practical study — does not by itself illuminate the distinctiveness of the traditional university if

we take the mediaeval university to lie at the heart of that tradition. Accordingly, the difference between university and other forms of education is less likely to be located in the difference between practical knowledge and theoretical inquiry than in the difference between, say, training as a mechanic and studying the law. However, to make much headway with uncovering this difference, which will not be addressed directly until section 3, we need to turn to more abstract topics.

When Plato wanted to explore the proper ordering of a human life he first examined the proper ordering of society, believing that if we can determine what is good and right on the larger social scale, we will be able to see more clearly what a properly ordered life for the individual might be. The idea that society should be an analogue for understanding the individual soul strikes us as curious because now, and for a long time, our tendency has been to think of these things the other way about. We are inclined to conceive of and talk about the conduct of society, and more especially the state, as if it were an individual agent, and we seek to understand it accordingly. There are good (if somewhat vexed) arguments to think that this is an important and far-reaching error, but these need not concern us directly here, though something more will be said about them in due course. It is enough, for the moment, to explore one aspect of this analogy and draw out some of the implications it is commonly thought to have for the idea of a university education. It can be shown, I think, that there is a good deal of confusion surrounding these implications, and that some of the confusion arises precisely from the employment of the analogy.

The useful and the valuable

The activities of any individual can be divided into two broad categories — work and leisure. There are other distinctions with which this can be (but ought not to be) confused. The distinction between work and leisure is not that between the dreary and the pleasurable, for instance. Some people find their work a source of great personal satisfaction and others find that leisure activities can pall. Nor is it a distinction between employment and non-employment. The possessor of vast inherited wealth, who is not employed, is working, in the relevant sense, when he keeps track of his millions or draws more money from the bank. Similarly, the unemployed in receipt of social security are working, in this same sense, when they stand in line to collect their benefit or fill in the forms bureaucracy requires. The distinction between work and leisure, then, is really between those activities which are necessary to live, and those which make living valuable or worthwhile. We might express this distinction as one between useful activities (work) and valuable activities (leisure). Any given activity, of course, even in the life of one individual, may be both useful and valuable, but there must always be some such distinction just because we can always ask of any activity (or object) that is useful — what is it useful for? — and because we can always ask this question, we need some further evaluative conception which will answer it, and which is not itself open to the very same question. It is this further conception that I am calling 'the valuable'. In short, every human life will contain actions and objects whose purpose is to sustain life, and others whose purpose is to make life worth sustaining.

If, returning to our analogy, we think of society as in some sense an entity on a par with individuals, we find, or seem to find, a similar distinction, sometimes thought of as the distinction between productive and non-productive activities, but better expressed as the distinction between wealth-creating and wealth-consuming activities. By analogy, then, just as an individual can only go to the theatre if he has done enough 'work' to give him the price of his ticket, so a society can only afford to support theatricals if it has produced the goods and services that will allow it to pay for them.

If this is indeed so, it appears to imply that social policy must give a certain priority to wealth-creation. We need to create wealth before we can consume it, and how much we have available for consumption will depend on how much we have created. It is on the basis of this implication, very often, that countries are said by their political leaders not to be able to afford this or that. The distinction between wealth-creation and wealth-consumption however, even in its own terms, is a little too simple. There are obviously activities which, though not directly wealth-creating, nevertheless contribute to wealth-creating capacity. Adam Smith regarded preaching and religious ministration in this way, as contributing to productive ability rather than directly to production. A more plausible example nowadays might be medicine; healthy people are more productive than sick people, and it is in this way doctors contribute to general well-being. Education and research can also be thought of along these lines. On this understanding, education and research are not themselves wealth-creating, but the former gives individuals the skills to create wealth, and the latter explores and opens up further possibilities of wealth-creation.

It is evident, to my mind, that the distinction I have been elaborating provides the terms in which many contemporary political and social questions are construed and discussed, most especially in the conduct of schools and universities. Just as an individual must ensure that his or her expenditure does not consistently and over a long period exceed income, so a society must ensure that the money and effort devoted to wealth-consuming activities do not consistently and over a long period exceed those devoted to wealth-creating activities. Further, if opportunities for wealth-consumption are to be expanded, wealth-creating capacity must be expanded also and, for a time at least, an adjustment made between the two activities — just as an individual will work overtime to pay for a more exciting holiday, or take evening classes to advance his wage- or salary-earning potential.

It is this idea of 'adjustment' which dominated government policy with respect to universities in Britain throughout most of the 1980s, and provided the framework in which almost all parties to the debate on this policy were inclined to think about it. If, adopting my earlier terminology, we call wealth-creating activities 'useful' and those activities in which wealth ought to be consumed 'valuable', we can describe the policy of adjustment as a shift from the valuable to the useful, and the political debate as a debate about the appropriate magnitude of this shift.

Now, viewed in this light, not all university subjects are useful. Some are, so to speak, 'practical', some are not, and others occupy an uncertain middle ground. Most who speak in this way would agree that civil engineering and computing science are useful subjects, while classics and archaeology, however valuable, are not, while economics and geography will have supporters and opponents on the ground of their usefulness. Similarly, research will be classified as 'applied' and 'pure', another version of the same distinction to be discussed more directly in a later section. And there will be disputes about which subjects (especially among the natural sciences) within the general category of the 'pure' have practical potential and which do not.

Transferable skills

Once the policy of 'adjustment' is accepted, not just as a policy to be applied within universities, or even education, but between different areas of public expenditure, it obviously becomes extremely important to distinguish between 'useful' and 'non-useful' subjects and areas of research. It also becomes tempting for academics to try to connect their subjects with the conception of 'usefulness' even at the cost of using rather strained (and occasionally, it must be said, contemptible) arguments. It is against this background in fact that the language of 'transferable skills' has gained the great credence it has. In the belief that education in some of the subjects universities teach is not in itself 'useful', and so not easily given a convincing public justification, very many institutions have come to require that course proposals should list the 'transferable skills' that students are expected to gain from them. So, for instance, courses in classics or philosophy or mediaeval history are advertised as worth taking in part because of the (generalized) intellectual discipline and literary skills they inculcate.

Now if we are to secure an adequate explanation of the value of university education, it is crucial to observe that justification in terms of transferable skills offers no support whatever for the *content* of these subjects. From the point of view of transferable skills, any 'useful' subject, such as engineering or pharmacology, which *also* teaches mental discipline, could, and should, replace classics or philosophy without remainder. The point is not that there are no transferable skills. It may indeed be the case, as has often been claimed, that a training in the classics inculcates habits of mind which are of great service in the sort of work that members of the higher civil service are required to do. The error in the appeal to transferable skills does not lie in its falsehood, but in the fact that it attempts to explain value in terms of use. A direct parallel is this: perhaps learning to play the piano makes people more adept at chopping vegetables, but it could only be a certain sort of desperation that made a musician explain the value of the former in terms of the usefulness of the latter. The general point is this: If the useful alone is valuable, subjects which are not in themselves useful can only have derivative, never intrinsic value, and hence such value as they possess can be derived in other, more directly useful ways.

The protagonists of classics, philosophy, Egyptology, Sanskrit or art history who adopt the language of transferable skills need to think again. But there are other ways in which they can think. The first step in formulating an alternative to this 'second-hand' justification of their existence is for practitioners of traditional 'academic' subjects to grasp that making these gestures of conciliation in the direction of the 'useful' is unnecessary. There is no need to make such a concession at all.

Usefulness

Are there any subjects which are, in themselves, useful or useless? The answer is 'No'. This is not because we never know what might turn out to be useful, though that is a thought on which the defence of 'pure' scientific inquiry has frequently relied. The real reason is rather that 'useful' is a relative term; something has to be useful *for* something or other. The contemporary obsession with usefulness in this respect mirrors the sixties obsession with 'relevance'. Subjects have to be relevant *to* something; there is no such thing as relevance *per se*. Similarly, since people's purposes differ, there is no such thing as 'usefulness' in the abstract; everything useful must be useful *for* something. This is easiest to see if we consider specific examples. Cancer research, for instance, is often taken to be paradigmatic of 'useful' scientific investigation. However, the results of cancer research are no use whatever to those whose business is improving agriculture or reducing the number of traffic accidents, though these are equally laudable aims from the point of view of ameliorating the human condition. Conversely, the mastery of ancient Greek is usually thought of as 'useless'. In fact, it is not merely useful, but essential, for those who want to study Plato in the original language.

These examples make the essentially relative character of usefulness thoroughly obvious, but they are sometimes resisted in the belief that the point is merely a verbal one, one about the meaning of the word 'useful'. Importantly, this is not so. We are concerned here with conceptual issues, not semantic ones. Compare the study of Latin with the study of French. A knowledge of French is often thought to have a usefulness that a knowledge of Latin does not, which in part explains why modern languages have displaced ancient ones in most schools. But it is a matter of incontestable fact that if one's purpose is to read Ovid, to enter the Roman Curia, or to be a teacher of classical literature, a knowledge of French is of no more use than a knowledge of Swahili. Claims about the usefulness of modern languages are sometimes sustained by the idea, or assumption perhaps, that a knowledge of French is *more* useful than a knowledge of Latin. If there cannot be usefulness in the abstract, however, there cannot be degrees of usefulness. Such claims can only be taken to mean that there are more purposes for which French is useful than there are for Latin.

It is hard to know how, for means of comparison, the number of purposes a specific body of knowledge or skill serves is to be counted up, but even if it is true that some serve more purposes than others, this fact is of no interest to actual people until it has been shown that this wider range of purposes contains more of the purposes that they may (or may reasonably be expected to) have. With a knowledge of French one can *both* holiday in France more satisfactorily *and* read the literature of the country, whereas with Latin one can only read the literature; it does not help with holidays in Italy. This is true, but it does not make French any more 'useful' to those who always holiday in the Highlands of Scotland and wish to read Latin poetry or study the origins of Roman law.

The conclusion to be drawn in the present context is that as far as individuals are concerned, it is not possible to generalize about usefulness in such a way that we could divide university subjects into the 'useful' and the 'useless'. The simple truth is that any subject may be useful to some people for certain purposes, and useless to others for others. What we can often say, for limited periods of time, is that certain subjects are more likely to be useful to a larger number of people than other subjects are. The central question for the topic of this section is why, in explaining the value of universities, special attention should be paid to this fact.

One answer is that the propensity of a subject to be useful to a larger number of people makes it socially more valuable. With this suggestion we move from the individual to society, and hence return to the analogy that is commonly made between them.

If the foregoing analysis is correct, some subjects at some times can be described as being more useful for more purposes to more people than others. It is under the influence of this thought that information processing, it is frequently suggested, is more useful than other subjects. IT is useful in very many different ways, whereas archaeology, for example, is useful to only a few people in a few ways. Thus expressly stated, however, we should not let this truth impress us unduly. There seems little doubt that the comparison of mortgage and other interest rates is likely to be of use to far more people than the study of Anglo-Saxon. Would this warrant our replacing the latter with the former in university curricula? Before we could reasonably draw this conclusion we would need, in addition to an assessment of the greater usefulness of a subject in the sense just specified, to arrive at some assessment of the value of the purposes for which it is useful.

Consider this example. In terms of multiplicity of uses, food science can be thought more useful than many other subjects. It often *is* more useful, in fact. But we cannot conclude that it is more *valuable* until we have put its investigations and results in a larger context. If the greater usefulness of food science were to lie in its ability to provide manufacturers with the means to increase the number of flavours of crisps, instant puddings or scented erasers, further argument is needed to show that these advances are especially valuable. Perhaps we have an enormous number of such flavours already (which indeed we do), and, as the (somewhat misnamed) principle of diminishing marginal utility tells us, further additions of more generate very little by way of added value. Where this is the case, we have good reason to resist all attempts to devote greater resources to food science. Largely, it has given us all it has to give and the admitted usefulness of yet more does not generate much, if anything at all, in the way of value.

These observations, plainly stated, seem self-evident, yet they fly in the face of a widely held belief that it is possible to employ a general basis of assessment which will enable us to distinguish between the more and the less useful. This general basis is usually thought to be wealth-creation. The widespread belief is that a subject may be described as more useful, that is to say, one which serves more purposes for more people, if it can be shown to be part of the social process of wealth-creation. Conversely it is less useful if it can be shown to be part of social consumption.

Wealth-creation

The concept of wealth-creation is complex. It is sufficient for present purposes, however, to draw attention to certain misunderstandings which surround it, and which are of the greatest importance for understanding the nature and value of a university education. First, it is clearly wrong to think that wealth-creation is the earning of money. To begin with, the creation of wealth is possible in a barter economy, and is even possible where there is no economy at all — a hermit may create wealth, that is, make his life richer than it was by means of his own labour. Secondly, it is wrong to think of wealth-creation as the manufacture of saleable goods. The life of the individual may also be enriched, in a perfectly straightforward sense, by the composition of music, the learning of games, the advancement of knowledge and understanding, and enjoyment of the natural environment. Thirdly, it is wrong to think of wealth-creation as an increase in the normal means of procuring goods and services. A society can have extensive financial reserves but its members, in the main, be unable to enrich their lives because the schools, roads, hospitals, universities, museums, theatres and sports facilities do not exist in which these reserves could be spent. Such has been the case in many Arab countries with immense oil revenues, but relatively little to spend them on.

In short, it is wrong to think of wealth-creation as the generation of income, even in the case of the individual in the abstract. In practice for many people income, provided it can be spent, *is* a measure of wealth, and an increase in income accordingly a measurable increase in wealth, but it is wrong to think of it in this way as far as society is concerned — for two reasons. Not only is an increase in purchasing power not of itself an increase in wealth, but a society is composed of many members amongst whom money and goods circulate, and between whom wealth is *exchanged*. The process of exchange, unlike the simple acquisition of the hermit, involves the creation and consumption of wealth simultaneously. To put it crudely, the very same five pound note which I spend, you earn, whenever we trade goods or services. Wealth-creation and wealth-consumption, in a *social* context, are simply the same action viewed from two different sides and since, as economists have told us for long enough, the very act of exchange may itself create additional wealth, it is senseless to speak of the two as in opposition.

What is the bearing of all this on the use and value of universities as social institutions? We have seen that from the point of view of specific individuals with certain purposes, some university subjects may be more useful than others. We have also seen that some subjects may be of use to more individuals than others, but that this, by itself, does not give us reason to value them more highly. To discriminate between subjects or educational institutions in the way that is commonly done, we need to be able to show that, just as an individual must work before he can play, a society must put wealth-creation before consumption, and that subjects are to be determined 'useful' as they contribute to wealth-creation. What the foregoing analysis shows is that this attempt rests upon a misunderstanding of wealth-creation in a social context. It follows that any attempt to discriminate in general between useful and useless subjects, or between wealth-creating and wealth-consuming intellectual activities is groundless. No subject can be declared useless (or useful) in the abstract, and all serious intellectual inquiry, I believe, can be declared valuable in terms of wealth-creation. This conclusion is confirmed, if we examine carefully some familiar objections to it.

Utilitarian suppositions

The points I have made in support of these contentions about usefulness and wealth creation do not rely on any very novel insights. On the contrary, it is an important part of the strategy of this section that they consist largely in commonplaces, albeit commonplaces which have been frequently overlooked. They have been overlooked because of the strongly utilitarian presuppositions that have governed the discussion of these issues for some considerable time. For instance, from a utilitarian point of view it seems obvious that we could all be farmers, but we could not all be philosophers and that consequently some occupations are necessary and others a luxury. But is this so obvious? Actually, once one thinks about it, it seems obviously *false*. 'Man cannot live by bread alone', since at a minimum he also needs stones that have been specially fashioned with which to grind the flour and firewood that has been gathered with which to bake the dough. This was not, of course, the point Moses was making, which was rather that there are other and perhaps more important forms of wealth than bread. 'Man cannot live by bread alone' need not be interpreted as a sententious or otherworldly appeal to the spiritual, however. A society in which all are hunters, herders and gatherers is, quite literally, a poorer society than one in which there are also musicians, philosophers and actors. The important point to grasp about this observation is that the music and the philosophy are not *bought* with a richer society's wealth, but are themselves *part* of it.

Might it not be said, nonetheless, that there is an undeniable difference between those things that are fundamentally necessary for human life and those that are not? Surely food is needed in a sense in which classical learning is not? The difference between food and knowledge is real, but it is not significant for the topic under discussion. No one could plausibly suggest that the difference between 'useful' and 'useless' subjects or activities lies in the capacity of the former to supply basic needs. We could live without classical learning, it is true, but so we could without computers, telephones, railway timetables and vaccines, all of them paradigmatically 'useful'. None of these things is needed just to keep life going. But any of them can play an essential part in making life qualitatively more valuable. Classical learning may be unnecessary from the point of view of basic subsistence, but it is not any more so than computational science. It follows that basic subsistence cannot provide a point of view from which to adjudicate between the value of these two subjects.

It is tempting, even while conceding these points, to cling to the belief that there is *some* difference here which, presumably, has not yet been properly articulated. This residual belief might be expressed, as it commonly is, in the claim that society needs farmers and mechanics, whereas it does not, strictly, need historians or sculptors. This is a claim of the greatest interest, I think, because while it is a way of thinking that powerfully influences public policy and discussion, it is also one that is deeply mistaken.

The needs of society

To begin with, the idea that we could need, say, engineers without needing non-engineers is absurd. We only need roads if we have reason to travel, and if our sole reason were to explore further possibilities for road building the whole exercise would be pointlessly circular. Road engineers are valuable because, amongst other things, we want to drive to the opera, visit friends or attend lectures on Egyptology. Similarly, electrical engineering is useful only in so far as it serves needs other than itself — lighting the places in which we live and work, making possible films and television programmes which have independent value. In short, society *needs* such skills only in so far as the individuals who comprise it *want* other things, things that non-engineers supply.

A second point to be made is this: the individuals who make up society have different wants and hence different needs. Earlier it was shown that some subjects serve some of these needs, and other subjects others. Consequently, to declare one group of subjects more useful than another is implicitly to declare a preference for the purposes they happen to serve. To put it bluntly: to maintain that electronic engineering is useful in comparison with musicology is to declare a preference for, amongst other things, video games over composition or concert going. Even this way of putting the point is misleading. The opposition between the two is quite factitious; one reason for valuing electronic engineering lies in its usefulness for the recording of music.

But in any case, on what are such selective preferences to be based? One answer, consonant with the utilitarian line of thought we have been examining, is that 'society', over and above the individuals who at any time comprise it, needs one more than the other. (If it did, then presumably it would pay them more. One reason to doubt the utilitarian assumption lies in the fact that it does not.) But to speak in this way is to think of society as an individual, the analogy with which we began, and to which we must now return. Margaret Thatcher's unguarded remark that 'There is no such thing as Society' met with much ridicule, in part rightly so, since it is easily shown that a society is not identical with the people who comprise it. The population of any society changes constantly, because of births and deaths, and though societies can indeed come to an end, they do not do so just because their population changes. If they did, their existence would be fleeting indeed. Still, it does not follow that 'Society' is the sort of entity that can be said to have needs or desires independently of the needs and desires of those who comprise it. It is only human beings who desire things, and hence only human beings who need the means to satisfy those desires. Whatever sort of thing society may properly be said to be, its 'needs' cannot be appealed to independently of the generalised needs of human beings. Besides, even if they could, 'Society' cannot sensibly be said, except metaphorically, to have a voice or hands. It takes individuals to declare the needs of 'Society' and to do its bidding. Who are we to take as its spokesmen?

Politicians are particularly prone to speak on behalf of 'Society', but industrialists and commercial interests, who more often speak of 'the economy', have been quick to do the same thing. Now it is these spokesmen, amongst others, who have for some time set the terms on which the social value of universities is assessed. Their view, however, is partial. This is not the same as saying it is prejudiced, though it may be. The point to be emphasized is that both politicians and industrialists have special interests, and that it is a mistake to think of their interests as being, or even indirectly representing, the interests of all. To arrive at a more adequate assessment and explanation of the social value of universities (or any other institution for that matter), we have to adopt a more general, less partial view.

Nearly everyone values health and longevity, hence the ease with which the claim that 'Society' needs doctors and health workers meets with general approval. Nearly everyone values recreation and pleasure. Hence the ease with which music and film, despite their largely non-utilitarian character, gain social support. Tastes differ of course, but commercially successful musicals and popular cinema that attracts spontaneous audiences are rarely called upon to justify themselves to others. Health and recreation are importantly different however. Freedom from disease and longevity are worth having only in as far as there are rewarding ways in which long and healthy lives can be spent. To be healthy and long-lived in solitary confinement without any source of stimulation or any means of recreation or diversion is, arguably, a fate worse than death. The importance of recreation and pleasure lies in their ability to supply such a deficiency. Health and longevity are means, amongst other things, to the end of pleasure and enjoyment. In other words, to employ an earlier distinction, health and longevity are useful; pleasure and enjoyment are valuable.

Pleasure, though important and intuitively attractive to most people, is not the only value that makes life worthwhile. Only out and out hedonists would think to the contrary. And this brings us to the principal issue around which the social value of universities turns. If, in the end, what society needs is what makes the individuals who comprise it better off, the question is: what *does* make human beings better off? It should be obvious that the list of those things which enrich a human life goes beyond the crudely utilitarian conception of 'basic' needs. It also goes beyond pleasure and enjoyment and includes knowledge and understanding. Though the slogan 'the value of knowledge for its own sake' is itself misleading, as we shall see in a later section, those, like Newman, who espouse it are pointing to an important truth. There is no reason to believe that, in the abstract, health or pleasure is any more enriching than knowledge. It follows that the producers of knowledge enrich human lives, and hence enrich society, no less than the producers of health and pleasure.

When industrialists, and in their wake, politicians, speak of what society needs they are usually referring to the means of increasing prosperity. There is nothing wrong, duplicitous, or necessarily philistine about this. But it needs to be said again and again that the concept of 'prosperity' conceived solely as purchasing power is logically incomplete. It says nothing about what that increased prosperity is to be spent on, and without additional *objects* of consumption, additional *means* of consumption are worthless. Wealth creation, properly understood, requires both. A society is truly richer only if it has *both* the means of securing better lives for its citizens *and* the availability of the objects which make lives better. The terms of the contemporary debate about the value of universities tends to have focused it on the contribution they might make to the means. It has generally ignored the contribution they make to the objects. And academics themselves have been lured into the argument about means, a context in which they can never do full justice to the institutions and activities in which they are engaged.

To assess the value of universities to society, then, we need to look at their contribution to wealth creation without distorting this to imply prosperity in the restricted and incomplete sense it so often has. Viewed in this light, there are two ways in which universities contribute to the societies of which they are a part. The first is education and the second is research. To say this, however, is not to answer the question of their social value, but only to set the context for answering it. This is because, so stated, their aims are not unique. Schools and colleges of technology also educate; commercial laboratories and pollsters also engage in research. So why should what goes on in universities be given special attention? If an answer is to be found it must lie in what is distinctive about university education and research. These are the respective topics of the next two sections.

3. University education

Right at the outset of *The Idea of a University*, Cardinal Newman states his main thesis in the plainest possible fashion.

> The view taken of a University in these Discourses is the following: — That it is a place of *teaching* universal *knowledge*. This implies that its object is … the diffusion and extension of knowledge rather than the advancement. If its object were scientific and philosophical discovery, I do not see why a University should have students … (Newman 1982: xxxvii, emphasis original).

This contention is at odds with the self-professed (and government encouraged) conception of the modern British university, in which research is seen as at least as important, and sometimes more so, than teaching. Yet with the exception of very special institutions such as All Souls College, Oxford, British universities exist in large measure to educate those who register in them as students, and depend heavily upon the support of the public purse as providers of university education, and generally it is this aspect that draws the most political attention and the most public debate. The question of 'access', the social and ethnic mix of student populations and the rightness and wrongness of tuition fees have figured far more prominently than the question of research agendas and their successful prosecution. Whatever the merits of research work on which university academics tend to focus more and more (the topic of the next section), public perception and political policy makers take educating students to be a central and ineliminable part of a university's function.

I use the term 'university education' for the topic of this section because the more common expression 'higher education' is unsatisfactory in at least one important respect; it does not attribute any distinctiveness to studying at university rather than other places of tertiary education. British English used to employ a terminological distinction that has largely been lost in contemporary parlance. At one time those who attended schools were known as pupils and those who attended institutions of higher education were known as students. Partly under the influence of American English, the two terms have recently converged and those attending schools are as likely to be referred to as students. The matter is not merely linguistic however. The adoption of the term 'student' to refer to those in secondary, and even primary education, also signals a change in educational philosophy, a belief that self-motivated inquiry is more appropriate for schoolchildren too, more appropriate that is to say than mere passive reception of 'lessons'.

The truth or falsity of this belief lies at the heart of contemporary concern with school education. It is not my purpose to examine the issue here, however. All that needs to be noticed for present purposes is that this important tenet of educational theory, whether cogent or not, can only be stated if it employs the same important difference which the older usage marked, namely that whereas pupils are taught, students study. Though nothing turns on mere terminology, I shall make use of the traditional distinction between pupils and students to explore what there is to be said about the distinctiveness of a university education.

Students and pupils

It is the *conceptual* difference between studying and being taught that is most worth uncovering for present purposes. Though it is not often made explicit in these terms, it is frequently evident in the practical experience of the individuals who cease to be pupils and become students. An important part of this practical experience is that students at colleges and universities find themselves much less subject to educational discipline than when they were pupils at school. It is true that in general the transition from school to higher education can be difficult, and this for a number of reasons. Chief among these, perhaps, is the fact that those making the transition are often leaving their parental homes for the first time. But the nature of their relation to their studies also changes in ways that can be unsettling. First, they are required to spend far less time in class. Second, their attendance is not subject to the scrutiny it was; there are (as yet) no university truant officers. Third, their work is far less directed. Of course there are great variations between institutions in this respect, and indeed between subjects and disciplines. Consequently, generalisation is fraught with risks. Nevertheless, it is broadly true that while *pupils* are for the most part directed by others, *students* are expected to be much more self-directed. There are deadlines for essays, lab reports and so on, to be met, and there are examinations to be passed. But just how these are prepared for is largely a matter for the student to decide.

This element of self-direction can be taken, in fact, as a crucial difference between pupils and students, and hence between schools and colleges. Here too, we might observe, British English and American English diverge somewhat, since, while some British schools are called colleges, it is common for Americans to refer to universities as 'schools', a usage which is still alien in Britain. There is also the fact already noted that many educational theorists would claim that those who are at school should be accorded the status of student (in my sense). Once again, nothing much turns on the words we use, and, to repeat, I do not propose to enter into debates about the objectives that are appropriate for primary and secondary education. I shall simply use the term 'school' to refer to primary and secondary education and 'tertiary education' to refer to the sector within which universities are to be found but which, importantly, they do not wholly encompass.

Tertiary education has a number of distinguishing features. First, participation in it is voluntary. Since the Education Act of 1870, some school education has been compulsory for all British children; only the length of time that must be spent at school has altered. In this respect Britain led the way since compulsory schooling is now to be found in all but the poorest countries. But everywhere, compulsion stops with tertiary education. Second, tertiary education has always been available, and increasingly so of late, to a variety of ages — not just to the school leaver. Third, and this point, already observed, is one of considerable significance, a large part of tertiary education not only relies upon but strives to inculcate self-directed study. Once more, the lines here are blurred. Colleges of Further Education prepare all ages for relatively low level examinations and modern educational practice in schools has encouraged the technique of active 'discovery' in preference to passive 'learning'. Whether this is for good or ill is an important question, but it is not the issue here. Many have come to reject, or at least question, the theory behind the practice. By contrast, no one seriously doubts that the mastery of autonomous inquiry is a crucial part of 'higher' education. In other words, it is widely agreed that there is a level of education at which a large part of the educator's task is to equip the student with the means to pursue inquiry on his or her own part.

If this is a central feature of tertiary education in general, it cannot be taken to mark out the peculiarities of university education *per se*. What then are these peculiarities? In answering this question we can still learn something from Newman.

Education versus instruction

Newman's distinction between 'education' and 'instruction' is drawn in order to mark this difference. In amplification of it he contrasts 'the philosophical' with 'the mechanical', the former being characterized by an introduction to 'general ideas', the latter with information 'that is exhausted upon what is particular and external'. Newman's language sounds odd to our ears, yet what he means to convey is familiar enough. It has to do with the different direction of thought that alternative forms of inquiry take. There is good reason to follow him in his use of the term 'philosophical' because it is philosophy properly so-called in which the direction of the first is most marked. Students (and others) often complain that philosophy is inconclusive. They mean that philosophical reflection never seems to lead to any firm and decisive result. Its direction is such that, far from matters being settled, the longer we engage in philosophical reflection, the more further and larger issues seem to open up. The complaint of inconclusiveness is overstated, in my view, because less attention is paid than it should be to the value of the negative no less than the positive. From the earliest times we find Socrates claiming, in the face of a similar objection, that if he knew nothing positive, he at least knew what he did not know; he knew just how *ignorant* he was. This put him, he thought, at an advantage over many of his contemporaries, who supposed that they knew what they believed, while in reality their beliefs, however firmly held, were groundless.

Knowledge of the negative is still knowledge. It is not just a mark of philosophy, however. Karl Popper made falsification, rather than verification, the mark of real science. He did so, in part, because of the history of science. One of the most telling events of this history is the overthrow of Newton by Einstein. Newton seemed to make, and did make, real advances in scientific understanding over the Aristotelian physics that had dominated European thinking for so long. Yet in their turn the conceptions of Newtonian mechanics were, eventually, rendered largely redundant by relativity theory. And we can expect, in due course, that Einstein will also be superseded. It seems that it is the apprehension of the false rather than the true in which progress in scientific understanding consists, which is why Popper chose falsification as the true test of science. It follows that no scientific hypothesis can be taken to be the last word.

We can say something similar of history. While the basic facts of the past can be established with certainty — Louis XIV died in 1715 — the larger story of any period is constantly under review — the full significance of the rule of 'Le Roi Soleil' is still open to revision. In the study of philosophy, natural science and history, then, students are encouraged, in a phrase of Michael Oakeshott's, to 'spread their sails to the argument' without knowing where or to what purpose this might lead. By contrast, the engineer and the pharmacist need to know 'hard' fact, truths which, when we know them are, in Newman's terminology, 'exhausted'. Only so can they be securely acted upon. It is not the business of the practical intelligence to raise general doubts and conceptual difficulties, but to ascertain what is needed for the purpose in hand. Water flows downhill. To know this is enough for the purposes of harnessing its power. Knowledge of the fact exhausts the inquiry. But why *does* water flow downhill? *Must* it be so? These questions lead in a different direction, and when we have a mind to inquire into them, the fact itself becomes one of relatively little interest.

Why, though, should we pursue such questions? What is the point if, in the end, they make us no better at constructing watermills, and hence no better at grinding flour and making bread? The answer, according to Newman, is that the desire to know is as basic a feature of human beings as the desire to do or to have. In my view it is a mistake to express his contention in terms of 'knowledge as its own end' but the defence of this claim must await section 4. For the moment it is enough to record that there is substance to his contrast between 'the philosophical' and 'the mechanical'.

Supposing it to be so, the import is this. Those who engage in learning as opposed to instruction are set upon a course — the investigation of general ideas — which in turn implies a different relation between learning and the mind which learns than the relation implied in a process of 'instruction'. There is neither reason nor occasion to mark this difference in terms of respective value. Newman does not claim — and no one needs to — that education is superior to instruction, only that it is different. The tendency to mark the difference with different evaluations has bedevilled debates about higher education. It is a mark of the British educational tradition that the 'academic' has been held in higher esteem than the 'practical', and this prejudice partly explains why polytechnics and colleges of technology were keen to change their names. At the same time prejudice is at work in the other direction also, which is why the 'purely' academic has often felt under a special pressure to justify itself.

It is questionable whether a preference for the 'academic' can be given any rational foundation, and equally questionable whether we should accept the value of the 'practical' at its own estimation. Something has already been said about this, but in any case it is not the issue here. What we want to know, rather, is what the nature and significance of the distinction is, and how it might reflect on the value of university education.

Liberal versus technical

In exploring these matters further we need to return to an observation made at the start of the last section. Since earliest times universities have included within their curricula subjects broadly called 'practical'. The training of priests, lawyers and doctors is as old a part of their purpose as an education in the liberal arts. This is why, unless we disregard a large part of its history, a place must be found within university education for training as well as for learning, for the practical as well as the liberal arts and pure sciences. The distinction we need to elaborate, accordingly, is one which will differentiate between lawyers and mechanics no less than between mechanics and philosophers. It will be useful, therefore, to replace the language of training *versus* education with a different terminology, one which contrasts technical with liberal education.

Newman contrasts 'liberal' in this context with 'servile' and, he says, 'by "servile" work is understood … bodily labour, mechanical employment and the like in which the mind has little or no part' (Newman 1982: 80). 'Servile' is an unattractive term to modern ears, but it is not one we need to invoke in order to acknowledge that there are some technical accomplishments which are almost entirely a matter of inarticulate knack or art. That is to say (in Socratic language), people can master practical techniques while being quite unable to 'give an account' of them, i.e. formulate, or even indicate, the principles that underlie them. There is no reason to denigrate such practical mastery, although Socrates (or Plato perhaps) tended to do so. Straightforward mastery of this sort accurately describes most people's linguistic ability; they can speak a language whose grammatical and linguistic structures they cannot articulate. In a similar fashion, it is generally true that mechanics, plumbers and electricians are masters of inarticulate skills. From the point of view of the purposes such skills are intended to serve, this is of no consequence. What we want is that our telephones, taps or lights work. Why should we care if those who can put them to rights cannot explain, except in elementary terms, how they have done so or give a theoretical explanation of why what they have done has been successful? Still less do we count it a deficiency that they have no knowledge of the higher sciences that underlie them. Conversely, as is well known, those versed in electro-dynamics may be quite unable to fix the power supply, botanists do not necessarily make good gardeners and nutritionists may be unable to cook.

Still, though there are these inarticulate skills that are no worse off for their inarticulacy, it is also the case that there are practical tasks the performance of which is improved by the addition of more intellectual accomplishments. In a world of rapidly changing and increasingly sophisticated technology — computer technology is a good example, biotechnology another — it is inconceivable that satisfactory results should be achieved through relatively unreflective techniques alone. And so it is that technological education has come more and more to involve its students in theoretical issues which prompt and encourage mental inquisitiveness and imagination. The very term 'technology' implies this, made up as it is of an amalgam of the Greek terms for both skill and explanation. Teachers of technology rightly deny that their task can be restricted to the instilling of mere techniques and accordingly any technology syllabus will have intellectual as well as technical components. This is true of electrical and mechanical engineering. It is even more so of service industry subjects like transportation, management or media studies which, though practical, are not generally thought of as technological.

Does the existence of technology and service industry subjects mean that the distinction between technical and liberal education has been breached, or needs to be abandoned even? In answer to this question it is worth recalling that Newman, the high priest of liberal education, did not deny the power of such subjects to provide intellectual stimulus. On the contrary, he says 'no one can deny that commerce and the professions afford scope for *the highest and most diversified powers of the mind*' (Newman 1982: 81). I have added the italics to emphasize how sharply what Newman actually says is to be contrasted with what he is so often thought to have said. But if commerce and the professions can fully engage our mental powers, does an education in them not also become liberal on Newman's own interpretation of the term? If it does, shouldn't we favour these over more academic subjects on the grounds that the former are *both* liberal *and* useful while the latter are liberal only?

This question returns us to a topic of the last section — transferable skills. In discussing the move to defend seemingly 'useless' subjects on the grounds of the transferable skills they teach, it was noted that no such defence could satisfactorily explain the value of those subjects with respect to their *content*. And yet it is in their content that an adequate explanation must lie. The same point can be made in other contexts. If we justify football on the strength of its ability to contribute to physical fitness, an ability it undoubtedly has, we say nothing about the special merits of the game itself. A proper approach, though there space here only to sketch it, must focus first upon the aims of game playing and then explain the distinctive ways in which football gives scope for them, or some of them. Physical fitness, we might say, is a *benefit* which comes of playing football, but it is not the *point* of playing it.

In the same way, literacy, numeracy, articulacy and facility with analysis are benefits (let us hope) of studying philosophy, linguistics, psychology, jurisprudence, comparative religion or cosmology; but it is not in these that we find their point. The point, rather, as I think Newman meant to say, is the exercise and enriching of the life of the mind for its own sake.

But are we any further forward in making this observation? If technological education is in part intellectual and affords 'scope for the highest and most diversified powers of the mind', what argument can be made for the independent value of non-technological subjects? The answer lies, I think, in the fact that the exercise of the powers of the mind which technology requires is *not* required for its own sake, but for the sake of another end. Consider a specific instance. Media studies goes beyond the technical mastery of camera work, editing and the like, and it does so because, if its purpose is to equip people for a lifetime's work in television and film studios, it must leave them with an intellectual ability to adapt to rapidly changing technology, and with the conceptual imagination to explore and exploit possibilities which simply were unavailable at the time of their training. All this is true, it seems to me, yet the point of such intellectual accomplishments nevertheless lies in their being of service to the (as yet unimagined) practical tasks of the television and film industry of the future. The life of the mind in such service can be both challenging and stimulating; it is a prejudice to think otherwise. For all that, it is subservient to an external purpose.

The distinguishing mark of liberal arts and pure sciences can now be said to be this. Their point is to enrich the mind, and their value lies in the success with which they do this. Importantly, however, they cannot be said to do this by means of the disciplines they inculcate. This, we have seen, is a feature they share with technological subjects. It follows that their peculiar powers of intellectual enrichment lie in their content. It is not that they provide occasions for thought, which they do, but that they provide the most worthwhile *objects* of thought. It is here that the rationale of university education properly so called lies; it is a source of wealth *per se*.

Is this true? The answer depends upon two propositions, first that intellectual enrichment is indeed a form of wealth. The second is that the liberal arts and pure sciences supply it. A defence of the first of these propositions will be postponed to the next section, since it arises in its most acute form when we try to give an account of the value of academic research. The defence of the second turns crucially upon matters of specific detail. Is it the case that all the subjects described as academic that have secured a place in the curriculum of the modern university are real sources of significant intellectual enrichment? They have (nearly) all had their detractors. Are social sciences, sciences? Is literary theory bogus? Is botany more than mere

classification? Is theology a real subject? Is women's studies a genuine discipline? These are all serious and important questions which have exercised minds both within
and without universities. Subjects come and go according
to political, social — and intellectual — fashion. We may
reasonably assume that impostors have sometimes joined
the ranks of the intellectual, that the redundant can for a
time go unnoticed, and that genuinely new subjects often
have a struggle to establish their credentials. Differentia-
tion between the many claimants to intellectual respectability requires a detailed examination of particulars that I
do not propose to engage in here. It is enough for my purposes to make the assumption that many traditional academic subjects would survive such scrutiny. Even when
they do, however, critical questions are not at an end. Of
any such subject it may yet be asked — how is its value as a
provider of intellectual wealth to be assessed?

The professional and the technical

Before turning to the question of assessment, there is a
residual issue to be addressed. Following Newman I have
drawn a distinction between liberal and technical/techno-
logical education. Where does this leave education in professions such as law, medicine and the church, all of which
have figured in university study since its earliest days?
The answer lies, I believe, in the recognition that legal,
medical and theological education is radically incomplete
if it remains at the level of the technical or even technological. Lawyers need to know how to prosecute cases successfully, doctors need to know how to cure people, and clergy
must master the 'mechanics' of liturgy and sacrament. If
these were all they came to know, however, there would
be a serious deficiency in their training. But it is not
enough that their practical skills are underwritten by more
theoretical learning in the way that technology under-

writes technique. Professionals also need an understanding of the significance of their profession. What is it to be
an administrator of justice? In what do healers differ from
witch-doctors? Why do we need priests and pastors?
Without some consideration of these questions, the
respective practitioners of these professions are mere
functionaries, reduced to servers, and not formers, of
social life. The profession of surgeon took some time to
emerge from that of barber. Its emergence, it seems to me,
had to do not merely with the mastery of different techniques, but with attaining a certain self-consciousness.
And this is where liberal education embellishes the technical and technological to create the professional. The idea
and significance of law, the social role of healing, the metaphysical (and moral) meaning of liturgy and sacrament
are necessary to the humanising, and one might say social-
izing, of these professions. Accordingly, jurisprudence
figures in law degrees, medical ethics is (rightly) com-
manding an increasingly larger role in the education of
doctors, and philosophical theology has always played a
part in training for the priesthood. It is these elements that
give professional training a place in university education
of the 'liberal' kind, and such training forms an important
bridge between the liberal and the technical. Even if it has
not always been explicit, though it often has been, it is this
self-consciousness that explains and justifies the traditional place such subjects have had in the curriculum of
universities. They are, we might say, the place where the
technical and the liberal meet because although their aim
is practical mastery it is no less important, in the Socratic
phrase, that they be able to give an account of themselves.
This double nature means that professional subjects cannot be assessed as technical subjects can, and that no less
than the arts and pure sciences, they raise issues about
how the quality and success of a university education is to
be judged. It is to this topic therefore that we now return.

Education and the language of commerce

Assessing the value of a technological education appears to have a relatively simple structure. Does it, literally, deliver the goods? In the last analysis, the point of technology is to solve practical problems, and though in any particular case it may be factually difficult to establish its success in doing so, conceptually the assessment of its success is a fairly simple matter. Technology does not set its own problems, except intermediately. Its ultimate problems are set for it by the social, commercial and industrial demands of the wider world in which it operates. It just is true that any technology can become outmoded — as the technology of gas lighting did — and at this point, whatever its intellectual interest, the technology has ceased to be of value. Its ceasing to be of value is not only marked, but established, by its failing in the market place. So, for instance, drugs that resulted from innovative research and have had huge success — Zantac (for ulcers) is a striking example — in their turn become no longer saleable, or, as in this case, have to find other, less prestigious outlets. Similarly students trained in a technology which becomes outmoded are no longer employable. With the advent of computer graphics the old skills and techniques of cartography are worthless. Typewriters and duplicators, hugely innovative and useful in their own day, are now quite without value. Home movies of the 32mm type have no place in a world with video cassettes, which have themselves largely disappeared with the advent of the DVD.

It seems then that assessing the value of a technological education is a matter that the world at large will take care of. The same cannot be said of university education. How are we to know when it provides something of real value? There is an answer to the question 'How many computer programmers does society need?' — and the answer is given when no more can find employment. But to the question 'How many historians or philosophers or sociologists does society need?' — there is no such ready answer since people educated in these subjects can more readily be expected to find employment in personnel management or the civil service than as historians, philosophers or sociologists. The issue rather is what the study of philosophy, history, and so on, can contribute to human good. But how is this contribution to be assessed?

In recent times a marked and sustained effort has been made to address this question in a fashion which, as I shall argue, is inappropriate to its being adequately answered. One way of describing this effort is to say that academic value has been subjected to the language of commerce, the language, that is to say, of supply and demand. The idea is this: what better measure could there be than the demand for such courses? If university education is to be valued, this will be reflected in the demand for it. And allied to this thought is the idea that the success of individual courses can best be estimated by surveying the views of those who take them. To adopt this approach to academic value is to view the student as the buyer or customer of the offerings university teachers have to make. Such a change in view marks a highly significant alteration in the relationship between university student and university teacher. It is one that needs to be explored in detail. That it has come to be conceived in this way is not in much doubt. The more important question is how it *ought* to be conceived.

The student as customer

The amalgamation of technological and academic institutions in a single system of higher education, together with an emphasis on increased participation and the continuing conception of tertiary education as essentially voluntary, has led to competition amongst institutions of higher education for students. One superficial consequence is the increasingly glamorous appearance of university prospectuses. Where formerly it was thought sufficient for these publications to inform, now they must attract, and promote a suitably fashionable image. As a result, university prospectuses are much more sumptuous than they used to be.

This is, as I say, a superficial consequence, though nonetheless indicative of a change of attitude and perception. Two things need to be disentangled here. The first is that it is no longer sufficient, and ought never to have been, for university teachers to dish out to students whatever they chose to offer, or worse, whatever they could be bothered to. There was certainly a period, though quite a short one I think, in which arrogance and indolence played no small part in the attitude of university academics to teaching. Part of the cause of this was the radical divorce that government support for higher education had created between supply and demand. Thanks to statutory grants, automatic fees and generous support for capital projects, university teachers were protected from those mechanisms of accountability that are a marked feature of the market.

Given the amount of state money that went into university education it was inevitable, and wholly reasonable, that those who received it should, sooner or later, be called to account. And indeed accountability has become a watchword of higher education. There are many systems of 'staff appraisal' and 'academic audit' now in place which aim to institutionalize accountability. But something in the nature of market forces has also come to play a highly important part. The simple financial need for contemporary universities to attract, please and keep students is incontestable. There is not, as yet, a direct relation between this need and the prospering of particular classes and teachers, but a standard budgetary device, generally known as a Resource Allocation Model or RAM, is now very widely used, and has the effect of connecting the size, prosperity, and even continued existence of departments and subjects to the number of students they attract directly. To a large extent then students have come to be conceived as customers (along with parents who pay for their upkeep).

This is the supply side of the equation. On the demand side, students are less obviously customers. There are costs attaching to being a student which must be borne directly and the reduction of student grants and the introduction of loans have intensified these considerably. Now, after protracted political debate, students at British universities have to pay tuition fees (though the system differs between Scotland and England). However, neither the indirect costs nor the tuition fee are under the control of the university, and though some flexibility is possible, generally students cannot 'shop around' to find the best value for money courses. Even with these recent changes, the relationship that exists, and is anticipated, is not as direct as it was at one point in Scottish universities when students paid, literally, at the door of the lecture room, and the professor who could not attract or keep students felt this to his cost.

The issue of tuition fees paid directly by university students will be discussed at greater length in section 6. But both before and after their introduction, an alternative system of measuring educational value through student response was introduced — student course evaluation — opinion polls in short. There is much more to be said about these than would be appropriate in the present context. What is specially relevant here are some of the assumptions on which they are based.

Student course evaluation

The vast majority of universities now require their staff to issue questionnaires by means of which students may express their opinions on the courses of study they have taken. Opinion amongst academics differs as to the value of these, but it should be recorded that though the administrative burden of processing them tends to be mildly resented, they are resisted in principle by relatively few. Yet, as it seems to me, the assumptions on which these course evaluations rest are much more interesting and important than the mechanics of their deployment.

On what is a student to base his or her opinion of a course? The answer, I think, can only be subjective preference, not an estimation of objective worth. Why this is and why it matters are topics which take us to the heart of the confusions surrounding contemporary university education.

The provider of a consumer good has one main aim — to satisfy the pre-existent desire of the purchaser. Accordingly, the manufacturer of CDs, the inventor of computer games, the restaurateur, the purveyor of holidays, must satisfy the desires of consumers. This is not to deny that consumer demand can be created and consumers introduced to new forms of enjoyment. Still, if the desire to be satisfied is *mine*, I am sovereign in deciding what does and does not satisfy it. No doubt there are worthy and unworthy desires, but it is not the business of the supplier to discriminate along these lines, except as a matter of personal restriction. Those who aim at successfully supplying the desires of the consumer can, for their own reasons, draw the line at being a pornographer or a prostitute. Commercialism *as such* places no such restriction.

The point to focus on is the sovereignty of the consumer's desires and preferences. There is no place for producers setting out terms on which the goods they produce *ought* to be wanted or are *worth* wanting. Now the position is different where the relationship between giver and receiver is one between the expert and the inexpert. This is typically the case in education, but to see it most clearly we should first examine a case of non-academic education. One of the most valuable things that a modern teenager learns is the ability to drive. In the contemporary world, while being able to drive is not essential, it is nonetheless of enormous value, not just for personal convenience but for employment prospects as well. Interestingly, it is also the one instance of education which is governed almost entirely by market relations. The test of successful education in this case is not personal satisfaction with the manner or method of the instructor, but with success as a result of his or her instruction. The good driving instructor knows what needs to be learned and how it is to be learned effectively. This is just what the pupil does not know, and hence the exchange is one between the expert and the inexpert. Though no doubt it is better, and may be more efficient, if the pupil enjoys the lessons, this is not the acid test.

Instruction in driving is illuminating, it seems to me, if we want to think clearly about the relation between teacher and pupil. It has these two important features, however. It is practical, and the measure of its success is a relatively straightforward test. Neither of these features is so evident in other more complex examples, and not evident at all perhaps in the case of university education. But we can go some way towards bridging the gap between driving and, say, English literature, by considering an intermediate case, namely learning a musical instrument.

The pupil who first comes to the piano has practical abilities to learn. However boring they may be, scales and finger exercises, and those rather mechanical 'studies' which many first-rate composers have devised, are an essential part of mastering the techniques without which great works of music cannot be played. But this technical mastery is only a foundation. The main business of the music teacher lies elsewhere, partly in the development of musicality and partly in a knowledge of which pieces of music are most worth playing. It is essential to the relationship between pupil and teacher that the teacher knows what the pupil does not. Accordingly, though (children being what they are) success will come more easily if pupils are quickly enabled to play the music they like, the purpose is to bring them to the point of playing music that is *worth* playing and being able to tell which music this is. It is at this point that they pass beyond the mere mastery of technique and are given a musical education. One way of putting this is to say that it is not merely the musical abilities but musical *taste* of pupils which must be educated.

The idea of educated taste is unfashionable. Yet its necessity in music, and the arts more generally, is undeniable. No good music teacher would take the preferences of the elementary pupil as sovereign; they await formation, and this is a major part of their musical education. Consequently, the test of a good teacher, and of a good course of instruction, is not that pupils are pleased, or have their pre-existent preferences satisfied, but that they become good musicians. To be inducted into the world of music is certainly to be inducted into a world of pleasure and enjoyment (though in my view it is not only this). But it is also a matter of being taught *which* pieces of music are most worth enjoying, and which it is best to take pleasure in. The crucial point to be observed is that the pupil/teacher relationship is one in which it is the knowledge and expertise of the teacher, not the pupil, which is sovereign.

Is there any reason not to say the same of academic subjects? Students for whatever reason decide to study, philosophy say. But what philosophers are worth studying? By the nature of the case the novice student cannot say. I can, thanks to my own teachers, and my special aptitude for the subject. If this were not the case, why would I warrant the position of a recognized teacher of philosophy? It follows that the content of the curriculum and the conduct of courses are matters on which my opinion matters much more than the students. It would be foolish as well as arrogant to deny that student questionnaires can be useful. Anyone may be unaware of defects that create obstacles to learning, and soliciting student opinion may reveal these. At the same time, to treat them like surveys of customer satisfaction is a profound error. A student, reasonably, may find Kant tedious and difficult, and find Alain de Botton more to their liking. Nevertheless, it is in Kant that far greater intellectual worth lies, which is not a judgement they are in a position to make, but one which they need to be taught how to make.

However cogent this line of thought, the anxiety it gives rise to is that academics are once more licensed to teach whatever they like in whatever manner they like. The authority of the academic can be abused. In an effort to allay this anxiety, and to guard against those excesses and abuses of academic independence which have undoubtedly marred university education in the past, there has come into existence a system of review originally known as 'academic audit' whose major innovation was 'Teaching Quality Assessment' known by its initials TQA. This has gone through several forms, and the name has changed more than once. I shall use the term 'teaching review', and the merits and demerits of teaching review are topics that any adequate account of university education must address. Before doing so, however, there is a further feature of recent university reform which needs to be considered, namely the modularization of courses. Important in its own right though this is, its examination is specially pertinent here since it has come about in large part because of the interest in meeting student demand, the same interest which has generated course evaluation.

Modularization

In the last two decades of the twentieth century most British universities modularized their courses. The issue of greatest interest is whether this has, overall, been a good or a bad thing. But to address it, it is necessary first to say what modularization is and why it has come about. The first of these questions is easier to answer than the second.

Modularization is the breaking down of structured degree courses into distinct and separate components, which are then assembled by the student in accordance with rules of 'credit accumulation' such that at the end of a period of study the credits accumulated entitle the student to a degree. This system is one that has been in operation in the United States since the beginning of the twentieth century, where it was first introduced in Harvard, and was subsequently copied in Canada and Australia. It facilitates what has been dubbed a 'cafeteria' system. Just as in a cafeteria, as opposed to a restaurant with a set menu, customers choose items from the dishes available in whatever combination or order they may prefer, so in a modular system the student puts together a course of study in which he or she has an interest. The change to modularization that has taken place in many British universities is still not quite the 'cafeteria' system that is typical of North America, but it nonetheless incorporates several important shifts. Formerly, it was exclusively dons who decided the combinations of subjects and the order of their study which were deemed to make most academic sense. Under the older system, which still prevails in certain places, students were largely told what to study and in which order to study it, though broadly speaking the Scottish degree had greater variety and flexibility within it than the traditional English degree. With modularization, it has become the students who decide these questions.

The considerations previously adduced about teachers and students and their relative expertise and inexpertness imply that there is reason to support a system of study structured by academics rather than by students. After all it is the academics who know and the students who have still to learn. Why then should such a change take place? The explanatory reasons are hard to uncover. University teachers undoubtedly felt under pressure to make the change, though why they felt this is obscure since there were no explicit central directives, or indeed any central body that could make them. Some were for the change, many against, but a sense of its inevitability seemed to grip the collective consciousness of the teachers in a large number of institutions. It is hard to say why this came about, but since our primary purpose here is to explore its rationale, the historical causes are ones on which we need not speculate. The rationale, fortunately, is easier to state. Student interest should dictate the choice of subject.

It is worth observing that though in a way British universities in this respect have come to ape North America, arguably the underlying motivation is significantly different. The American system, at least in the most important universities, was dictated by the interests of professors, not students. The modular system allowed teachers to offer courses specially tailored to their research interests and academic enthusiasms. It was then up to the student to combine these in ways which would add up to a cogent degree. This overstates the case a little. North American universities have always been subject to consumer demand in a way that British universities have not. As a result of a cultural belief in the value of liberal education and an accommodation between the competing interests of student and teacher, a system resulted in the US, and Canada, which could not be replicated exactly in the UK. The fact is that history and tradition make a difference.

In the UK the modularization of courses was driven by the idea that the student is a customer whose requirements must be met. Flexibility was the watchword, but it may be questioned, in my view, just how important a determining factor the belief in the educational value of flexibility really was. What made the difference was anxiety about successful student recruitment. However this may be, the result is that the conception of student as customer has been substantially strengthened. It is not my purpose here to inveigh against modularization, even if there is reason to do so, but to observe that it has contributed substantially to the cogency of the language of commerce. University students are not only enabled, but encouraged, to pick and choose between the academic courses on offer as one chooses between the goods in a supermarket. The question is: Is this to their benefit? Or more precisely: Is this to the benefit of their education?

It should be evident that the answer is that it is unlikely to be. The root of the word 'education' carries the meaning of being led, and this implies a subservient relation between those who are being educated and those who are educating them. Some educational theorists have set themselves to deny this. They speak of university education as though it were a matter of mutual exploration, and they do this partly under the inspiration of a certain kind of egalitarianism, which regards with suspicion *any* talk of superior and inferior, and with it any conception of elitism. This egalitarianism is misplaced, and still recognised to be so in many contexts. Surgeons do not, and are not expected, to regard their students as their medical equals. Lawyers still trade upon special expertise. The same is true in sport and in music. The egalitarians suppose, I think, that claims to educational or intellectual superiority inevitably carry with them claims to moral, social or political superiority. Perhaps, in point of fact, they not infrequently do. This is a difficult matter to generalise about. But whatever unwarranted airs educational superiority may be inclined to give itself, it seems plain that teachers *ought* to be better at their subjects than pupils or students, or else their claims to be teachers are fraudulent. If education, at university or any other level, truly were a matter of mutual exploration between equal minds, why should some of those minds enjoy a salary and others not?

The fact is that university teachers either have superior knowledge and understanding to offer their students, or they have nothing. Student course evaluation may have its uses, and modularization may have brought advantages. It certainly seems that neither is likely to disappear in the immediate, or even intermediate, future. It is nevertheless the case that in large measure they both rely on and strengthen presuppositions about university education which, upon no very close examination, can be shown to be conceptually confused.

It would be misleading however to represent the present state of university education in Britain as though the conception of student as customer had carried all in its way. Despite the significant power shift which it has occasioned, it is still the case that within modules, and to a considerable extent within degree structures, the authority of the expert is the principal determinant. This autonomy in its turn is bolstered by the relative security of university teachers. Although tenure of position has been weakened in a number of ways, not least in changes in the law designed to end it, and though pseudo-commercial pressures have come to be felt as they have rarely been felt before, academics are still not subject to simple market forces in the way that the shopkeeper or the plumber is, and hence not really subject to the student as customer. For the most part their salaries are paid and their facilities provided by the public purse. This gives them a considerable measure of protection against the fluctuating fashions of student demand. Added to this is the fact that university teachers are not directly the employees of government bodies, as teachers in state schools are. The contemporary concern with accountability is such, however, this does not mean that within this protected sphere they are left alone to do as they think best. Alongside the 'checks' of

course evaluation and student demand there has come
into existence another form of scrutiny, namely peer
review. Both university education and university research
work are now regularly reviewed. The purpose of central,
Funding Council sponsored, peer review is to determine
whether what the tax payer is paying for is being done
properly. In this section it is the first that concerns us. The
precise form this has taken, and ought to take, has been
subject to change and dispute, first there was internal Academic Audit then external Teaching Quality Assessment,
and finally external Quality Assurance of internal audit
procedures.

Academic audit

The term 'academic audit' itself signals something of the
idea that has informed it, since it is an expression modeled
on commercial practice. What it means, broadly speaking,
is the introduction of systems of inspection that are
designed to ensure that the courses on offer in a university
all meet certain standards of acceptability. This way of
stating it is slightly misleading. It has never been the case,
except in rare and special cases, that individual academics
or departments have been free to offer to students whatever they wanted to offer. Before academic audit all British
universities (in contrast to some in America) had Boards of
Studies, or some equivalent, whose approval had to be
sought before new courses could be entered in the official
list of educational provision. The awarding of degrees was
subject to Boards of Examiners, usually including at least
one external examiner from another institution. Normally
these Boards were effectively committees of the Senate or
Academic Council, the governing academic body of the
university.

   The novelty of academic audit lies rather in its making
the system of approval much more formal and more uni-

form. The pursuit of uniformity has had two significant effects. The first is that academic audit does not concern itself directly with the intellectual *content* of courses, but with their form and presentation. The requirement is not that a course proposal should justify the intellectual worth of what it proposes to offer, but that it should meet general standards of a more abstract kind. Thus, courses have to set out clearly their educational aims and objectives, the ways in which these will be realised, the additional transferable skills they can be expected to secure for the students who take them, and the methods by which the attaining of these objectives is to be assessed. Generally, the effect of this attempt to 'audit' all courses uniformly has led to a high degree of abstraction because of the great variety of subjects to which it must be applied. In turn this has led to a somewhat superficial, and arguably fatuous, style of scrutiny. Thus a course in, say Harmony and Counterpoint, will meet the first of these requirements by stating that its objective is to teach students the elements of harmony and counterpoint. What else could its objective be? And is anything accomplished by requiring it to be formally stated? To the more telling question — is Harmony and Counterpoint worth teaching? — academic audit does not address itself.

There is reason for it not to do so. Academic freedom is to be prized greatly. Academic opinions tend to be held strongly. Standards of intellectual worth are themselves matters of genuine intellectual dispute. Consequently, to raise the deepest questions about intellectual worth is, usually, to open a hornets' nest, and one that very often admits of no practical resolution. Still, there are occasions on which it is just this question that needs to be asked. What matters about certain courses — sport science, post modernist literary theory, creationist biology, peace studies, hotel management are plausible examples in my view — is whether they have the intellectual substance that warrants a place in a university. This is not to say that they do not, only that the question can reasonably be asked of them, unlike long-standing subjects such as physics, philosophy, pure mathematics, or political history,

The effect of academic audit as it has been introduced is to leave no place for such questions to be raised. Any subject, in fact, could meet its requirements. Courses in astrology could state aims and objectives, methods of study and transferable skills, and could be assessed according to how they achieved them. The gross intellectual defects of astrology would not be revealed in this way. If this is correct, it implies that the system of academic audit is seriously inadequate with respect to the purposes of universities, and, I think, any educational enterprise. A large part of the reason for this is that academic audit is built upon a commercial model. Assessment of efficiency and productivity can be as easily applied to candy floss as to computers. Efficiency and productivity say nothing about intrinsic worth.

The second effect of academic audit is a huge increase in the multiplication of bureaucracy. To prove this would require the assembly of substantial empirical evidence. Here I shall simply assert it, though I think the experience of most academics would lead them to concur. But at any rate, it is true that academic audit does not include any audit of itself. And yet any rational human activity should include some assessment of relative cost and benefit. What has, as yet, not been adequately addressed is this question: has the introduction of academic audit reduced the number of poor courses? As I have suggested, there is an interpretation of 'poor', i.e. intellectually lightweight, which the system by its nature cannot assess. But even if we restrict ourselves to the more superficial measure of effectiveness, there is still a question whether the introduction of academic audit has done enough in this respect to outweigh its undoubted costs. If my claim of hugely increased bureaucracy is correct, then these costs have been great, and it would be difficult to show, in my opinion, that the corresponding benefits, which are not negligible, have outweighed them.

However, I think it would be true to say that academic audit was not introduced in an entirely disinterested spirit. A large part of its motivation was the belief that external review by the Funding Councils was inevitable and that putting such systems in place, if it did not forestall it, would at least demonstrate a willingness to comply. Academic audit was in effect, the forerunner to Teaching Quality Assessment, which was itself replaced by Quality Assurance, and then by Educational Enhancement.

Teaching Quality Assessment and its successors

How are we to assess whether the teaching of a subject is being adequately done? This is a matter, let it be acknowledged, which it is wholly proper for the custodians of public finance to raise. The answer that the Higher Education Funding Councils came to initially was this: ask other teachers. In short, institute peer review. What needs to be questioned is not whether they have any right to raise this question, but whether this is the appropriate, and an effective, way to address it. In the face of the sort of systems of teaching review that were employed through most of the 1990s and into the twenty-first century, the most important question to ask is whether *formal* institution of peer review is the right way to secure accountability. In my experience academics are almost obsessively self-critical as teachers. Long before TQA or QAA, there was constant review and assessment of teaching, motivated by the concerns of university teachers themselves. Even if it is unlikely to be believed by a sceptical reading public, the fact is that during my career as a university teacher (which started in 1975) there has never been a year in which I have not been involved in long, and often tedious, meetings whose sole purpose was to question the educational adequacy and intellectual relevance of courses on offer. This has been more true of undergraduate than postgraduate provision. Nevertheless, the image of the careless and indolent, not to say callous, academic which the popular images recorded in section 1 so entertainingly describe, is generally at odds with the truth. Certainly it has *some* basis in fact, but at best it is a caricature and for the most part a figment of the imagination. There have indeed been indifferent and careless teachers in universities, throughout their long history no doubt. Yet in what occupation is something of the same not the case? Careless and indifferent doctors, worldly priests, unscrupulous lawyers, corrupt policemen, fraudulent businessmen, bullying teachers, self-serving politicians are the stock in trade of literature and the other arts since the time of Chaucer. But that the type, and the attitude, not merely occur, but are so prevalent in any given occupation that it needs instituted, systematic, central, assessment, is an inference requiring substantial additional justification. In the case of British universities in the last hundred years it is, as I believe, lacking.

However, lacking or not, the most important (and most telling) question to ask is whether, as it has been instituted, teaching review performs a real and valuable service which works to the educational interests of students. Investigation of this question, I think, is a matter of effect not ideas. The idea of inter-university peer review is interesting, and there is no reason in the abstract to object to the suggestion that expert teachers from one institution (or a number of institutions), should be asked to look critically at the educational provision of another. It all depends how it works.

How has it worked? No straightforward answer can be given to this question because, as I have already noted, 'it'

has undergone almost continuous change over a decade. Teaching Quality Assessment (TQA) was replaced by Quality Assurance under the direction of a Quality Assurance Agency (QAA). Quality Assurance later collapsed partly under the weight of its own paperwork, partly because the results were so positive that they raised a doubt about its necessity, but chiefly because the system was so manifestly failing to secure the support, still less enthusiasm, of universities. In its place came continuous Enhancement Learned Institutional Review or ELIR, the latest acronym. Some of the essential elements of the earlier systems remain in ELIR since these continue to form the basis of the internal 'subject review' that ELIR requires.

In both TQA and QAA, 'subject review' — the examination and comparison of teaching provisions for specific subjects — was conducted on a nationwide basis. This system required departments to submit a document describing what they do and offering a 'self-assessment'. The panel of reviewers then made a short visit, of three days or so, during which classes were visited and staff, students and support staff were interviewed. There was an accompanying examination of prescribed documentation — reading lists, sample essays and exam scripts, student questionnaires, external examiners' reports etc. At the end of this process the assessing team was invited to award a rating on a large number of different aspects. These were summarised into a single grade that might be expressed linguistically — from unsatisfactory to excellent, say — or by a number — 1–5 in TQA, marks out of 24 in QAA. This grade was then made public. Such grades were, as a matter of fact, used extensively in the construction by the media of university league tables, and (where they were good enough) on the websites and promotional material put out by universities.

Now the first point to be made about any system wide method of assessment is that centralisation brings with it a large measure of standardisation. As in the case of academic audit this works against in-depth (and indeed accurate) assessment. Although there are shared educational objectives which can be stated in the abstract, in reality the degree of abstraction that is necessary obscures or ignores important differences between subjects and renders the application of these abstract criteria too remote to deliver meaningful and valuable judgements. How likely is it that, say, the teaching of building methods, biochemistry, and art history can be subject to the same criteria? Not very likely, reason suggests. If, in addition, the judgements are supposedly content indifferent and aimed at assessing, not the intellectual worth of the subject matter, but the degree to which the 'objectives' that different subjects and departments have set themselves are achieved, the resulting overall judgement tells us very little indeed, next to nothing in fact.

A further point of some importance is that the final grade, since it is very coarse-grained, can, and has usually, disguised real areas of merit. Thus the existence of good and talented teachers can be overshadowed by poor teaching rooms, below average computing facilities and less than adequate career advisory services. It is not that these should not be criticized. Rather, the overall assessment, to those who do not read the details, leaves a mistaken impression with respect to many features of the institution in question. QAA tried to get around this by allocating sets of points — up to four in six different aspects of provision. But these were universally aggregated so that they could be expressed as a single result for the purposes of institutional comparison, thereby rendering the new system just as course grained as the old.

A third and perhaps most important point is that the emphasis on documentation led to a culture in which a paper trail was more important than the thing itself. In a few extreme cases, the required paper was invented; minutes of staff/student consultative committees that had never been held, for example. But in the majority of cases, where there was no attempt to 'cheat', the need to produce a paper trail meant that huge amounts of time were spent on doing so, with the ironic result that teaching was reduced in order to allow time to prepare for 'the QAA'. In short, the seemingly reasonable suggestion that universities be held accountable for the quality of their teaching, rapidly led to a bureaucratic monster that was the enemy of time spent in the lecture hall and seminar room.

Finally — and this it was that finished off QAA — subject review revealed, what might have been surmised anyway, that most university courses in Britain are conscientiously taught, and that though there is room for improvement no doubt, there is little point in persisting with a cumbersome and costly system of regular inspection. Accordingly, the next phase was ushered in — Enhancement Led Institutional Review or ELIR — which aims to shift the focus from snapshot review, to institutional processes for 'quality enhancement'.

ELIR aims to incorporate some of the lessons learned from the systems that preceded it. First, it restores a large measure of importance to internal Academic Audit. Rather than review the educational provision of a given university in a given subject area, the idea of ELIR is to review the university's own system of review and identify the places where it needs 'strengthened'. However, this not only leaves internal teaching review in place, but powerfully re-inforces its institutionalization. Yet if external teaching review is flawed, the effect of its internalization must be to perpetuate those flaws. Second, the external system focusses on 'trouble shooting'. That is to say, in recognition of the pointlessness of scrutinizing a perfectly good institution, ELIR makes a welcome assumption that all is well unless periodic review (every six years) suggests that it is not. However, ever fearful of complacency, and haunted by the spectre of those slackers and idlers with which Amis, Sharpe and Bradbury had such fun, ELIR (as its name suggests) introduces a new element – continuous enhancement – the perpetual improvement of courses and teaching.

We might call this the 'no standing still' conception of excellence. It denies what otherwise we might suppose to be true – that like other things, if well constructed and well taught, university courses can reach a standard beyond which no further improvement can reasonably be expected. Or to be more accurate: such further improvements as might be possible would not be worth the additional effort put into achieving them; that the courses under review are, in short, as good as they can be for all practical purposes. Now as it seems to me, the 'no standing still' conception of excellence flies in the face of experience. Sometimes things are as good as we are going to get them, and to recognize this is not a matter of complacency but of realism. In fact, *continuous* enhancement may be an incoherent ideal. If we have realistic standards of what can be achieved, then we should be able to achieve them. To achieve them is to have done the best we can, in which case there is no scope for still further 'enhancement'. Of course, we could reasonably suppose this to be the case if what is at issue is not educational attainment, but customer satisfaction, and it is striking that in introducing Enhancement as a replacement for Quality Assurance, government ministers were quick to assert that student satisfaction would play an important part in its implementation. Indeed 'enhancing the student experience' is the catchphrase by which many initiatives in this new phase of teaching review are described. But this signals a shift from an educational to a consumerist conception of universities which I have already discussed under the heading of student course evaluation, as well as a shift beyond the laboratory and the lecture hall to the 'whole student experience'. In this case, regular teaching review should be supplemented with 'catering review', 'accommodation review', 'sporting review' etc. and something truly novel — 'administration review'.

It seems, then, that the developing sequence of academic audit, TQA, QAA and ELIR has probably not yet reached a satisfactory resting place, and at least something of the cost, inefficiency and misconception of earlier phases remains in the latest of these systems. In order to appreciate the force of this conclusion it is important to stress that nothing has been said here against the idea of assessment as such. Nor is it claimed that the world of universities before TQA, QAA and so on was perfect. The point is whether the huge amount of effort and considerable sum of money that has been spent on the introduction of formal systems of assessment, has been well spent. Just how much worse would an unregulated system be? To leave university teachers free to determine what is best for their students carries its risks certainly. There will be carelessness, inefficiency and indifference. Such things will never be eliminated entirely. The only interesting question is whether academic audit and teaching review have reduced them to a degree that warrants the costs in time and money that they themselves have incurred. I think that a dispassionate approach to them will conclude that they have not.

The same issue, not necessarily with the same result, arises with respect to the other main function of universities — research. But before this issue can be considered directly, we need to ask whether and why universities should be involved in research at all.

4. University research

Teaching students is not the only purpose of the contemporary university. Even if Newman were right in the abstract that the sole (or at any rate principal) purpose of a university is to provide for the education of students, his reflections on the nature of a university would still be at some remove from contemporary reality. This is because today's university teachers are committed to, and convinced of, the importance of scientific and academic research. They regard this, not just as an adjunct or a spin off, but as an essential part of their function. Indeed, the Robbins Report declared the dual purpose of the transmission and extension of knowledge to be fundamental to a university, and this has not been seriously called into question.

Whether or not it was right to do so seems to me an essentially idle question, since this is how things are, and consequently it is a question I shall not inquire into. It has this further importance. Even if the arguments of the preceding section, which aimed to elicit something distinctive about university education are deemed to fail, a secondary claim can be that university teachers, unlike those in other institutions, have a duty to extend knowledge and not merely to transmit it. However, any claim for the importance of research in universities raises a second issue about justification. A university that educates students can at least call upon the respect and resources of the society in which it exists: university *education* benefits those who undergo it and thus enriches society more generally. What claim does university *research* have to public support? This question can seem specially pressing when applied to the more esoteric subjects that academics inquire into. It may be granted that research in pharmacology benefits us all, but why is it a good thing if, for example, someone somewhere discovers how the Abbey at Bury St Edmunds was run in the time of the Abbot Samson? And why is historical research of this sort more appropriate to a university, and in general more valuable, than studying railway timetables or calculating the frequency of winning numbers in the National Lottery?

Pure and applied science

To answer these questions we should start with natural science. The reason for doing so is this. Whereas people find it hard to see just why the public purse (or any purse, perhaps) should support the investigations of, for instance, Egyptology, the grammar of Middle High German, or the anthropology of the Trobriand Islands, most people imagine that scientific inquiry is a good thing. This, as I hope to show, is an indefensible prejudice, but it is nonetheless real. Thus it is important, for rhetorical purposes, to begin with the case of science, and if we can make a case for the value of research in pure science, and extend this to the arts and social studies we will have established the value of intellectual research in general.

There is a familiar and widely employed distinction in natural science (and in the discussion of its public funding) between pure (or basic) research and applied research. This distinction reflects, I think, a further, underlying distinction between alternative explanations of the value of scientific inquiry, namely explanations by appeal to knowledge and to utility, an opposition we have already encountered in the discussion of the value of universities in general. It is a distinction needing to be examined more closely in the more specific context of scientific research.

According to this common way of thinking the value of pure or basic research lies in the furtherance of human knowledge for its own sake, whereas the value of applied research lies in its usefulness. There is no exclusiveness about this distinction, of course. Wherever we think the most cogent justification of science lies, we need not deny that basic research can turn up hypotheses which, in the future, prove to have been useful discoveries. James Clerk Maxwell's discovery of electromagnetism is a good example. It was not until sometime after his death that radio waves were exploited for practical purposes. Conversely, applied research can add substantially to our knowledge. Galileo's invention of the telescope had huge consequences for astronomy. But the *aim* of pure and applied research is different. In the former the knowledge we hope to gain is sought for its own sake, while in the latter it is sought for a further end.

This at least is how the generally accepted picture goes. But it does not take very much reflection to see that, at best, this view of the matter, familiar though it is, could only be part of the story. Consider first applied research. That its aim is utility is true. However, this is a truth that tells us very little. 'Utility' is a more abstract concept than is often supposed and when we appeal to something's utility we have not in fact said anything substantial about its value, until, that is, we have answered the question — 'Utility to what end?'. Here, everyday speech is somewhat misleading. 'Useful', as it is commonly meant, is a positively charged word; it is conversationally taken to mean 'useful for some good purpose'. Logically, however, a discovery is useful if it serves *any* purpose, good or otherwise. When people commend applied research they normally have in mind research which results in, for example, improved ways of promoting health, producing food, increasing the efficiency of transport or reducing the cost of communications. In short, the utility of applied research is tacitly associated with additions to the sum of human welfare (though we have no reason to restrict it to exclusively *human* welfare; utility explains the value of veterinary science). This tacit assumption closes the gap between utility and value because welfare is readily intelligible and widely accepted as a suitable goal both for scientific inquiry and for public support, the sort of goal, moreover, which is generally thought to require no further justification.

Whether it does or not — whether, that is to say, an increase in welfare always justifies the thing that produces it — is a question to which we shall have to return. For the moment the main point is to observe that the utility of applied research explains its value only and in so far as it is utility for some *good* end and not merely for some end. Applied research, in short, can be useful without by that fact alone being justified, because its usefulness may as easily be to harmful as to beneficial ends. Those who take a dim view of the arms industry would not deny that scientific research can develop better weapons, but they would deny that such research is for the general good.

Knowledge for its own sake

This contention about the normative emptiness of 'utility' is not a novel or even very surprising conclusion, but it has an implication other than that which it is sometimes believed to have. It is often thought that defending scientific inquiry on the basis of its usefulness is selling it short, because utility is an instrumental, not an intrinsic, value. The appeal to utility does not really explain the value of science *as such*, but only of the value of the *consequences* that scientific knowledge and inquiry may have. If true, this suggests that an adequate explanation of the value of science must locate the value in science *itself*. It is at this point that knowledge as opposed to utility enters the argument, because the further value to which any adequate justification of science must point is normally thought to be knowledge for its own sake.

The value of knowledge in and for itself is a point upon which Newman's argument in *The Idea of a University* turns. His defence is of 'knowledge as its own end'. Now although nothing said so far conflicts with Newman's contention, the claim that knowledge *in itself* is valuable is one which we need reason to make. Otherwise, it amounts to no more than a slogan. To accept that utility is not a complete explanation of the value of research, even where utility is in fact *served*, is to agree that there must be some other value involved which makes it usefulness *to a good end*. But what this value (or range of values) actually *is*, is a further issue. It can certainly be welfare, as the conversational implication of 'useful' generally assumes it to be, understanding welfare to mean, broadly, health, happiness and prosperity. What the argument so far has shown is this: we can mount a satisfactory explanation of the value of applied research, even if welfare is the only value that utility serves. However, while such an explanation does attribute value to the acquisition of knowledge as a means, it makes no appeal to its intrinsic value.

Now it follows from this that to demonstrate the insufficiency of pure utility, is *not* to show that the pursuit of knowledge for its own sake must enter the discussion. The promotion of welfare, human or animal, is an end logically sufficient for a complete explanation of its value. For all that has been said so far, it may be the only one. Why do we need to add knowledge to the calculation? It is all very well to *assert* the value of 'knowledge its own end' or to *declare* 'pure' research more fundamental to the scientific enterprise. But anyone persuaded that utility to the end of welfare is the best explanation of the value of research, is at liberty to argue that, since *only* the value of applied research could be explained in this way, the pursuit of pure or basic science which has no connexion with application cannot be lent any special value or importance, except perhaps in terms of the personal curiosity of the scientist. The point to stress is that the argument about the insufficiency of utility in the abstract does nothing to counteract this contention, because it is not an argument for the sufficiency of knowledge alone.

The value of knowledge

Popular opinion finds utilitarian justifications for the pursuit of knowledge attractive. They also appeal especially to those responsible for the public financing of scientific research, partly because of the ease with which an explanation in terms of general welfare can command public support. If scientific research can indeed be shown to contribute to an increase in the well-being of society as a whole, expenditure upon it is easy to defend. Scientists themselves are sometimes led to concur with this line of thought just because they acknowledge the same pressure for the sort of political justification which will win credibility in the competition for limited resources. Usually, however, whatever they may say by way of public defence of their work, personally they remain convinced of the importance of basic research. It is just that they do not know how to make this personal conviction publicly persuasive. Yet by harnessing the justification of pure research to that of applied research, they are making a concession that strikes many people, and not just scientists, as defective.

If the explanation of the value of pure research is that it will, eventually, through technical application, promote the goal of welfare, this has two implications, and neither of them seems satisfactory. First, it makes pure research secondary to applied research. This appears to be contrary to the essential character of science as an independent human endeavour, one of very ancient lineage indeed. Since the time of the ancient Greeks, knowledge of the natural world has been pursued for its own sake. Secondly, it implicitly admits that if we were ever to know, or at least be reasonably sure, that some piece of research would *not* lead to technological innovation, we could attribute no objective, socially defensible value to it. To put applicability at the heart of the defence of research is thus to declare that research which is useless (from the point of view of welfare) is valueless. We have already seen reason to doubt any identification of the valuable with the useful. The case against doing so may now be strengthened by the observation that a great deal of research in physics, astronomy and biology (amongst which we find theories commonly regarded as being amongst the greatest of scientific discoveries, those of Copernicus, Newton, Darwin and Einstein for instance), has no known practical application. This seems an odd and unfortunate implication.

Its odd and unfortunate character, however, does not render it false. A thoroughgoing utilitarian, concerned solely with public welfare, as many public policy makers are, can consistently maintain that only research which can be shown actually or with a reasonable probability to contribute usefully to welfare can be said to have value. (Those who are drawn to utilitarianism as a basis for social policy rather than a general approach to evaluation might restrict their conclusion to the claim that *public* expenditure can only be justified on useful science. Private donors can do as they wish, in accordance with their interests.) But even if this contention can be held consistently, it is one that scientists and many others feel strongly inclined to reject. They do so because intuitive conviction tells them that something essential is missing.

'Intuitive conviction' is sometimes a politer name for prejudice, of course, so whether this intuitive conviction is rationally defensible or not must be a legitimate subject for further discussion. This is the point of wondering if 'knowledge its own end' is anything more than a slogan. Nevertheless it is in the context of this further discussion that appeals to knowledge for its own sake are most often made. The scientific utilitarian's error, it is alleged, is to conflate the useful with the valuable (which has indeed been shown to be an error) and hence to ignore the value of knowledge for its own sake (which has yet to be shown). Now this response, which we have reason to think would be Newman's, is only half right, it seems to me. I have argued that it is certainly erroneous to suppose that nothing other than the useful is valuable, where by 'useful' we mean 'that which promotes welfare'. But it is equally mistaken to suppose that knowledge is always valuable. This is because it is easy to show that there can be genuine knowledge which is wholly worthless.

It is not hard to think of examples. There is a fact of the matter as to how many people listed in a telephone directory between, say, pages 171 and 294 have surnames beginning with the same letter as the street in which they live, and quite some time could be spent ascertaining this fact. But the knowledge that we came to possess as a result of doing so would be quite worthless and the time spent in gaining it completely wasted. This is because the knowledge we would acquire is not worth having. Nor is this a matter of the relatively pedestrian character of the inquiry. Suppose, to take another example, I am cutting grass. There is a fact of the matter as to how many blades of grass I cut in the space of five minutes and whether the rate at which I cut it falls in some regular proportion to the length of time I spend at the task increases. This is not a case for simple counting, and we can imagine sophisticated mathematical methods by which I might try to ascertain these facts. But the sophistication of the methods does not make the knowledge of these facts worth possessing. As this example shows, there can be worthless knowledge that only someone possessing considerable skill and displaying methodological imagination can arrive at; but it is still worthless.

If it is easy to think of such examples, however, it is equally easy to amend them in ways that give the worthless knowledge some value. Take the first example of the telephone directory. Imagine that an eccentric millionaire has established a large cash prize for the first person to come up with the answer. The knowledge that was formerly worthless has now become worth obtaining, if I obtain it quickly enough, and the use of my time in doing so has become a plausible investment of effort. Or, to take the second case, I may be engaged in some sort of cost-benefit analysis, aimed at helping me decide whether I would not be better to employ a gardener than to do the work myself. In this case the knowledge I seek is not worthless, but is, rather, information required for rational decision making.

These two emendations present slightly different cases. In the first, the connexion between the knowledge and the value of knowing it is a wholly fortuitous one. It happens that this detail about the telephone directory is worth knowing because someone has whimsically made it so — any other randomly chosen fact might have served as well. In the second, there is a more internal connexion; the knowledge is required by the particular decision in hand — an accurate cost-benefit analysis of my efforts at gardening requires knowledge about those efforts and not about any other randomly chosen fact. In both emendations, knowledge that was hitherto valueless, is given a value, by being put in a context. But in the second example the context lends significance to the knowledge in a less than wholly fortuitous way. It explains why *that* item of knowledge, as opposed to any other, was required.

This is a difference of some importance, and I shall return to it. But before doing so, for present purposes there is a feature of both examples that is worth noting. I have argued that the appeal to knowledge for its own sake as a justification of scientific endeavour is unsatisfactory because there is knowledge that is quite valueless. Any piece of valueless knowledge, however, may become valuable if we place it in an appropriate context. Thus the distinction between valueless and valuable knowledge is a distinction between contextless knowing and knowing within the context of some further purpose. In the examples given this further purpose turns out upon inquiry to be connected with welfare. In the first it is crudely so — monetary benefit — and in the second less crudely but no less obviously so — the minimization of wasted effort. What this shows is that where a resulting increase in knowledge is inadequate as a justification of research, the remedying of this inadequacy is most easily accomplished by a further appeal to welfare. But if so, we are back where we began; the appeal to knowledge has not allowed us escape from the primacy of applied research or the over-riding end of welfare promotion.

This is true only of these examples, of course. What they demonstrate is not the pre-eminent value of welfare, but that valuable knowledge requires a context in which it is sought. The examples chosen also show that this context may indeed be the promotion of welfare. But it need not be. We can readily think of other contexts that will do as well. Take for example, the pursuit of pleasure. Train spotters and cricket buffs accumulate large quantities of otherwise trivial and worthless fact in the pursuit of a hobby they enjoy. Taken in isolation what they know is of little significance, but they derive pleasure from the fact of knowing it, however odd this may seem to those who do not share their enthusiasms. Engaging in a hobby provides a relevant context in which knowledge comes to have value.

This sort of example may not be thought to advance the argument much. Should we not regard the pursuit of pleasure as an aspect of the promotion of welfare? I do not think that we should, because people can and frequently do pursue pleasure at the expense of their own welfare — the pleasure of drugs or sex, for example, may jeopardise their health or happiness. Persistent drug taking is most easily explained by the pursuit of pleasure over the promotion of health and well-being. However, I do not propose to argue this particular case in detail here. The very possibility of making a distinction between pleasure and welfare shows that attributing value to the acquisition of knowledge by locating it in the context of promoting welfare only proves that *some* such context is needed; it does not follow that welfare promotion is the only one. And if the pursuit of pleasure is not regarded as a convincingly distinct context, others are easily thought of. The administration of justice, for instance, is one such non-welfare alternative. 'Where was so-and-so on the night of the such-and-such?' is, in itself, a question of idle curiosity. It is transformed into a matter of consequence when the context in which it is asked is one concerned with punishing guilt and protecting innocence.

The argument so far has shown this, then. The distinction between pure and applied scientific research suggests that we should seek different explanations of their value. It is a common and tempting thought that while applied research is justified by its usefulness, the justification of pure scientific inquiry lies in the contribution it makes to human knowledge. But however tempting this thought may be, it is deficient in both particulars. On the one hand the utility of a discovery is not an adequate explanation of its value until we know what purpose its utility serves; research may be as useful to a bad as to a good end. On the other hand, since there can be genuine knowledge that is nonetheless trivial, the mere acquisition of knowledge is not an achievement unless it serves some larger purpose. What we have seen is that this larger purpose need not be the promotion of welfare, even if in the case of applied science it often is. There are other purposes which provide a context for knowledge that would otherwise be valueless. It is in these contexts that it takes on a value. The question now arises as to whether there is some such purpose which science in itself peculiarly serves and within which the knowledge produced by its inquiries is lent value.

Knowledge and understanding

There seems to me an obvious answer to this question, and one that I propose to explore and defend. This is the suggestion that pure science is not the acquisition of *knowledge* for its own sake, but rather the pursuit of *understanding*, within which the acquisition of knowledge has a central part to play.

It is not altogether easy to know how to defend the claim that understanding is valuable for its own sake. Here it will be useful to consider further the question I promised to return to, namely whether welfare can be considered valuable in its own right. This is because the same sort of difficulty arises for welfare as for understanding; it is a value so basic that it is difficult to establish a firmer ground upon which we might secure its justification.

At this point we can profitably turn, I think, to ancient classical ideas. Let us mean by welfare something like Aristotle's concept of *eudaemonia* or human flourishing. Within the Aristotelian scheme of thinking, human beings, like plants and other animals, have a nature which can flourish or be stunted, and the nature of a thing determines what its flourishing will consist in. So, just as some plants thrive where it is hot and dry, others thrive only where it is wet and cold. It is in this sense that we can speak of a plant's welfare and the conditions which help or hinder it. So too with animals, and with human beings. Poor diet, poor health, poor living conditions and poor human relationships prevent human beings from developing the potential that their natural aptitudes and capacities make possible. Human beings deprived of certain conditions end up physically and psychologically stunted. Conversely good diet, health and so on, allow them to flourish as human beings and can thus be regarded as important aspects of their welfare which there is reason to promote.

Aristotle's notion of *eudaemonia* has rather broader connotations than the modern concept of welfare which is its most obvious contemporary counterpart, and often its literal translation in fact. For us, welfare is primarily a matter of material, and to a lesser extent psychological, flourishing. To the modern mind health and prosperity are most readily thought of as constituent elements of welfare, though personal happiness (or psychological adjustment) is generally included as well. But Aristotle takes a fuller picture of human nature. He means to encompass the intellectual and the artistic no less than the material and the psychological. For Aristotle, a person whose mind is unextended and who has no artistic sensibility is no less stunted than someone who is physically disabled or psychologically disordered. We need not argue about the respective adequacy of these two conceptions, however, for there is no matter of real contention here. Even if we restrict the concept of welfare to the material and the psychological, as common contemporary usage does, we can allow that human beings have other aspects to their nature besides these — the life of the mind and of creative endeavour being obvious candidates. Once this truth is accepted, it follows that these other aspects of human nature also have their flourishing, or perhaps it would be best to say, in these respects too we can plausibly speak of excellences and ideals.

Aristotle himself gives the exercise of intelligence a central role in the development of a fully rounded human life, though there is some uncertainty amongst scholars over the interpretation of his thinking as to its precise role. Still, he distinguishes a number of different ways in which human intelligence may exhibit itself and for most of the *Nicomachean Ethics*, the central work in his exposition of these ideas, *phronesis* or practical intelligence seems to be the mental faculty that binds human virtues into a unity. At the end of this work (which probably consists in notes on, rather than the text of his lectures), it seems to be *theoria*, a more contemplative intelligence akin to pure intellectual inquiry, that is given pride of place as the crowning achievement of the life of the mind. We do not have to resolve this interpretative tension here, however. It is sufficient for present purposes to note the following implications of this Aristotelian way of thinking. First, even if we make welfare or happiness (in the more narrow modern sense) the supreme value, we thereby automatically attribute value to understanding. This is because we can only realize welfare in so far as we understand the nature of the things whose welfare it is. To fail to understand their nature is to be rendered incapable of promoting their good. We need to *know* about plants, for instance, in order to *make* them thrive. The goal of intelligence, therefore, is understanding. Secondly, though understanding has a crucial role to play in the promotion of welfare, it can also be found in forms independent of it. The mind can exercise itself in ways that do not contribute to material or psychological well-being. If such exercises are to be valued the reason cannot therefore lie in such a contribution. Where then does it lie?

The value of understanding

In answering this question it should first be repeated and emphasized that the life of the mind is as much a part of the nature of human beings as the life of the body or the emotions and *a priori*, that is, without illicit presupposition, there is just as much reason to value the full development of mind as of body or personality. To restrict the development of mind to its activity in the service of welfare seems a quite arbitrary limitation, consequently. Of course it is true that in endeavouring to arrive at and improve our understanding of the content and promotion of welfare we do indeed require extensive and sophisticated mental processes; modern technology (something to which we will return) is perhaps the most impressive demonstration of the extent to which practical reasoning is able not only to satisfy recurring human ends but also to widen human horizons about how those ends might be extended and integrated. The marvels of information technology are a good demonstration of this.

Still, impressive though the development of technology has been, the almost equally long-standing human project of understanding both the natural and the social world to the end not of increasing welfare but of reducing ignorance, confusion and misconception, is no less impressive an outcome of intellectual analysis, reflection and inquiry. It is in connexion with this second project that we find a context in which research that has no practical application, which is useless in the normal, everyday sense, may nevertheless have value, a context, that is to say, in which the acquisition of knowledge takes on the right sort of significance. If we take the promotion of welfare to be a justifiable end for human endeavour, on the grounds that welfare is to be understood as nothing other than a central part of human flourishing, we can equally well argue for the promotion of understanding, on the grounds that it too is an aspect of human flourishing. A concern with welfare is a concern to ameliorate the human condition from the point of view of suffering and hardship; a concern with understanding is a parallel concern to ameliorate the human condition from the point of view of ignorance and misunderstanding.

This could hardly be said to be a dramatic conclusion. Nor is it meant to be. Despite all the (necessary) effort that has been put into arriving at it, it is rather mundane. The point, however, has been to arrive at it as the result of an argument which, I think, has the following important feature. In public discussions of the respective value of science and technology, the defence of applied research is generally taken to be easy and the defence of pure research more difficult. This is because the connexion between

applied research and welfare is presupposed and its justi-
ficatory adequacy assumed, and because claims on behalf
of knowledge for its own sake have a less than convincing
ring. But once we ask for the ground upon which welfare is
to be valued, we arrive at an explanation in terms of
human flourishing from which a precisely parallel
defence of the value of understanding may be mounted.
The point to emphasize in this way of thinking is not so
much the conclusion that understanding is to be valued,
but that its value is to be explained, or perhaps more accurately, clarified, *in just the same way* that the value of welfare is. This means that, contrary to common opinion,
appeals to welfare enjoy no advantages over appeals to
understanding, and for this reason the defence of pure
inquiry need not be made subservient to the defence of
applied research.

The useful and the enriching

There is, perhaps, some point in reiterating here conclusions that were drawn in section 2. The argument of this
section, which purports to show that increases in understanding for its own sake are to be valued no less than
increases in economic prosperity, is sometimes thought
less than convincing because of a tendency to confuse the
concepts of prosperity and enrichment, concepts closely
allied to those of purchasing power and wealth creation.
Some of the points that were made in section 2 are worth
repeating. Let us agree that applied research is valuable
because it increases prosperity, at least potentially, and
that prosperity is a universally recognized good. People
are inclined to think of prosperity in terms of material
resources, and in many instances this is no doubt correct.
Yet it is not hard to see that the value of some material
resources lies in the further goods they are able to secure.
For example, while an increase in the supply and variety of

food may be a straightforward material benefit, improvements in methods of transport more often take their value from the existence of valuable places to go. Better roads and bridges are to be valued in large part because of the holiday resorts, sports centres, concert halls and so on that they enable us to travel to. On their own, in fact, they have very limited value. In this way, the value of such material benefits can often be seen to derive from the value of a non-material benefit, the composition and performance of music, for instance. To suppose otherwise is like supposing that the value of books lies primarily, not in their being items for intellectual appropriation, but in the fact that they generate employment in paper production and printing. The truth is the reverse; paper production and printing take their value from the interest that lies in books, magazines and newspapers.

Conversely, not all increases in strictly material prosperity can reasonably be regarded as real benefits, because here, as elsewhere, the law of diminishing marginal utility applies. The application of food science to produce a second flavour of potato crisp may be said to be the provision of a benefit, while its application to produce a thirty-second flavour can hardly be. The same can be said of more significant cases. The development of a drug for the alleviation of a serious illness is a great benefit; the development of a second drug whose sole advantage is marginally reduced side effects is much less obviously so.

It follows from both these considerations that increasing the material resources of a society is not the same as enriching it, and that the enrichment of society not only allows but requires the promotion of non-material ends. Scientific research, even if it serves no other end than the enhancement of human understanding, may therefore, along with art, sport and entertainment, play as important part in the enrichment of human life as does more 'practical' or utilitarian inquiry. More importantly, perhaps, it does so in an integral way. Whereas the justification of applied research requires reference to a further end before its utility can be said to be truly valuable, understanding enriches the life of the mind directly. The mind flourishes, we might say, in so far as it understands, and academic research is to be valued, therefore, in so far as it contributes to this understanding.

Research assessment

Though the relevant facts may be hard to amass, conceptually speaking the utilitarian assessment of applied research is relatively easy. Does it increase the stock of human welfare or not? The answer lies very largely in the satisfaction of consumer demand. But what about the pure research of scholars and scientists? The question here is whether human understanding has been increased and this is very much more difficult. How is it to be assessed? How are we to know whether the researches in which universities engage are genuine additions to human understanding? On the assumption that there is no real role for demand here, an assumption which we will consider a little later, the answer which has been arrived at by the University Funding Councils is 'research assessment'. As with the various forms by which the assessment of teaching has been attempted, research assessment is a system of peer review, and a proper estimation of its value, in my view, also turns on how it works in practice. As far as the *idea* of research assessment is concerned, there can hardly be an objection to exercises in which those who claim to be advancing human understanding with respect to some subject are required to convince the experts in that subject that an advance has indeed been made. There can hardly be any objection because this is precisely what happens anyway with submissions to academic journals and publishing houses. If I wish to have an essay enter the currency of the journals, I need to convince an expert editor that it is intellectually worthy enough to appear there. This is a parallel which we will find reason to consider further.

In short, although the term 'research assessment' is relatively recent, the practice is probably as old as academic publishing. What is new is the introduction of one off, standard, across the board, national assessment exercises for the purposes of distributing financial resources in support of academic research. What is most worth examining, therefore, is the *institutionalization* of research assessment in this form. Whether it is a good idea is not the main question therefore, but whether it really has secured greater accountability in this area of public expenditure, and ensured better value for money. This is, in the end, its purpose and sole rationale.

There have now been several such exercises and their results have had important consequences for the distribution of finance. However this is not our direct concern. To examine the merits of the system it should first be explained how it works. The rules have varied between different exercises, but the basic method is the same, and the Roberts Report in 2003 seems to have confirmed that the same broad pattern will continue indefinitely. Universities are required to list those members of staff who are 'research active'. Research activity is understood in terms of successful publication. For each member of research active staff a quantity of published material is submitted. This work is then subjected to the critical scrutiny of a panel of expert judges. The judges are required to decide how far the work submitted matches up to standards of national and international 'standing'. Depending on the proportion of staff for each subject in each institution meeting these standards a result is declared. For exercises up to that of 2001, this result took the form of a single grade, and it was upon this grade that the Funding Councils decided the level of financial support that was to be given to academic research in the institutions under review in proportion to the number of research active staff. From 2007, the result will take the form of a 'profile', and the translation of this profile into the allocation of funds has yet to be decided.

There is no doubt that British universities have taken these Research Assessment Exercises (RAEs) very seriously and continue to do so. The recruitment and rewarding of staff and the allocation of resources within universities have all been heavily influenced by the desire for improved RAE ratings. There is indeed good reason other than mere financial considerations for them to do so, since the measure of a university's success in terms of RAE grades has very largely determined its academic standing within the university system as a whole. Just which is cause and which is effect is difficult to assess here, however. It may be that RAE ratings are taken at face value, and intellectual status accorded in line with them. Alternatively, it may be that there is a sort of circularity. In the stock market a firm's share price can fall not so much because its balance sheet makes investors believe it is doing badly, but because investors believe that its balance sheet will make *others* believe it is doing badly. In a similar fashion, it may be that particular departments come to be held in high regard because everyone believes that everyone else believes that their high RAE rating will lead to this result.

If it is this second more complex relationship between RAE rating and academic standing which truly prevails, there is a danger that institutionalized RAE has the nature of a race in which no one believes, but in which everyone has reason to take part, and to do so vigorously and with the appearance of enthusiasm. This makes it all the more important, in my view, to attempt as impartial an examination as possible of its merits and demerits. To do so we

need to look first at its procedures and then at its consequences.

One thing to be said about RAE is that it is a snapshot
procedure. The quality of research is assessed according to
the staff in post at a certain date. For instance, one such
RAE took as its basis selected publications of academic
staff in post on the 31st March of the year in which the exercise took place. Now this permitted the following. Universities were able to recruit staff (with publications) very
shortly before this date, while the same staff, having been
given flexible contracts, were able to leave not long after,
in some cases even before the results of the assessment had
been announced. This had the consequence that the RAE
grade awarded was in part based upon work done elsewhere by people who only fleetingly belonged to the institution in question. In short, the published grade included
an estimation of people and publications that had very little to do with the institution whose grade it was. Of course,
something of this sort is possible with any snapshot procedure, and perhaps it cannot be avoided. The point of drawing attention to it, however, is to try to arrive at a true
estimation of RAE — just what does it tell us about the
institutions that are assessed?

A second procedural point is this. In an effort to avoid
crude estimation of worth in terms of mere *quantity*, RAEs
have come to rely upon judgements of *quality* by the
assessing panels. Together with division of labour within
panels, necessitated by the formidable size of the task, this
has meant that the grade awarded to any given institution
for any given subject has not infrequently rested heavily
(though never, as far as I know, exclusively) on the judgement of a single individual. Now as the editor of any academic journal knows, there can be radical differences of
genuinely held opinion between equally well qualified
referees over the intellectual worth of material submitted
for publication. These differences continue after publica-

tion of course — poor reviews are evidence of this possibility. And they may be expected to persist when the published material is used for the purposes of RAE. It follows that, while the desire to avoid an abject worship of quantity is commendable, reliance upon judgements of quality must give special authority to the opinions of some over others when there is good reason not to do so. The resulting system, in fact, is one in which academic worth is identified with *opinions about* worth. To see the error in this, consider again the case of academic journals. When an article is submitted, the editor, with the assistance of referees, must form a judgement about the worth of the piece, and on the strength of this judgement accept it or reject it. But though there can be good judges and bad, the opinion of even the best does not *determine* that an essay accepted for publication is intellectually substantial or important. Whether it is or not, is determined by its reception and influence in the wider world and the longer term. Editorial judgement is inescapable, but it does not *make* something good or bad.

If this is correct it follows that a proper process of research assessment would not consider the *content* of published work, but the *effect* of its publication on the subject to which it is a contribution. The trouble is that though there are some very clear cases in which this can be done — who could seriously deny that Darwin, Mendel, Einstein, Fleming, Namier, Leavis or Wittgenstein were major contributors to the growth of human understanding — to do so on a systematic regular nation-wide basis introduces a range of intangibles and imponderables that would render any clear outcome impossible.

An illustration of the difficulty involved in doing this is to be found in the use of citation indices, which have been deployed for similar purposes mostly in the United States, but in other places also. Citation indices record the number of times a book or published paper is referred to by other writers. The problem is that the counting of citations is indiscriminate. That is to say, they do not register the reasons for or the source of the citation. Consequently, a paper which is cited largely for the errors and misunderstandings it contains will appear as readily as one that is commended, and individuals and groups can inflate their appearance in the index by citing their own work. In principle these problems can be circumvented, but in practice the task of producing a count of 'quality' citations is almost impossible. In any case, there is the question of time-scale. A work which causes an immediate stir may, after a time, come to be regarded as of little lasting significance. Conversely, it may be some years before the value of truly pioneering research is recognized.

An even greater difficulty is this. Some highly influential intellectual work gets rapidly absorbed into its subject. This is specially true where its influence is chiefly on methods of study rather than by its results or conclusions. A good example of this is to be found in my own subject, philosophy. J.L. Austin, who taught in Oxford in the 1950s, published relatively little, but his influence over many years on how philosophy was studied — the so-called ordinary language method — was immense. I doubt if any citation index would reveal the extent of this influence because most of the papers and books which adopted his method did not expressly acknowledge the fact.

Finally, there is the phenomenon of the unpublished contribution to scholarship and scientific inquiry. Intellectual exchange is not limited to the printed page. Academics meet in conferences, special seminars, visitor programmes and the like. The important contributions that may be made to a subject on such occasions sometimes show up in footnotes and acknowledgments. More often, I would guess, they do not. Any measure of the intellectual worth which does not capture these, omits a highly significant factor in the growth and development of human understanding, and of course, measures which focus exclusively on publication or the citation of publication will not do so. To arrive at an accurate assessment of research we need to go beyond the printed page.

Recent versions of the RAE have tried to incorporate some of these other factors, and now, in addition to 'Research Outputs' (publications), 'Research Environment' (research grants obtained, research students recruited, etc.) and 'Esteem Indicators' (invitations to lecture, election to learned societies etc.) are accorded a percentage value in the overall assessment.

However, so many factors influence postgraduate students in the choice of where to study that it is difficult to see how any statistic of this sort could reveal much about the quality of research being undertaken. The appeal to success in research grant application as a mark of excellence is different, since these are usually awarded on a competitive basis. This raises the question, though, whether, given the doubts and difficulties I have raised about direct qualitative judgement, successful research grant application might not be a *better* standard, rather than simply an additional indicator. It is a topic I shall take up again later. For the moment, though, it is worth noting that figures on research students and research grants are referred to in the jargon of the RAE as 'minor volume indicators'. This in itself is significant, because it reflects an often unspoken assumption — that academic achievement is properly regarded as a kind of production.

The language of production

RAEs employ the concept of the 'research active' academic. This has been identified almost entirely with the concept of those who are 'productive' and in turn this is measured in terms of 'output', which is to say published books and papers. Nor is it uncommon for university reports to speak of their aims and purposes in terms of 'deliverables'. This is the natural language of industry, not of academia, of course, but its use has become widespread and its employment has a number of important consequences.

First, any system of assessment which places exclusive emphasis on published 'output' has no place for according merit to individuals who are truly masters of their subject but who do not commit their thoughts to print, or do so only rarely. This is an evident error. It would be absurd to deny that Socrates was a major figure in the philosophy of the ancient Greeks, yet it is only from Plato's published writings that we know this.

But it is not only the exclusion of contemporary Socrates that matters. Academics who keep up with their subject and who are truly expert cannot figure in such assessments. Yet they may be uniquely well placed to supervise postgraduate research and through that supervision contribute to the advancement of their subject. This has a double defect. First, if we really are concerned with whether public (or other) funds are being well used, we ought to know about such people, and a focus upon published output will not tell us. Secondly, a heavy or even exclusive emphasis on publication easily works against the judgement of the truly expert. Someone who is thoroughly versed in a subject may judge, with good reason, that the prospects of contributing something really novel to it are small and likely to be realized only occasionally. Professional judgement in these circumstances dictates that worthwhile publication will be relatively rare. A constant pressure to publish works against this better judgement.

The declared intention of RAEs to assess research in terms of quality rather than quantity is a commendable attempt to resist this pressure. But the pressure comes from several sources and not just official Research Assessment Exercises. One of these is individual career prospects. 'Publish or perish' has been a familiar maxim in the United States for some considerable time and has come to figure in British university life to a degree that was never previously the case. There are exceptions of course, but by and large, it is no longer enough for a British academic to be a good scholar, a conscientious teacher and an efficient administrator in order to secure promotion and advancement. It is also necessary to have published reasonably extensively. I have no doubt that this has come about in part as a reaction to an earlier condition in which universities were more or less a law unto themselves, where relatively little was demanded in the way of accountability and where, accordingly laziness and carelessness were unduly protected.

Just how rife these were is debatable. They were not, in my experience, as rife as the popular satires listed in section 1 make them out to be. But be this as it may, our interest here is not in the past, or with the justice of these complaints, or even with the principle of accountability. Let it be acknowledged that universities can reasonably be asked to justify public expenditure by promoting rich and energetic research work. The question then is: have the new conditions under which they operate brought it about that they do this?

It is difficult to answer this question decisively, but there is some reason to think that the emphasis on productivity and output is in fact *counter*productive. If so, however, it is in an especially interesting way, and one that throws a different light on the concept of accountability.

At one time the European Common Agricultural Policy gave rise to very large surpluses, familiarly known as the butter mountain, the wine lake and so on. Arguably, the pressure to publish has given rise a similar phenomenon which we might dub 'the book mountain'. There has been a huge (and still rising) increase in the number of academic books and journals. Interestingly, the explanation of this increase bears a similarity to its agricultural counterparts, namely an artificial gap between producer and consumer. In both cases a system has come about that creates incentives to producers that have little, if anything, to do with the demands of the consumer.

The growth in the number of academic books and periodicals has not come about because of rising demand from scholars and readers, or at least not primarily. It is a result of the relatively independent requirement that academics be 'productive' and the fact that their productivity is measured in 'output', which is to say, published books and essays.

The two incentives driving the supply side of this 'productivity' have already been noted, first, research assessment exercises, and second the fact that recognition and promotion within the universities is decided almost entirely on the number of publications an academic can list. Both have been exacerbated by research grant awarding bodies and commercial publishers. The awarding authorities want to see the results of scholarly and scientific inquiry issuing in a tangible form, and in the award of such grants, success promotes success. At the same time publishers are willing to produce tiny runs of books and periodicals since, to make the exercise profitable, it takes only a small number of libraries to subscribe at very high prices.

These conditions ensure that there is a large but hidden subsidy to academic 'output'. Academics are paid, in part, to write books and articles. Consequently, the financial return on the sales of the books themselves is not of any great moment. Any academic who makes money by writing regards this as a very welcome bonus; academics are not *required* to earn money by producing books in response to consumer demand. They are only required to write.

To a degree this is as it should be, of course. Many of the best academic books inevitably have slow sales and a very long shelf life, and many of the great academic presses were set up in recognition of this fact. But as incentives unrelated to demand have grown, the subsidizing of authors and publishers has now reached unprecedented levels. The result is that the proportion of books and articles making up this 'output' which virtually no one has any interest in reading almost certainly exceeds the number which enter the currency of academic inquiry. As a result they simply reside on library shelves.

There are at least two deleterious effects of this. First, genuine academic book buying has virtually collapsed. Since limited print runs push up prices considerably beyond the rate at which academic salaries have risen, there are few true consumers. Most purchases are made by means of recommendations to libraries. In contrast to individual purchase, it is relatively easy for academics to recommend that their libraries acquire new books and journals (though library budgets too are seriously stretched by the book mountain). However, these recommendations are generally based, not on a direct desire to read the recommended title, but on a more abstract idea of what the library 'ought' to have.

Second, even if most new titles could be, and were, purchased directly by potential readers, only a tiny proportion of what is produced could actually be read. There simply is too much. A strange condition has come about in which academics are writing hard, but reading only a very small proportion of the vast outpouring relevant to their subject. In the early 1990s it was estimated in philosophy, for instance, that *on average*, each journal article attracts about four readers. Since this was an average, it follows that very many articles are read only by editors and those who write them. We can obtain more accurate statistics in the era of on-line access to journals through *Ingenta* and the like, though of course these relate to visiting and down loading which may not always mean reading. But the emerging statistics from this source show that while many philosophy articles pick up more readers now, for the majority the number is very small indeed. It is an inevitable consequence of such a condition, that real and substantial contributions to knowledge stand a very high chance of disappearing without trace.

This emphasis on the tangible creates an indefensible preference for publication. There is no rationale to this, in my view. A published paper that attracts as few as four readers will be preferred to paper delivered to a conference before thirty expert listeners, whose author moreover, has the opportunity to engage in exchange and discussion. But if it is not published it does not enter the reckoning which RAEs and career advancement require. This is why it is common to try to publish conference proceedings even when it is unlikely that they will interest anyone who could not have chosen to go to the conference.

It is no longer enough that a university should have amongst its number scholars expert in a subject, who may or may not publish when they have something of special interest to say. The result is that supply hugely exceeds demand. Since anyone seeking advance, or even security, in the profession, must secure a national, or better international 'reputation', and the way to prove that this has been done is to be able to cite large numbers of published works, these works appear irrespective of the value of their publication to potential readers. This is not to say that most of what is published is worthless dross. Some of it may be, but most of it is probably of very high quality. The point is rather that the chance of genuine intellectual value surfacing in such a way as to make a difference to human knowledge and understanding in general is very seriously diminished.

If this is true, the conclusion to be drawn is that present trends have not actually served the interests of public accountability construed in terms of benefits being relative to costs. Money is well spent on the promotion of academic research if the result is that human knowledge and understanding is increased and enriched. The emphasis on 'output' and 'productivity' seems to serve this end because it requires tangible evidence. Influence and enrichment in this context, however, is essentially intangible (which is not to say inestimable), and the language of production, drawn as it is from the relatively alien context of commerce and industry, in fact works against it. The point is not that more means worse, though it may do, but that more means less, paradoxical though this may sound. The more books and papers that are produced, the less they contribute to the real enrichment of knowledge and understanding.

Research proposals

This leaves us with a question. How is intellectual enrichment to be assessed? How are we to know that money spent on intellectual research is money well spent? This is a question that can be raised by a private trust or donor, as much as by the state and the taxpayer. One alternative to RAE would be (in the jargon) to make one of the 'minor volume factors' the major criterion of assessment and make greater use of the system of competitive research proposals. The RAEs purpose is to provide a basis for the distribution of block grants to whole institutions for the continuing support of research in general. How it is distributed within universities is a matter for them. Many have in fact adopted small-scale schemes modelled along the same lines as the system used by the Research Councils (as opposed to the Funding Councils). This system aims to assess the merits of intellectual research not in retrospect and on the basis work already done, but in prospect, on the basis of research someone proposes to undertake. Under this alternative scheme, individuals and groups of researchers present research proposals which are scrutinized by experts, and sums of money, greatly varying in size, are awarded accordingly — for release from teaching and administrative commitments, the employment of assistants, the purchase of equipment, the cost of expeditions, and so on. Might such a scheme not be adopted in general such that all or almost all support for research took this form?

Its strengths are as follows. Under RAEs the assessment is based on work already done, while the funds it secures are for future research. There is of course no guarantee that future work will reach the same standards as past work, and hence no way of assuring that what is being paid for is in fact worth paying for. Under the system of research proposals, the work paid for is the work done, and past research figures, more intelligibly, as a guide to future success on the basis of a track record. Second, under this system the money awarded goes to the institutions where the work is done, thus avoiding some of the problems of the 'snapshot' nature of RAEs. Third, since research proposals have to be costed by those who will undertake the research, there is a closer, more easily monitored relation between reasonable cost and actual expenditure.

These strengths, many would argue, are more apparent than real, however. The most that can be judged in advance is the plausibility of the proposal. There is still no guarantee that the money will be well spent, that is, that in return for it there will be genuine intellectual enrichment or advance. Another objection is that reliance on track record inevitably weights the system against newcomers, whereas it is often the case that the best intellectual work is done by younger minds whom block grants more easily support. Third the system is cumbersome and expensive; the cost in terms of the administrative and academic time consumed by writing, processing and assessing research proposals is very great, much greater than a block grant system such as RAEs. But most importantly, as with RAEs, the idea itself is importantly flawed. Even if the monitoring of cost and expenditure is better under a proposals system, this is still far removed from the idea of getting value for money, because the value of the outcome cannot, by the nature of the case, be estimated in these terms. Modern scientific research is expensive and historical research is relatively cheap. But who is to say whether the pursuit of a deeper understanding of the Dead Sea Scrolls is more or less valuable than the pursuit of a deeper understanding of galaxy formation? The very idea of comparing them along these lines makes no sense in fact. Both are worthwhile because both are intellectually substantial issues whose significance derives from their relevance to long-standing traditions of inquiry. That is as far as we can go with the question of their value. Research proposals, it seems, are no better in the abstract or in their implementation than general research assessment.

When, as in this case, the conclusions are all negative, they give rise to an understandable impatience. Don't we need *some* system, however flawed, by which relatively scarce resources can be distributed in a reasonably intelligent and equitable way, albeit one which inevitably falls short, perhaps very far short, of the ideal? The question itself implies the answer 'Yes', and many will find in it sufficient licence to set on one side the conceptual issues with which the last few parts of this section have been concerned. What we have, and are likely to go on having, the argument runs, is a mix of RAEs by the Funding Councils and research proposal schemes administered by Research Councils and charitable trusts. The only interest, from a practical point of view, seems to be that these are run with reasonable administrative efficiency and subject to regular cost/benefit review.

While I am myself sympathetic to this retreat to the practical, it reveals, I think how far the present world of universities has come from an idea of the university which it is the principal purpose of this book to recover. Consider again the question: who is to say whether the pursuit of a deeper understanding of the Dead Sea Scrolls is more or less valuable than the pursuit of a deeper understanding of galaxy formation? One possible answer is — those who are *entrusted* with decisions of this sort. The same point can be made about the distribution of scarce resources. The best way to ensure that money is well spent is to leave the decision to those who have a serious commitment to the values its expenditure is intended to realize and the expertise to adjudicate between them. It is along these lines that Sports Councils, Arts Councils and the like are constituted.

In short, one way in which we might seek to ensure that public money on research is well spent is to allocate it through institutions that embody a serious commitment to intellectual values, and whose commitment in this respect is endorsed by the express desire of individuals to study in them and to seek the outcome of their activities. It is important to see that this possibility addresses the practical as well as the conceptual questions we have been discussing. The university as the institution of intellectual values is a conception that combines realism and idealism. The realism lies in the defects that we have detected in existing formal systems of assessment and research fund allocation, and the idealism lies in the intellectual values to which such an institution is committed by its nature and constitution.

This is, of course, a solution easily stated in the abstract. So stated it may indeed express an ideal, superior to the alternative mixed system the merits and demerits of which we have been examining. But its realism is less obvious.

How are we to know that it is realized in practice? The answer to this second question turns, I believe, on how universities are run, and how people come to study in them. These are the topics of the next two sections. We will then return to the first — the realism of the ideal — and ask how far something of this sort could be recovered and what recovering it would imply.

5. University management

If what has been said so far is correct we have uncovered good reason for a society to value institutions which are engaged in both university education and the pursuit of research. But how can we ensure that they perform these functions well? Though systems of central review have come into being and remain in place, the last section argued that in the face of their defects, an alternative answer to the need for accountability lies in the kind of institutions they are and how they are run. This brings us to the topic of university management.

Collegiality

The etymological root of the word 'college' implies a 'gathering together'. The dictionary defines a college as 'a society of persons joined together for a literary or scientific purpose'. Accordingly, collegiality is a form of governance by which decisions are taken collectively for the benefit of the society's purposes. Broadly speaking, collegiality in this sense marked the government of universities for a long time, which is why their governing bodies were generally made up of 'councils' of 'fellows', that is, bodies comprised of all those directly concerned with promoting their objectives.

Such bodies were invariably headed by rectors, presidents, provosts, or principals. It is worth noting that the express function of such people was not to act in an independent executive capacity, but to convene and to chair the collective decision making body. Of course, every human organization requires, and generates, those who lead and those who follow. Imagination, initiative and decisiveness are characteristics of some human beings and not of others. It is the imaginative and decisive who initiate and so set the pace and determine the course and character of development in all institutions and organizations. Because these are recurrent (if not abiding) features of human nature, there is a danger that favourable allusions to 'collegiality' and nostalgic references to its demise, draw upon a romantic rather than a realistic conception of the past. As a general truth, I am inclined to say, if there is no 'brave new world', equally there were no 'good old days'. Nevertheless, there *are* different understandings of how leadership and control fit into patterns of organization. These different understandings generate important differences in constitution, status and relationship, and some of these differences are reflected in the changed and changing character of university management.

Whatever the past may have been like, the contemporary position of universities, most of which have large operating budgets and considerable numbers of employees, is one in which it is plausible for provosts, principals and vice-chancellors to style themselves 'chief executives' (another borrowing from the world of commerce and industry) and to be concerned not merely with presiding over, but *running* the institutions they head. The difference is not merely one of designation; it signals a striking change in the understanding of their role.

Another important point of contrast between past and present is this. There were always bureaucratic tasks to be undertaken in the life of colleges and universities — the registration of students, the recording of graduation, the provision of accommodation and the keeping of accounts — tasks which fell, as it were, below the immediate concerns of the collegiate body. And so, from the earliest days, universities and colleges employed clerks and bursars, registrars and secretaries — administrators in short — whose business was with these more mundane matters. No doubt there were always some elements of what would nowadays be recognized as management, just as college councils always had their 'politics'. However, it is plausible to claim that the conduct of colleges and universities was generally understood to be divided between these two groups — those whose who decided the aims and objectives — the academics or fellows — and those who secured the effective means to them — the bursars or administrators. The lines were often blurred, of course, and it seems likely that this general understanding only imperfectly mirrored the reality. For all that, the recent period is marked by the emergence of another class in universities — self-conscious managers.

To understand this change something needs to be said about the *idea* of collegiality. Collegiality is a deeply egalitarian system of government. To be admitted as a fellow or member of a college was to be one amongst equals, charged with equal responsibility and bestowed with equal power for the approving of courses of study, awarding of degrees, maintenance of standards, provision of facilities and use of resources. Though the word is much overused nowadays, the permanent members of a traditional university comprised a *community* of scholars, originally sharing a communal existence as well as a common purpose. Within the ranks of the college there is no division between 'bosses' and 'workers'. The only 'workers' in the picture were the secretaries, cooks, gardeners, cleaners and so on which the college as a whole employed.

It was inevitable, perhaps, that as the life of universities became more complex, partly because of the involvement of the state, but also because of their internal growth, serious problems should arise for the workings of collegiality, but it is striking that the demise of this understanding in the universities of Britain is of very recent date. College councils and university senates were always subject to 'politicking' and the true distribution of power, it seems safe to say, was never as egalitarian as the ideal of collegiality implied. Those who are good at their subjects are not necessarily good at decision making, or manipulating decision making procedures. Conversely, those whose interest in their subject has faded somewhat may find other sources of stimulation in the intricacies of college life. Both facts made a difference to how university government worked in practice. Nevertheless, despite these natural tendencies and the growing complexity of the institutions, the idea of collegial government remained largely intact, and it is interesting to uncover the causes of its recent demise.

Necessarily this involves a good measure of speculation and surmise, but the following features seem to me especially pertinent. There is first the structural limitation of government by committee and its inability to respond speedily and flexibly to rapidly changed circumstances and moments of crisis. Even the most ardent defender of collegiality would have to admit that in British universities (and elsewhere no doubt) the multiplication of committees reached absurd proportions. Correspondingly, the conduct of their affairs took on a labyrinthine quality in which clear and fixed decisions on matters of policy were hard to arrive at. In relatively tranquil and generally favourable conditions this limitation, though often frustrating to those who must work within it, is not critical. It becomes critical when circumstances are less favourable. When, in the 1980s, British universities were faced with substantial cuts in government finance, universities were required to take major decisions, and the system of committee government militated against decisive action. Its intrinsic cumbersomeness was not its only problem. A committee can only arrive at firm decisions if there is some measure of a common mind. The problem with the 'crisis' of the 1980s was that it dispersed any common mind. It was, in short, divisive, and in these circumstances, the effect of committee government is to produce outcomes based on the lowest common denominator and on political fudge.

Still, this would not of itself explain the emergence of a different conception. At many periods in their chequered history, British universities have faced financial and other crises, and somehow staggered through them without any fundamental revision in the ideas underlying them. What made the difference in this case, in my view, was the dramatically altered social role in which they had been cast and the additional effects this had. Having been educational institutions they became competitive suppliers of education. It is in this alteration that origins of university management lie.

Institutions versus organizations

Between Oxford and Cambridge, since time beyond memory, there has been a measure of rivalry. This was not true, so far as I can tell, of the ancient Scottish universities, or was not true to any very marked extent, though to some degree they may have vied with each other. But rivalry is not competition. Rivals may do equally well. The success of one does not imply the failure of the other, and rivals may in fact spur each other to greater heights. The mark of competition, by contrast, is that, at some point or other the success of some of those taking part is won at the expense of others. This is most evident in sporting competitions. For one competitor to win, the others must lose. It is also evident in the market place. Markets grow, however, so contestants in a commercial market cannot be conceived of as engaged in what is known as a strictly zero-sum game.

The advertising campaigns of two car manufacturers, for example, may increase the total number of cars purchased. Consequently, the competition between two companies may be for market share, rather than absolute volume. Nevertheless market share is in the end a matter of volume, and at some point the more cars one manufacturer sells, the fewer the other succeeds in selling. A manufacturer who succeeds in selling too few, in the extreme case none at all, goes out of business.

Two considerations are forever salient in the world of commerce — keeping pace with consumer demand and minimizing the costs of supply. When consumers no longer want the kind of thing you manufacture, or when the costs of producing it exceed what they are willing to pay, you go out of business, unless subsidies or other distorting factors come into play. This has two further implications, both of which were mentioned in passing in section 3 where we considered the idea of student as consumer. The end which an industry serves is independent of those who serve it, and the principal constraint upon them is to find ever more efficient ways of serving it. This is not to deny that there is an important role in manufacture for innovation, design and promotion. The desires of consumers can to some degree be influenced by those who supply them. And of course design and innovation have central parts to play in the process of manufacture.

One way of characterizing this relationship between outcome and activity is to say that a manufacturing company is an organization, not an institution. The function of an organization is to supply an end, and the mark of its success is to supply it more extensively by means of greater efficiency. The function of an institution by contrast, is to fulfil a distinctive purpose, and the mark of its success lies in the manner rather than the degree to which it does this. For example, the institutions of justice — police, courts, prisons — cannot be judged in terms of pro-

ductivity, despite some recent, absurd attempts to think of them in this way. Policemen who make no arrests, courts which convict no one, and prisons that are empty, are not *necessarily* failures. In fact this might be the mark of their success. In the normal course of things it would be a mark of failure, certainly, but this is because we live in an imperfect world. A world in which there were no crimes, and hence no convictions or prisoners, *could* be one in which the effectiveness of policing and the impeccable justice system forestalled all inclination to criminality. Would-be criminals in such a world would know that they were certain to be caught and certain to be convicted. Conversely, no one who had *not* committed a crime would be convicted, and hence there would be no innocent people in prison either. Notice that in theory the same result — no criminals, no convictions — could be secured by a reign of state terror. The important difference is that though in such circumstances the same condition would obtain, it would have been achieved in the wrong way. But since the outcome in both is the same, the wrongness of the means cannot be characterized in terms of inefficiency.

The crimeless world is a fantasy, one in which we will never live, this side of the grave. But the very fact that it is conceivable is sufficient to illustrate one important conceptual difference between two sorts of social entity, a difference I have labelled with the terms 'organization' and 'institution'. It also serves to illustrate a feature of more likely worlds, that a diminishing number of arrests, convictions and imprisonment can on occasions be regarded as a measure of *success* in the administration of justice. By contrast, it could *never* be a mark of their success that shops had no sales and factories produced nothing. *Organizations* that are largely inactive, or have diminishing levels of activity, are failures. *Institutions* of which this is true may well be succeeding.

It is not difficult to find other examples of social institutions. Although it is the case that most modern legislatures pass more and more legislation, a Parliament might be successful just in so far as it was less productive in this respect, failing to pass most bills into law because it found them to be inappropriate or unnecessary. Arguably, in fact, greater legislative 'productivity' is not a mark of good government, but a sign of failure to govern well.

The administration of justice and the manufacture of cars fall clearly on one side and the other if we differentiate between institutions and organizations in the way I have done. It is not a distinction that is always easy to apply, however. Consider for example the Christian Church. On the one hand, the *manner* in which it conducts its business is everything; there is no (religious) point in winning converts or boosting the numbers of worshippers by means of payment, the promise of political advantage, or social respectability, though all of these have played their part in the Church's history from time to time. On the other hand, an important part of its mission is to 'win souls for Christ' and if no souls are won, or the number is dropping steadily, this has to be cause for concern. Full churches are no guarantee of success — it depends how they came to be full — but empty ones are indeed marks of failure. The Church, it seems, has a dual nature at least with respect to the terms we have been employing. This 'mixed' character is found elsewhere. Take the case of a health service. Does it efficiently make more people well? This is obviously a relevant question. At the same time, its productivity depends upon there being sick people, and this is not something we want to see on the increase. It follows that we cannot operate with a simple notion of productivity. What now of universities? Are they organizations, or institutions, or some mixture of the two?

Administration versus management

The distinction between organizations and institutions is obviously not exhaustive. Nor is it intended to be, but it helps, I think, to provide a framework within which to think about some important issues in which contemporary universities are embroiled. There is a case to be made for the claim that mediaeval and early modern universities were, in my sense, institutions not organizations. Their function was to promote certain purposes, not to supply a demand. Their students were not customers and their fellows were not suppliers. This, though plausible, is in my view too simple an account of their position, because they functioned in the wider context of the church and legal system both of which did make extraneous demands upon the universities. However this may be, it is evident that in the twentieth century the position is radically altered. It may be still be wrong, or at least seriously misleading, to think of students as customers (though there *is* something more to be said about this shortly), but there is a customer, namely the government. Central government sees itself, and is seen by the public, as at least in large part the purchaser of a good — higher education — and accordingly universities are seen as more or less efficient suppliers of it. This change has come about because, rightly or wrongly, governments are believed to have the duty to secure a population sufficiently educated to provide the high level of prosperity that any modern economy is expected to achieve, and this includes tertiary no less than primary and secondary education. It is this change in perception which alone makes sense of familiar remarks about providing Britain (or Ireland or India or wherever) with the skilled personnel it requires to compete in the world of the twenty-first century. From the 1920s on governments have increasingly been thought of as not merely supporting, but *investing in* universities. The difference is crucial to understanding the change that has come about. Moreover, the return from this investment is believed to depend to a considerable degree on increased participation levels, hence the dramatic expansion in the number of institutions and the numbers of people attending them. The huge scale of this expansion is not always appreciated. As recently as 1945 only 2.5% of the relevant age group went to university in the UK. By 1995 it was well over 30%.

Not surprisingly this has had a number of important consequences. First, universities are now very large institutions responsible for the expenditure of equally large sums of money. Second, with this increase in scale, and its near total dependence on government finance, a much more strenuous attention to public accountability is only to be expected. But third, and most important, universities *are* now competitors and not merely rivals. Competition exists at two levels. Since the resources of the state are not unlimited, there is competition for government finance, albeit one mediated through the Funding and Research Councils, a competition which is itself conditioned by the existence of other major claimants on the public purse. Furthermore, however, and somewhat oddly perhaps, as the level of participation has risen there is competition for students. There are now so many universities so completely dependent on student finance in one way or another, that the flourishing, if not the survival, of almost all depends upon their attracting and retaining students, and this competition is exacerbated by changing population structure. Accordingly, there is a range of decisions to be made that did not have to be made before — how to pursue and promote the successful and not merely the worthwhile, how best to distribute a large recurrent, but varying, income, how to manage extensive portfolios of property and equipment, and how to oversee long lists of employees of very varied kinds. In their turn these questions generate a need for marketing, personnel management including hiring and firing, and a conception of corporate responsibility which, if not in itself new, is greatly altered.

One way of putting this is to say that universities have become big business. The limitations on this way of speaking are yet to be explored, but it is easy to see that it has sufficient substance to render the old model of collegial government served by administrators outmoded, and this explains the move from administration to management.

It was for this reason and in this spirit that the Jarrett review of university administration was undertaken in 1985, commissioned not by government but by the universities themselves. Jarrett recommended wider use of 'on-line' management, modelled in good measure on contemporary business practice, or what was believed to be business practice. Following its recommendations major changes were set in train. The import of these changes cannot be outlined completely, because, in my view, not enough time has yet elapsed for them to be assessed fully. What they plainly did do, however, was to conflate the hitherto broadly distinct classes of academic and administrator. Formerly university employees could be divided into two almost exclusive classes — those who were academics full time and whose role in running affairs was restricted to meetings, and those who were full time administrators (or other functionaries), charged with carrying out the policies and procedures determined by committees of academics. There now came into being a class of people who were academics by education and background, but who were seconded full time, sometimes for limited periods sometimes permanently, to manage.

Such academic managers were the pattern in North America long before they came to prominence in Britain. Their emergence has coincided with — perhaps it has caused — an increasing use of the language of business in the conduct of universities. Universities now issue 'mission statements' according to which their role is to 'deliver' education, they engage in 'strategic planning', adopt 'logos' in an attempt to create a 'corporate image', 'market' their 'products' and issue glossy annual reports in the same way that banks, insurance companies or airlines do. It is also true that in the discussion of terms and conditions, and especially rates of pay for academics as well as all the other ranks of employees, principals and vice-chancellors have come to be referred to (though to a lesser degree actually thought of) as 'the employers'. The Association of University Teachers (AUT), unlike the Law Society or the British Medical Association, has become a union, affiliated to the TUC. Even the application and review of academic standards has been affected, as we saw earlier, with the introduction of 'audit'. All these are ways of thinking and speaking which were alien and would have been universally regarded as quite out of place only a very short time ago.

To reach a judicious assessment of the merits and demerits of this change is a difficult matter. Because the language of business is still alien to many of those teaching in universities, it attracts a measure of ridicule and resentment from them. Others, who believe themselves to be more abreast of the radically altered world of the university and who have taken more readily to the new form of management, have adopted the new ways of speaking and thinking with almost slavish enthusiasm. These two responses tend to exhaust the field, and leave little scope for any 'on the one hand this, on the other that' approach. Yet, as I shall argue, it is only this measured approach that will allow us *both* to take full account of altered circumstances *and* to continue to pursue those purposes which alone can make sense of the university as a distinctively valuable idea.

The corporate image

How far is the language of business appropriate to a modern university? It is hard to answer this question dispassionately because the presence of much of it in university reports and proposals seems to owe its appearance to a quite uncritical attitude to its appropriateness, and an indifference to its cumbersome ugliness. Ugly and unhelpful language is found in many places of course — social work and psychiatry are notable examples perhaps — but such critical indifference to its use is unquestionably a fault on the part of academics and educationalists, and properly declared to be so. The truth of this does not mean, however, that the adoption of new ways of speaking and writing is not a genuine indication of a necessary change, and it is the necessity of this change, rather than more superficial questions of style, into which it is most important to inquire.

Certain facts seem to me incontestable. The modern university is large and does require structures and mechanisms for the effective pursuit of its affairs and for the successful management of a great many personnel, structures that older and smaller universities did not need. Furthermore, it has to compete for state finance and for students as units of resource. Its success in this is probably assisted by a more professional approach to publicity and public relations than was hitherto the case. There are saleable skills and facilities which can find buyers beyond the world of education strictly conceived — hence the conference, catering and holiday markets in which many universities now engage, some (though by no means all) very profitably. These are genuinely business pursuits, whose profits can contribute significantly if not substantially to the central purposes of the university. It is perfectly acceptable, therefore, that they should be run along business lines, and this may require a measure of consequent change in other parts of a university's organization.

However, these facts do nothing to support the much more ambitious contention that universities are themselves businesses. Important social and economic changes have brought it about that much of the style of the modern British university, both of management and presentation, is appropriately modelled on commerce and industry. To deny that this is so, it seems to me, is indeed to fly in the face of reality, an accusation that can reasonably be levelled at some academic critics of recent developments. The crucial mistake which many of their opponents make, on the other hand, is to think that the spirit of commerce and industry should, or could, enter into the conception of its principal purpose as well, that, so to speak, the heart of the university must itself be adapted to the corporate image.

To see that this is a mistake, we have only to rehearse another set of incontestable facts, several of which have been mentioned in previous sections. Education and research are not valuable solely for the material benefits they may bring; man cannot live by bread alone, or at least it would be a much poorer life in which we wanted or were required to. Educational accomplishment cannot be measured in any straightforwardly quantitative way. It is not a 'product' as some other things are. The value of different educational accomplishments is incommensurable. It makes no sense to try to compare advances in cosmological theory with more subtle literary criticism or improvements in surgical procedures. There is no balance in which the value of a Newton can be set against the value of a Wittgenstein. In education the 'customer' is never king. Students need not only to learn, but to be taught what is worth learning. They are thus not the equal of their teachers, and their teachers, or the institutions in which they work, do not 'serve' the needs or desires of students in any plain meaning of the word. Government policy cannot settle which intellectual avenues are promising and which are not; only intellectuals who are free to engage actively in their subjects can do this. And so on.

Because parallel observations to these cannot be made for manufacturing or insurance, there is solid reason to conclude that, while it is wrong to refuse to adopt it at all, it is also profoundly mistaken to go too far in applying the language and practice of commerce and industry to the conduct of universities. Such a modest conclusion, I imagine, would find few detractors. This is because it leaves unanswered the critical question — how far is too far? — and plausible answers to this question will surely vary from context to context. There is one place however where a general line can be drawn with reasonable clarity, and this relates to the topic of the present section — university management.

Workers and bosses

Whatever steps may be taken to blur it, or to ameliorate the strife it can give rise too, most businesses embody the distinction between bosses and workers. In the Victorian period, in which Marx wrote, the bosses were usually also the owners. An important change between then and now (one which has serious implications for Marxist theory in my opinion), is that the identification of bosses with owners has more or less ended, thanks in large part to the enormous expansion of institutional stock holders. Today, for almost any business of any size (though there are notable exceptions), it is the managers not the owners per se who are the bosses, though it is common for senior managers to hold shares in the company they manage. That is to say, it is managers who take all the most important decisions about how the business is run, including the power of hiring and firing, promotion and demotion. They also determine its aims and direction and hence its success or failure. Economists and others have done a lot of interesting work on co-operative enterprise and the social market, but whatever is to be said about the desirability and practicability of these in theory, it is a fact that they form a very small part of contemporary commerce and industry, the organization of which is still structured mainly around this fundamental division.

Modern management is partly a matter of style. It is chiefly this part that the shift from administration to management in universities has copied. A different, more substantial question is this: should university managers also be viewed as bosses? It is worth observing that in answer to it, contemporary realities send mixed signals. Most universities are now headed by 'executives' or 'senior management groups' comprising the principal or vice-chancellor and his (or her) most senior assistants, and these are bodies with great decision making powers. On the other hand there are still Councils, Courts and Senates with some form of representative composition in whom the ultimate authority resides, in theory at least. Although academic tenure was ended by law in the late 1980s and it is now possible for any university management to institute redundancies on grounds of financial exigency alone, in reality those university academics who have permanent contracts enjoy a security of employment very rare in twenty-first-century Britain. The distribution of financial resources within universities takes much more account of income generation than it used to, and there is a substantial measure of devolved financial responsibility and accountability. But 'profit and loss' do not in fact have the immediate or even intermediate effects they would have elsewhere.

One oddity of the present position is that on those rare occasions when academics, frustrated by negotiations over pay and conditions, have taken 'industrial action' it is quite unclear against whom this industrial action is taken, because those represented as being on the other side — the principals and vice-chancellors — are in fact equally members and employees of the same institutions, as well as being eligible, and in many cases actual, members of the union (AUT) which called the strike or work to rule. The important point, I think, is that it is difficult to see just how this oddity might be straightened out.

It reveals in fact, something of the truly dual nature of the 'academic manager', especially where the 'managers' are seconded as managers only for a period, as the Rectors of Nordic universities are (though this is changing). Even in those cases (increasing in number) where university heads and deans of faculties are appointed from a non-academic background, academic managers do not in fact stand in relation to teaching academics as bosses to workers, and it is hard to see how they could. This is because, however much they may control the use of resources, they cannot control production. University managers are not able to determine the value or consequence of a university's 'production' any more than anyone else because of the nature of that production. Moreover, in so far as they are academics themselves, they are committed to the maintenance of a regime of intellectual freedom that works against any idea of such control. The activity and the success of a university depends directly on its academic 'workers' in a way that is not true of commerce and industry. Consequently, the only intelligible role of those who manage its resources, and its personnel for that matter, is not to *direct* this activity, but to *support* it.

It is not important that this be shown to be a characteristic peculiar to universities. Almost certainly it is not. The same thing can be said of other types of institution. But it is a salient difference between universities and manufacturing or service industries. Moreover it sheds a different light on management in universities, which must be more continuous with the older style of administration than innovative differences in style might suggest. Universities nowadays are involved in competition in a way in which they were not formerly, but the application of the language and practice of business is significantly limited by the fact that this competition does not take the form of producing and selling commensurable goods in a single market. Universities can flourish or flounder, but not by better meeting the needs or the desires of the consumer. This is not how it is, nor could it be.

There is no denying, however, that universities have to be paid for, and that in some way or other the opportunities and advantages they offer must match the resources they consume. Here too, but at a different level, there is competition, the competition between universities and other calls upon the public purse, and between the alternative forms of expenditure which the individuals who study in them must forego. To examine the questions this observation raises, however, requires us to move away from issues relating to the internal workings of universities and consider them in a larger social context. In particular it requires us to ask how, in general, universities are to be financed. This is the topic of the next section.

6. Financing the system

Universal access

One of the four main aims for British universities espoused by the Robbins Report was that they should offer the opportunity for personal development to all those who had the ability to benefit. This was taken to imply that the benefits of university education should not be confined to those who were able to pay for it. Intellectual aptitude, as measured by examination passes required for university entrance, was to be the sole criterion of admission. Thus it was that a generous system of student support came into existence. The local authority in whose area a student resided was obliged to pay his or her tuition fee, though this was largely an administrative matter, since the local authorities reclaimed the cost from central government. Alongside this, students were awarded maintenance grants. These were means tested against the income of the student's parents, but even so a good proportion of students received 'full' grants, that is, grants sufficient to support them through university without additional parental assistance. Before this system of grants was introduced, students, with or without the assistance of their parents, had paid their own way through university. In the older universities bursaries were available and endowments accumulated over time met a considerable part of salary and running costs. Students could also make application to educational trusts and charities of various kinds, of which a great many existed. However, even with the existence of bursaries, scholarships and endowments, a good part of the cost of university education fell on the individual student, and correspondingly a sizeable proportion of the cost of running universities came directly from those who studied in them.

The idea of grants and bursaries that would enable relatively poor students to devote themselves to study is an old one. In the mid-fifteenth century, for instance, the first students to attend St Salvator's College in the University of St Andrews were choristers who received scholarships in return for a duty to sing at masses for the repose of the soul of the founder. Many other scholarships with different provisions were established over the years, as indeed they were at all the ancient universities. The early existence of bursaries is not surprising. It is a fact that serious study is incompatible with regular work, and in a world in which those who do not work cannot live, special provision must be made to enable some to devote themselves to study.

The creation of many new universities following the Robbins report brought into existence a large number of universities which had neither bursaries nor endowments. This meant that the realization of the ideal of universal access — higher education without financial restriction — required that the state should pay almost all of the cost of tuition, student maintenance, capital expenditure and overheads. One consequent effect was that existing systems of bursaries withered away. It was not that they disappeared so much as that they ceased to make a serious contribution to the cost of education. Since every student could expect free tuition and some measure of assistance with living costs, bursaries no longer played an essential role. The result was that their real value shrank to the sorts of sum more appropriate to academic prizes. Another casualty of state funded study was the expectation that the cost of education would have to be met by parents, or by earnings through part-time and casual employment. This expectation has continued to play an important part in the United States, but in Britain it ceased to figure as a consideration for those contemplating university study.

While the absolute number of students attending universities remained fairly low, this generous system of support was manageable within the public purse. Few other countries have offered anything similar. On the continent of Europe university tuition has generally been free, but with far larger numbers the quality of provision has been less satisfactory for the individual student. (This is one of the factors that has led to a major imbalance in the movement of students between Britain and the rest of the European Union under ERASMUS and similar schemes. There are far more students from France, Italy, Germany and Greece and Spain studying in Britain, than there are British students studying in these other countries.) In the United States, a college education is cheap at less good institutions, and at better institutions substantial philanthropic support offers fee support to large numbers of poorer students. In Britain, post-Robbins, relatively small numbers of students from poor backgrounds with good school qualifications were exceptionally well provided for.

The attempt to reduce state spending in general which was undertaken in the 1980s meant less money for university education along with everything else, but it was not this so much as its subsequent huge expansion which threw the system into financial crisis. The fact that tax revenues are necessarily limited means no government can support a system of funding, whether of health, social security, defence, legal aid or education, that requires virtually unlimited expenditure. It was possible to give wholesale financial support to a highly selective higher education system such as existed in the 25 years following Robbins. With the arrival of a mass system of education, this was no longer a possibility. The question, despite the wishful thinking of many academics and some politicians, is not how it can be restored, but how it can be replaced, and what restrictions and requirements should be put upon its replacement.

Other systems exist in many parts of the world. These include direct tuition fees with and without subsidized loans, a graduate tax, the injection of private capital, competitive allocation of tax revenues. The elements of some of these were always present and have come to greater prominence in Britain also, and after extended and often heated debate, both the Scottish Parliament and Westminster have approved the charging of tuition fees direct to students, though in different amounts and in different ways.

All methods of financing systems of mass higher education have their difficulties. Their practical merits have been subject to close scrutiny and the issues surrounding them are complex. The purpose of this section is not to examine these various schemes afresh but to explore some of the background ideas and presuppositions against which their pros and cons are normally measured. Chief among these is the principle of universal access. This was a notable part of the Robbins report, but 40 years on it is an idea that finds widespread support among people who have never heard of Robbins, and far beyond the confines of Britain. A first necessary step in assessing it, however, is to clarify what it means, or more accurately, what it might mean.

At first sight this seems fairly plain. Universal access means that everyone who has the ability to undertake a course of higher education should be able to do so, and should not be prevented from doing so by lack of financial resources. Hidden in this principle, of course, is an uncertainty over what is meant by 'ability'. Universal access does not mean open access. There are university systems which lay down no conditions of entry whatever. Anyone can enrol, and if they pass the examinations and tests required by the courses they take and accumulate the necessary credits, they graduate with a degree or other qualification. This is true for the most part on the continent of Europe and for state universities in North America. Until the late nineteenth century it was true of Scottish universities, but with the exception of the Open University, for well over a hundred years has not been the case in Britain, where all universities have, in theory at least, laid down academic requirements for entry. Universal access does not mean open to everyone, but open to anyone with the right qualifications.

Academic entry requirements can be higher or lower, and have as a matter of fact varied very considerably even between subjects and faculties within the same university. Moreover, in so far as they are measured in terms of high school examination passes, there is further scope for variation, because the standards of these examining boards are known to fluctuate. If the academic entry standard is high enough, and perhaps as high as it ought to be, very many school leavers will not qualify. Universal access is thus something of a misnomer. It means universal access within a limited (i.e. non-universal) ability group.

There is a further feature of the Robbins principle to be considered. The provision of financial resources for the purposes of study is not the same as compensation for financial burdens associated with it. In fact, there is always at least one such burden, namely opportunity cost. In a vigorous economy with high employment, anyone who opts out of the labour market in order to study is foregoing potential earnings. Where these are appreciable, the financial burden of study is accordingly large. Opportunity cost is not a consideration that weighs very much with contemporary students, for two reasons. Most of them think, first that the potential earnings they forego are probably limited, and second that the increased earnings potential which higher education will bring will more than compensate for these. This is a calculation that has to be made in each particular case, of course, but it is worth observing that the advent of a mass higher education system, by producing very many more graduates, is likely to diminish the economic advantages of possessing a degree, and has already done so according to some studies. A familiar, but flawed, argument cites the earning potential of graduates (who have hitherto been in a minority) as a motivation for all school leavers to go to university (but in numbers that would radically alter the size of that minority). Furthermore, making higher education the norm can lead to shortages in manual occupations such as electricians, mechanics and plumbers, resulting in significantly increased earning potential for non-graduates. Trades in very short supply can offer earnings greatly in excess of those of the graduates whose numbers are plentiful.

The general point is that the decision to go to university rather than take a job, even with free tuition and some state support for living costs, is *not*, despite the common belief to the contrary, one that can be made irrespective of financial circumstances. Another way of putting this same point is to say that, even where there is a system of financial support in place, anyone contemplating university study still has reason to ask whether it will result in financial loss or benefit. It is thus misleading to suggest that it is only with the introduction of direct charging that this question arises..

Universal access, then, is a misleading term, and perhaps as a result a somewhat misleading ideal. It does not in fact mean open access to all, and it does not mean that financial considerations are eliminated with respect to higher education. For the moment however, we can leave aside the issue of what it means, and ask whether there is indeed good reason to regard universal access as an ideal.

Education as a right

Why should it be thought that university education, or any personal good for that matter, should be cost free for those who benefit from it? One answer is that it is their right. To explore this idea it is useful to consider a less contentious case — criminal justice. Everyone accused of a crime, it is widely accepted, has a right to a fair trial. In reality, a fair trial requires good representation, and good representation costs money. The principle behind legal aid is that the right to a fair trial should not be denied to those who cannot afford good representation. Why not? The explanation lies in the fact that the conviction of the innocent is a violation of a basic right, one which in turn derives from a fundamental principle of natural justice — the innocent ought not to be punished.

To understand the basis of this right we need to see that the administration of justice by the state requires a system of compensation before it can be said to have adequate justification. If all citizens are to be subject to the rule of law, regardless of whether they have or have not given consent to such a rule, and if, consequently, they are to be made to run the risk of false accusations and, worse, false imprisonment, society must compensate for this risk by subsidizing the cost of minimizing it. That is to say, citizens must not be subject to these risks *and* required to meet the cost of averting them. In short, if justice is to be done, and the rights of the individual in society are to be protected properly, the cost of securing justice must be met by the society which imposes it. The fundamental idea is that failure to secure justice for any individual constitutes the violation of a right. Consequently public funds must be used to prevent such violations, hence the system of legal aid.

Could education be considered a right in the same way? To justify a positive answer we need to be able to say that anyone who fails to obtain a higher education, and who could have benefited from it, has had their rights violated. On the face of it this seems implausible. The first point to be noted — and it is one that is often overlooked in a general atmosphere of welfarism — is this; not all benefits are rights. I can benefit greatly from your friendship, but it does not follow that I have a right to it. Friendship is a gift relationship, not a contractual one. I can buy advice, and having paid my fee, have a right to it. But the advice of a friend is not something I can buy. So the mere fact that higher education works to my benefit is not *in itself* a reason for thinking that I have a right to it.

Of course, some benefits *are* rights, as in the case of a fair trial, which is both a benefit to the accused and their right. But there are important disanalogies between the cases of education and justice. First among these is compulsion. The modern state takes to itself the exclusive administration of justice and forbids its citizens to use force (either their own or that of private agencies hired by them) to secure it. We are not permitted, in the familiar phrase, to take the law into our own hands. It is this element of compulsion that necessitates the principle of compensatory subsidy. Now an argument can be made for thinking that a similar principle of compensatory subsidy should apply to citizens who are *compelled* to undergo courses of study. Thus, where primary and secondary education are compulsory, as, broadly speaking, they have been in Britain for over one hundred years, it is reasonable that those who are forced to attend educational institutions (or more accurately their parents and guardians) should not be put at a disadvantage by adverse or constricted financial circumstances. Setting out this argument more fully would show grounds, I think, both for the use of tax revenues to meet the cost and for the legal implementation of systems of accountability and control designed to secure a fairly uniform level of provision. Both claims can be derived from the contention that those who are compelled to undergo courses of education should not be unequally, and hence unfairly, penalised by the compulsion. They have right to be treated on a par.

These points are easily illustrated by circumstances prevailing in this country when compulsory schooling was first introduced, and by circumstances in many developing countries today. For the poor in 1870 (the year of Forster's Elementary Education Act) to be required to send their children to schools rather than have them work was a considerable sacrifice to material well-being. For the rich, who generally sent their children to school anyway, it was not. One recompense to the poor was the increased earning potential of educated children, but this was (and is) true only in so far as the education was good enough actually to increase earning potential. Parents who are obliged not only to forego the limited supplementation their children's earnings can make to family income but *also* obliged to pay for an education that does little to improve those children's prospects, are multiply disadvantaged. It is thus that the requirements to subsidize education and ensure its quality are generated.

Just what the underlying rationale for compulsory education is, is a different question. It could rest either on the advantage to the individual who undergoes it, or on the general social benefit that results from a better educated population, or possibly some combination of the two. All that needs to be noted here, however, is that a system over which individual citizens and families have no choice, is one which, it is plausible to claim, requires the use of tax revenues to redistributive ends, and in which the language of rights has a place. It is also a separate question whether a system of private fee-paying education can coherently exist alongside a compulsory state one, and what, if it does, this implies about the requirements that may legitimately be placed upon those who pay for their own or their children's education directly. But neither of these questions concerns us here.

The position is different when we turn our attention from primary and secondary to tertiary education which, as far as I know, has never been compulsory anywhere. If we are free *not* to take part in the system, how could there be a right to have it subsidized when we do? The decision to undertake a course of higher education is like any other choice. Whether it is worth doing requires an estimation of anticipated costs and benefits. Whether the costs, including the opportunity costs, are worth incurring, is no different in principle to the decision whether to buy a better car at the expense of a longer holiday. So it would seem at any rate. To draw this parallel, of course, is to construe higher education as a good like any other. Is there any reason not to do so?

Here it is common, and often thought instructive, to explore yet another parallel — with health care. Paying for health care raises many of the same questions as paying for education does. Should all health care be free at the point of delivery? Systems of socialized health care are based upon the idea that it should. What justification is there for this idea?

Illness is incapacitating. If people are to function properly in the normal affairs of life and to compete equally for (and contribute usefully to) the goods and opportunities which social life makes available, they need to be in good health. Accordingly, it is right that the state should ensure what has come to be known as 'a level playing field', both among its citizens and on their behalf. Health, and hence healthcare, are preconditions which need to be supplied if people within society are to be equal.

Such, at any rate, is a familiar line of argument. However, thus broadly expressed, it is too general. Some illnesses are indeed seriously incapacitating, but others much less so, and some not at all. Pneumonia renders its victims incapable of living and working normally. Duodenal ulcers, however unpleasant, are not of the same order. Mild skin irritations do not incapacitate in any significant way. By contrast, adequate care of the dying, which is something we should expect any civilized society to provide for, cannot be explained in 'level playing field' terms.

In real life, even where, as in Britain, there is a National Health Service which provides treatment free at the point of delivery, we do not regard health care as of just one kind. Remedies for minor ailments (bandages, aspirins and so on) are purchasable, and purchased, in the way that other goods and services are, and decisions relating to their purchase are subject to the usual cost/benefit analyses and trade offs that other decisions are. Nor is this just the case for minor matters. Some complex and expensive medical procedures — in vitro fertilization, sex change operations, psychiatric treatment of some neuroses, plastic surgery, for example — are not always available from the public health system, and must also enter the competition which governs the use of an individual's resources. If there is a good argument for health care being made free at the point of delivery, it must be tempered by the overall cost to the public purse, and discriminations must be made between the essential and the inessential.

Without entering into deeper issues of social justice, efficiency and so on, the most that a parallel between health and educational provision will show is that there is a basic level of each which the state has a duty to supply, and the cost of which it can legitimately require the taxpayer to meet. This suggests that while an argument can be made for basic education being a right irrespective of the financial circumstances of those who enjoy its benefits, there is less likely to be an argument to this effect for higher education, a conclusion which is re-inforced by introducing yet another set of rights into the discussion — the rights of the taxpayer.

The rights of the taxpayer

To those broadly persuaded of the merits of the welfare state on grounds of social justice, the expression 'the rights of the taxpayer' has an unwelcome ring. This is, I think, because of an unspoken assumption that any appeal to the rights of the taxpayer ranges the interests of the rich against the interests of the poor. It is assumed, in other words, that the rights of the taxpayer are to be indentified with the interests of the rich, which in turn presupposes that taxpayers are (relatively) rich. There is in this assumption, however, a mistaken perception of the realities of the modern tax system, and the errors in thinking which it leads to are perhaps more easily uncovered when we consider the case of higher education than in some other areas of social expenditure.

The first point to be emphasized is that the burden of increased taxation falls more heavily on those who are liable for less tax than those who are liable for more. This sounds paradoxical, but it is in fact correct, and its accuracy can be easily demonstrated by the use of illustrative figures. If I have an income of £1 million a tax rate of 50% leaves me with £500,000 — a very good income by contemporary standards. If I have an income of £11,000 the same tax rate reduces my income very seriously, pushing me into poverty. Even if we leave aside the impact of indirect taxation, and suppose that a steeply progressive income tax system operates, as it does in most modern economies, so that those on this lower level are only liable, let us say, to 10% tax, the burden on the lower taxpayer is still higher in real terms. This is because, as the law of diminishing marginal utility shows, £1,100 out of an income of £11,000 is a much more substantial loss than £500,000 out of an income of £1m. In terms of spending power, i.e. in terms of resources available for the purchase of whatever goods and services are needed or desired, people on lower incomes feel the loss of small sums more than those on higher incomes feel the loss of large ones. What this demonstrates is that higher taxes can be, and usually are, a greater burden on the poor than the rich, even when the absolute amounts taken in tax from the rich are many times higher.

The second point to be emphasized is that where taxes are used to subsidize certain activities in preference to others, this means in effect that some people are paying for benefits that others enjoy. A much cited example is the subsidizing of opera against the non-subsidy of soccer. If tax revenues reduce the cost of an opera ticket from say £60 to £35, those who go to the opera are being subsidized in part by those who do not. If such subsidies are not paid to football teams, soccer fans are paying for the pleasures of opera fans. If we add this to the first point about diminishing marginal utility and assume, reasonably, that the cost of opera tickets is still high enough to make it the recreation of wealthier sections of society, we can see plainly that when tax revenues are used to support opera rather than football, one recreational activity is arbitrarily being preferred over another, and the relatively poor are in fact subsidizing the relatively rich.

In itself this does not mean that subsidies to the arts cannot be justified. Nor does it mean that opera and soccer are to be treated on a par as equal forms of entertainment. There may be good reasons to think otherwise. But at a minimum it means that a true concern with fairness and equality, and with protecting the interests of the poor, will approach such subsidies with great care and circumspection, because it is clearly possible that they should constitute an indefensible redistribution of wealth from poor to rich, and one for which consequent social goods — the flourishing of the arts — do not adequately compensate. We might all agree that it is important for the cultural inheritance of a society to be preserved, more important (possibly) than the preservation of sports and entertainments, and further that only public subsidy can be expected to do this. Even so, there is a point past which the consequent burden on the relatively poor cannot justify doing so.

A similar point can be made about higher education. To use substantial amounts of tax revenue to support it can mean, and in practice often does mean, that the preferences and choices of some are being paid for at the expense of others, and that the relatively rich are being subsidized by the relatively poor. It is certainly true that the financial as well as the intellectual capital of past ages is embodied in many universities, that present generations benefit from the consumption which earlier ages were willing or forced to forego, and that we in our turn must invest in a future which we will not ourselves benefit from directly. Nevertheless, as in so many other things, balances and trade-offs must be struck. In this case the continued flourishing of universities can justify public expenditure only in so far as it combines *both* the concern with institutional investment *and* a reasonably equitable contemporaneous distribution of its benefits. Those who do not themselves benefit, and whose children and grandchildren are less likely to benefit, cannot be expected to make an equal, still less a greater, contribution to current cost and to future investment.

Serious doubts may thus be raised and sustained about the desirability of 'universal access' funded by the state. But there is yet another consideration to be adduced, and this raises an even more substantial doubt about the justice of systems of higher education financed very largely from the public purse. This is the fact that, though higher education produces general social benefits in the form of skilled personnel — the doctors, lawyers, engineers, food scientists and so on whose existence increases overall social prosperity — it is also true that financial benefits of higher education often accrue directly to the individuals who have received it in the form of higher earnings. The same people, we should add, can also expect to benefit in the form of a more varied and interesting life than they would otherwise have had. In such circumstances, on the worst scenario, *the relatively poor are paying for the relatively rich to have a yet more prosperous and a better life*. It is against the background of this possibility that we should approach questions of rights and justice as they apply to fees paid directly by students. There are also the rights of the taxpayer to be taken into account and, in the circumstances described, these rights are more concerned with protecting the interests of the poor than the interests of the rich. But before addressing this question directly, and in order to forestall a certain sort of criticism, we should first consider the financial support of higher education in a more social, less individualistic context.

Public benefit and public expenditure

The arguments we have been considering do not show conclusively in the case of opera and other arts that a case cannot be made for public subsidy from tax revenues. Similarly, they do not show that a case cannot be made for the support of universities from general taxation. As we saw in section 2, it is wrong to think of prosperity as exclusively a matter of generating increased purchasing power. Without goods, services and other benefits to purchase, those who have increased purchasing power are not any richer. Accordingly, if it is reasonable to look to the state to increase disposable income, it is equally reasonable to look to it to encourage and maintain sources of enrichment. These include cultural enrichment, and it is in this way that we can lend to the state a proper role in the support and encouragement of the arts and higher learning. Moreover, we need to remember the point considered briefly in the last section, that social responsibility does not begin and end with the present generation. Indeed it is questionable whether it is even coherent to suppose that it could. We have duties to those who have lived before us (the sort of duties that are legally embodied in wills and laws of inheritance) and we have responsibilities for future generations. Consequently, the fact that the present generation wants or does not want some social good is *a* reason, but not a conclusive one, for supporting or withholding support from the good in question. The consumption (or desires) of contemporary citizens is not the only focus of social and political responsibility.

However, when all such considerations are taken into account, there is still the practical matter of managing public finance. It is never possible to meet all the demands that may legitimately be made upon the public purse. There must be trade-offs between equally good claims, and compromises between competing interests. Let us agree that higher learning has a legitimate claim to the financial support of the state, that a convincing case can be made for thinking that tax revenues can properly be used to maintain universities as well as nursery, primary, secondary and special schools. Any radical claim to the contrary would both be hard to sustain in my view, and unlikely to carry much credence in present or foreseeable future circumstances. The question then is not whether public money should go to universities, but only how much. This is not a question we can answer with a figure, obviously, for arriving at a sensible figure depends upon complex contingent facts which it is not our business to examine here. The point of posing the question is to reveal the impossibility of one principled answer to it, namely, 'as much as is required for as good a system of university education as possible'.

This is an answer, probably, that could not be sustained for any area of public expenditure. Even systems of defence, irrigation, the water supply, or the protection of the environment, upon which arguably the very continued existence of a society might depend, can always be improved upon, and choices have to be made between these highly important, but competing, functions of government in the face of limited resources. In the case of universities it would be impossible ever to argue, I think, that the continued existence of a society depended upon them. Certainly they can contribute substantially to the prosperity and wellbeing of a society, and their loss or neglect can be felt in striking ways and across a wide spectrum. Nevertheless it seems plain that important though they generally are, universities cannot claim special privileges, even within the realm of educational expenditure. Their claims must take their place among the many claims that the general cause of education makes upon government support and hence upon the taxpayer. Moreover, education as a whole must take its place alongside the equally good claims of health, social services and law.

With the colossal expansion of the British university system in recent years, the amount of money that is available has necessarily implied a reduction in the quality of provision that is possible, with the result that not only is the system less good than it might be, but it is less good than it was. How are its deficiencies to be remedied? Assuming that the requisite level of state finance will not, because realistically it cannot, be restored, one plain answer seems to be the introduction of fees by which students pay directly, in part, not only for the education they receive, but to support the continued existence and well-being of the institutions from which they receive it. This was the answer, in fact, of the Labour government elected in 1997, under whom a flat rate tuition fee payable 'up front' by students was introduced. Subsequently, this flat rate was replaced by a variable range, though capped by government and set around with other conditions. In Scotland, following the re-establishment of the Scottish Parliament in 1999, this system was altered so that students pay a flat tuition fee, not 'up front', but after graduation.

The introduction (or more accurately re-introduction) of student tuition fees led to very considerable opposition and debate. It is a debate that rumbles on, and their abolition remains the intention of some political parties and groups within them. What objections sustain this continuing opposition? This brings us back to the idea of universal access.

Objections to fees

If we leave aside the morally ambitious claim that university students, if they are sufficiently able, have a *right* to free higher education, a claim we have seen reason to question on the very grounds on which it is often advanced, namely social justice, the principal objection to direct fees seems to be that they present an obstacle to per-

sonal betterment, and further, that this obstacle will operate unevenly, and hence unfairly, across different socio-
economic groups. It was to address this fear that the introduction of variable fees in Britain was accompanied by a
government appointed 'regulator' whose task would be to
set and police access 'targets'.

These two points, as it seems to me, need to be answered
differently, the first by direct confrontation, the second by
greater imagination. Take the first. Why should the fact
that direct costs present an obstacle to personal betterment
carry the implication that they should be met by someone
other than the person whose betterment it is? In almost
every other context than health and education, no one
thinks this. My life is better if I have personally available
means of transport — a car in short. But no one, to my
knowledge has ever taken this to be a reason for providing
cars free of charge to those who use them, and the same
applies to music centres, holidays, gymnasiums and a host
of other goods. It applies to the most basic goods of all in
fact — food and drink.

Even in the case of education our thinking on this matter
is highly selective. Countless people pay for music, danc-
ing, driving, elocution or sports lessons. These are all, they
calculate, for their betterment, and hence worth paying
for. Why should the same connection not hold for lessons
in philosophy, accountancy, medicine, agriculture or art
history? This is a rhetorical question, for the answer to it is
plain: there is no reason why they should not. The only
qualification to be entered is that the institutions which
provide intellectual goods cannot be called into and out of
existence at will or in the course of a short period, and
hence must rely upon the capital of ages and make provision for the future. There is thus reason to think that present beneficiaries of these goods cannot reasonably be
expected to meet their full cost. This is especially true for
laboratory based subjects because of the very high cost of

modern science. But from the fact that it is unreasonable to make the present generation bear the *full* cost, it does not follow that they cannot be expected to meet *any* of the costs. In support of this logical leap we have only the backing of (recent) habit and custom. Yet the fact that this is how it has been since Robbins obviously does not show that this is how it ought always to be, regardless of greatly altered circumstances.

Everything turns then on the second objection, that direct fees would result in an unequal distribution of the benefits of higher education across socio-economic classes. On this point two observations need to be made. First, it is a prediction about likely consequences, and only experience can show what does in fact result. There is an unpleasant tendency for some who discuss these questions to adopt a paternalistic (not to say patrician) attitude to members of lower socio-economic classes, to regard them as 'the feckless poor'. This assumes that when they calculate what use of their resources would be best for them or for their children, they *ought* to come out in favour of higher education, but left to their own devices probably will not. We do not know this, but in any case, a true belief in equality attaches great importance to leaving them to make their own decisions. If relatively poor people reckon higher education to cost more than it is worth to them, this is a decision that ought to be respected.

The second point is that genuine response to the needs and aspirations of the relatively poor does not imply the universal rejection of fees. Those who are truly able, and desirous, but unable to meet the cost, can be assisted by bursaries, as they were at almost every period in the past. This is where imagination comes in. The level of fees for those who can reasonably be expected to pay can be set precisely in order to underwrite bursaries for those who cannot. The debate about fees is sometimes dogged by the assumption that what is under discussion is the imposition of full cost fees for all. Such a thing is most unlikely and almost impossible to bring about. What is possible, however, is a highly flexible and varied scheme of fees and bursaries which would make a substantial contribution to the high costs in the contemporary world of good quality higher education. Such a system is common in the more prestigious colleges and universities in the US, where sometimes up to 50% of students are on fee support.

But would this be desirable as well as possible? Two lines of argument open up. The first responds with another question. Is there really any alternative, except the slow, and perhaps not so slow, erosion of the opportunities universities offer both their students and the intellects they ought to attract? The second draws attention to the positive aspect of fees levied directly by universities, namely a measure of financial autonomy without which academic autonomy means little. This second point relates, in fact, to a larger issue — value for money.

Value for money

Thought about how to finance universities, like financing the arts, has been distorted by a certain high-mindedness. Where truth and beauty are concerned it is easy to pull off a rhetorical trick which casts concern with money in a rather Philistine light. Surely, this way of thinking goes, our first concern should be with promoting the best, not the cheapest. It is a line of thought that seems to gather a good deal of support from the (true) perception that educational (and artistic) goods cannot be quantified. Universities trade in intangible values, and cannot therefore be expected to prove themselves in profit and loss accounts. There is here an association of ideas, which, however common, produces confusion rather than enlightenment. It is correct to say that truth, understanding and learning cannot be given numerical values. It does not follow however that their value cannot be assessed, or that the assessment of this value cannot be conducted along the ordinary lines of what is and is not worth spending money on.

On the contrary, such assessment is unavoidable. In the competition between goods and services, individuals have no alternative but to make judgements about how to spend their time and money. Nobody really thinks otherwise. In choosing between an evening at the cinema, the concert hall, or the restaurant, we readily and easily decide in terms of relative cost and limited resources. What could it be that would incapacitate us when it comes to other intangible goods? To make some of them free at the point of consumption simply disguises, and distorts, the fact that we are choosing. It was the belief that this was so which made the Scottish universities at the start of the twentieth century turn down Andrew Carnegie's offer to pay the fees of every student in Scotland. Free higher education, the university authorities argued, would erode its value amongst students, since they would not be compelled to make a choice between it and other goods. What they could have for free they would not value. More importantly in a way, they would not trouble to assess its value, and so higher education would cease to be under the critical scrutiny of those it was intended (at least in part) to serve.

Arguably, the cumbersome machinery of accountability which has grown up in recent years — teaching review, staff appraisal, course evaluation, academic audit — all of which were discussed in an earlier section, are merely indirect and less effective ways of introducing what would more easily be accomplished by students voting with their feet and hence with their fees. To decide whether universities give value for money, which is what all these procedures are intended to do, there is no simpler way than making them in large part (though not exclusively) dependent on convincing potential students that what they have to offer is money well spent. In short, the existence of direct student fees, across the country, is a simple and effective means of securing the outcome that currently large numbers of bureaucrats are paid to achieve — value for money.

A second assumption at work in much of the discussion surrounding the question of student fees is that universities would thereby be improperly imposed upon by market forces. The truth is, however, that the danger of this, which is not negligible, is unlikely to be greater than the degree to which they have been improperly opposed upon by government bureaucracy. It is a salutary fact that British universities have proved easy targets for state intervention, in part it has to be said, because of the ready compliance of academics within them. Recent experience should lead us to combine real concern with the independence of universities to pursue their appointed activities according to their lights and judgement, with a reluctance to give preference to reliance on state funding.

This is the other aspect of value for money. How do we determine that money spent on higher education is money well spent? The question requires a two sided answer. First, though not foremost, those who study in them must be able to satisfy themselves that the resources they could have used to other ends are best used in higher education. There is no simpler power than the power to spend their money elsewhere. Second, and equally important, those who can tell the intellectually superior from the intellectually inferior, must have the resources to pursue the former. There is no guarantee that this will happen when those resources have to be secured from the state, as recent experience confirms. There is then a lot to be welcomed in the introduction of changes which, though they do not eliminate, seriously reduce the power of the middleman, the middleman in this case being government and its quangos.

Unfortunately, the way in which directly payable tuition fees have been introduced militates against the advantages that their introduction might have. Indeed, it may be said to have completely eliminated it. If the payment of fees is to have an impact on the quality of provision through something looking a little like the market place, then universities must be free to charge in accordance with the quality of what they offer, and students pay in accordance with the quality of what they get. Flat rate fees set by central government or even variable fees within government prescribed ranges represent a different income stream, but not one that gives universities greater control over supply and demand. Fee levels (or ranges) determined by what is politically acceptable bear no necessary relation to the cost of the education provided. Moreover, in so far as they are the same everywhere (which can result easily enough within permissible variation) they bear no relation to the quality of what any given university offers. In almost every other walk of life, I can exercise some control by paying for what I hold to be good value, and getting what I pay for. Not so university education in contemporary Britain (and many other European countries). In this case, I pay what central government tells me to pay, irrespective of what I get or what I think worth paying for. To offset this assault on my autonomy there is the opportunity to fill out indefinitely many student course evaluation forms.

From the point of the student, then, a politically determined fee system (whether flat or variable) is simply an additional financial burden with no detectable benefits. From the point of view of the universities it is a source of student resentment and bad debts that are expensive and difficult to collect. (The level of debt to universities has risen dramatically since the introduction of fees.) In short, no one on either the supply or the demand side of the university system is better off.

The government middleman, I shall assert, threatens academic, and more importantly intellectual independence far more than the fee bearing student would do. Suppose this is true. To make it a convincing move in the argument it needs to be shown that academic freedom — intellectual independence — is a central value for anything called a university. To demonstrate this we need, in my view, to recover an idea of the university that has almost been lost. This is the topic of next, and final, section of this essay.

7. Recovering the idea

In his 1996 Sir Robert Menzies Oration on Higher Education, delivered at the University of Melbourne, Professor Sir Stewart Sutherland (now Lord Sutherland) then Principal of the University of Edinburgh, argues that British universities (and perhaps universities more widely) have been guilty of 'a failure to redefine [their] identity in a new diverse world of higher education'. Unlike so many critics of the universities, however, he speaks as an insider. 'The most essential task' he says 'is to recreate a sense of our own worth by refashioning our understanding of our identity — our understanding of what the word "university" means'. Though his analysis of the contemporary university seems to me both timely and pertinent, the call for redefinition is in some important respects different to the advertised topic of this section — the recovery of an idea.

University — name or conception?

Sutherland's chief contention, with which there can be little to dispute, is that the changes which British universities have undergone have called into existence a system of

mass higher education sharply in contrast to the relatively small scale and much more selective system that prevailed before. The previous condition of British universities was one in which, though there were differences between them, there was also a basic equality — at all levels. Every university could expect to admit students of roughly equal abilities, and hence could apply broadly equal educational standards. All could expect to have in their employment at least a good number of outstanding intellects. All could claim the ability to make provision to the highest level, namely doctoral studies, and all could reasonably profess a commitment to first class research. The emergence of a greatly expanded system put an end to this uniformity. There are wide differences in ability between both students and staff at different universities, and accordingly, as a matter of fact, standards of educational accomplishment vary considerably. The cost of research in many subjects, the ages of different libraries and similar resources, and the naturally limited pool of talent to pursue truly substantial science and scholarship, has rendered impossible an equal distribution of valuable research across the system. For the same reasons, serious questions have arisen about the quality, even possibility, of doctoral programmes in many places.

Comparison with another mass system, the one that has been in place in the United States for a long time, is instructive. As Sutherland observes: 'Whereas in Britain every institution with the right to award degrees has subsumed within that the right to award PhD's, in the USA the proportion with the latter right is about ten per cent.' A similar point can be made about research. Many small, and excellent, US universities and degree awarding colleges are teaching institutions, committed to the highest standards of liberal education, but making no demands on their staff to engage in what we might call 'front-line' research. By contrast, every institution in Britain that goes by the name of 'university' must at least pretend to a vigorous programme of research.

Sutherland rightly says that the differences which exist between universities in the United States exist in Britain also. But they cannot be openly admitted. The myths that all universities are of equal standing, that a chair in one is equal to a chair in another, that a degree from one is of the same standard as a degree from another, are claims which it is impolitic to deny, and hence which are rarely denied. Until some measure of honesty is publicly possible in this matter, the confusion, uncertainty and insecurity which dogs universities and which makes them susceptible to every puff of educational policy will continue. The truth is that the word university does not mean what it did, hence the need for redefinition.

In my view Sutherland is incontestably right in insisting that these dramatic changes must be acknowledged by universities themselves before a proper self-confidence can return. Yet if the arguments and analyses we have explored up to this point have any substance, the ultimate issue cannot be one of the meaning of a word. A natural language will take whatever course it does. It is a living thing, largely unconstrained by self-conscious regulation of the use of words in accordance with conceptual theorising or principled reflection. Those institutions which have been granted the legal title of a university are unlikely to lose it in the foreseeable future, and will go on being called 'universities' even in those cases where there is little prospect of their attaining the kind of education and level of scholarship which will mark others. The most illuminating description of these circumstances is not that the word university has taken on a new meaning, though perhaps it has, but that the name 'university' now applies to institutions with widely different functions and characters. The crucial task is not to find a common concept to cover them all, but to distinguish in thought between the different ideals each can plausibly aspire to. To exploit the strengths and avoid the weaknesses of such institutions it is essential to understand the range of values and purposes which can give them coherence. History embodies these values, and consequently it is essential to understand the continuity of past with present, as well as to accommodate discontinuities. A relatively narrow *idea* or conception of a university — something like Newman's — figures in this understanding, and it is as much a recovery of this idea that present circumstances require as an appreciation of the variety of institutions which the *label* or name 'university' now covers. This distinction relates directly to the question of worth. An institution cannot have a satisfactory sense of its worth if it has no conception of what its purpose is. But equally, no sense of worth will ever be forthcoming if it aspires to an ideal which it cannot attain, or, just as importantly, if it thinks in terms which fall short of what it might justifiably aspire to. This is why the recovery of an idea, and not merely the redefinition of a name, is of critical importance.

Ideas of the university

However this crucial question arises — which idea? In the opening section we saw that the development of universities in Europe, and from there across the world, has been marked by at least three different ideas. The first and oldest of these is that of the mediaeval university. Originally tied to the Christian Church and governed by its purposes, this type of institution slowly gathered independence for purposes of its own. Nevertheless, its distinguishing characteristics were largely unaltered over a long period of time. These can be identified as four. First, a major rationale for the mediaeval university was the provision of a general, liberal education, not simply for its own sake or for some strictly utilitarian end, but as a foundation for

citizenship at large and for training in the professions of
law, medicine and divinity. Second, the mediaeval university was home to the scholar, the simple 'inquirer after
truth', and was committed to the promotion of what we
might call the *spirit* of truth. Third, its core concerns —
what ought to be taught, what was worth studying and
what counted as 'mastery' of a subject — were conducted
in relative autonomy by a community of scholars modeled
on a monastic community, and sometimes identical with
it. (Traditional academic dress is a modification of monastic garb.) This community determined the curriculum of
study, awarded degrees and established chairs of instruction (or their equivalent). Fourth, in the service of its activities it collected, preserved and made available, the
materials of learning, most notably in the form of a library
of course, but also in the creation and maintenance of
buildings, fellowships and scholarships. What has been
called the 'modern' university did not essentially deviate
from this idea. It simply loosened the ties with church and
theology, and added experimental science to its activities.

A real alternative arose as a result of the French Revolution. The Napoleonic university, initially styled a 'polytechnic', is a department of state in pretty much the way
that institutions of primary and secondary education usually are. As such it is not self-governing, even in principle,
but like these other levels of education, subject to political
control whose exercise is determined by the needs of the
society which it is its purpose to serve. This leads to a
heavy though not exclusive emphasis on 'useful' subjects,
and social need.

The third model, perhaps a conscious reaction to the
Napoleonic, is the university as conceived by Wilhelm von
Humboldt — a community of scholars and scientists
devoted to the pursuit of knowledge for its own sake and
primarily devoted to research. This model has figured
very prominently in people's idea of a university, but it

has rarely been put into effect. The North American liberal arts college with which it is sometimes confused, is a natural development of the mediaeval university, and Newman's ideal, though it shares some of von Humboldt's 'purism' is essentially of a teaching institution.

History, of course, does not often accord with the ideal. These models are conceptions only, and the actual character of most institutions called 'universities' has been an amalgam of these and other elements. The question then is not which model is the 'true' one, but which of them is most worth keeping firmly in view in the social, political and economic currents that the contemporary university must navigate, and which aspect of that model is the most important to focus upon.

My own preference is for the mediaeval university. Humboldtian 'purism' about the pursuit of knowledge for its own sake is wholly unrealistic in a world where universities must defend a massive call on the public purse. And in any case, since the most ancient of universities gave important attention to professional training, 'purism' of this kind excludes an enduring purpose. At the same time, the Napoleonic conception, in its spirit, lays little store by the liberal education that the ancient universities regarded as foundational. To pursue this ideal in its essentials would be to convert universities to polytechnics — institutions teaching and researching into every kind of useful knowledge. This has not been the course of their development in fact. The Napoleonic institutions resumed the name of 'university' in the end, and as section 1 recorded, British polytechnics without exception opted to change their names in the same direction.

The reason, in part, is that within these institutions, non-vocational subjects had made their appearance. There are some strictly technological universities in Europe, but polytechnics in France and Britain included the humanities and the natural and social sciences in their curriculum, some of them from the start. A similar development can be found in the US agricultural and mechanical (A & M) universities. Founded with the idea of lending equal important to strictly practical subjects, their very success led to the addition of non-practical subjects.

Is it the case then, that between the mediaeval university, which always had a place for vocational training, and the Napoleonic university which rapidly found a place for the non-vocational, there is really no difference, or at least only a difference of emphasis? The answer is that the truly salient difference lies not in subject mix, but in constitution. The mediaeval university is (in theory) autonomous; the Napoleonic university is a Department of State. It is on this difference that the mediaeval and the Humboldtian ideals converge. Both want to secure a certain kind of autonomy. The crucial issue is not whether they teach and research theoretical or practical subjects — astronomy *versus* hotel management — fashionable or unfashionable — theology *versus* film studies — useful or arcane — accountancy *versus* feminist theory. The issue is whether this is a matter for the university itself to decide, and whether the criteria by which both teaching and research are judged good, bad and indifferent, are matters reserved to teachers and researchers. Crucial to healthy inquiry (the protagonists of all models agree) is academic freedom, and academic freedom requires a measure of constitutional autonomy. It is autonomy, in my view that lies at the heart of the idea of the university.

Recovering the idea

[I]t is certain that modernity is as little modern as are the attacks on modernity. The melancholic 'Ah, nowadays …,' 'there is no longer,' 'in the olden days' and similar expressions contrasting the corrupted present with the splendor of the past are probably as old as the human race … I can well imagine Paleolithic nomads angrily resisting the foolish idea that it would be better for people to have

> permanent dwellings or predicting the imminent degen-
> eration of mankind as a result of the nefarious invention
> of the wheel.

So writes Leszek Kolakowski in his brilliant essay 'Modernity on endless trial', and we do indeed need to guard
against simply falling into the mentality that amounts to
no more than lamenting change. In the present context,
and with this danger in view, it is salutary to read Max
Weber's essay 'Science as a Vocation' originally delivered
as a speech to the University of Munich in 1918. The
changes Weber detects in German universities — the public perception, the attitude of students, the conditions of
employment, the success of the mediocre at the expense of
the excellent — might have been re-iterated almost without amendment by British academics 70 years later. One
striking difference is this. Weber remarks that however
excellent a researcher someone might be, it is professional
death to be declared a poor teacher. The pendulum has
swung powerfully in precisely the opposite direction.
Leaving this detail aside, however, what conclusion
should we draw from the fact that many of Weber's anxieties are similar to those that might be expressed today?

It is tempting to conclude that such anxieties are patho-
logical rather than rational and should be passed over or
ignored. But this rests upon an underlying error. It is true
that there was no golden age of universities or anything
else, and that, despite this fact, in every period there could
be found those who deplored its passing. There never was
a golden age because 'the idea of the university' is not the
sort of thing that can be fully realized and permanently
secured. Rather, it is a regulative ideal that gives us our
bearings and against which trends and tendencies are to
be judged. But though it is a mistake to think that such ideals could be secured for ever, it is equally a mistake to
think that their articulation is therefore unnecessary. Intellectual ideals need constant renewal. Otherwise they

disappear and die. But their renewal depends crucially on their intellectual articulation. This means setting out what makes them ideal and why they are worth adhering to and pursuing, despite the fact that the vicissitudes of real life will forever prevent their full realization. Viewed in this way, the task is to explain the value of institutional autonomy and why it matters to more than the institution that enjoys it.

Societies can be structured around different kinds of institution. A society could, for instance, include institutions that provide specially protected fora in which there is freedom to float, explore, criticize and teach theories and ideas of all sorts, fashionable and unfashionable, useful and useless. Or there might be no such institutions. It is a notable fact that totalitarian regimes have generally made it one of their first tasks to take institutions of 'ideological formation' under their control.

To make autonomy central to the idea of the university is to construe it as an institution of this kind. It does not have to have any special place in the formation of public policy, as Western universities generally do not. Nor is it to be conceived as the repository of truth, the place where intellectual objectivity ensures that all and only that which is taught or published is true. The pursuit of inquiry and understanding of a wide range of disparate issues requires freedom, the freedom to come up with the erroneous as well as the well grounded. The university is an institution not marked by its possession of the truth, but its commitment to the *spirit* of truth, which is to say the belief that intellectual inquiry should be allowed to go where it will at the instigation of those gifted in intellectual research and teaching. Commitment to the *spirit* of truth sets no boundaries. It does not confine itself to the useless or disdain the useful. But neither does it worship the useful above all else. Some ideas are potentially of great use; some are simply of great interest; any of them may turn out to be false or misconceived, and that includes ideas that are taught to new generations whether at their own or the tax payers' expense. What matters is the character of mind required for their acquisition and invested in their investigation and exhibited in their transmission.

In short, a university can be conceived as first and foremost a place in which freedom of inquiry is regarded as — literally — a *sine qua non*, something without which the institution is not worth having. This is not the same as saying that universities should act as centres of social criticism. Possibly one role for universities is to subject the policies of governments and state agencies to critical scrutiny. But if it is, it is peripheral rather than central. Universities can be expected to devote part of their energies to social criticism, without this being their aim, or even their most desirable function. Often too high a profile in this respect is destructive, as when students imbued with this ideal, take to the streets in rioting. The criticism of social policies and political parties will inevitably arise in a context where there is a more general commitment to the pursuit of truth and to freedom of inquiry, but universities would do well, in my view, not to insist on their autonomy in virtue of a role as centres of social and political criticism. To do so would inevitably attract even more intervention from the State than at present. Far more importantly, it would imply subscription to the very utilitarianism which universities ought to seek to escape. Critiques of public policy may be commendable, but they are of passing significance, and the enduring interest of cosmology, classical archeology, Roman law and German literature have little to contribute to them.

At the same time in seeking to escape a crude utilitarianism, there is no need for universities aggressively to assert their indifference to personal and social utility. 'Here's to pure mathematics: may it never be any use to anyone', is said to be a traditional toast at some ancient universities, and though it says nothing about usefulness, it can none-theless convey an attitude that disdains, or even *despises* the useful. If the arguments of preceding sections are taken seriously, however, such an attitude is misleading. It deflects attention from an essential role that universities have. They are sources of enrichment. No small part of this is what might be called their cultural custodianship. Universities as centres of scholarship have a key role to play in maintaining and continuously revitalizing cultural inheritances. Actively studied, it is the disciplines of literature, philosophy, history (including the history of science and technology), theology and languages that prevent cultural heritage from becoming nothing more than the passively observed content of the museum and the art gallery. They do this by the constant pursuit of new evidence and critically revised interpretation. It is an area in which, as it seems to me, the distinction between research and teaching is at its thinnest. Universities prevent mere cultural tourism by supplying the critical minds that can engage with cultural inheritance.

In summary, one idea of the university is as a place in which the pursuit of truth and undertanding are given special protection, not to the exclusion of useful or socially relevant subjects, but not principally in their service either. Experience suggests that such an institution is unlikely to emerge (or if it does, unlikely to survive) in circumstances in which those who pay for it are subject to the opinion of electorates or, more vaguely, popular support. Such pay-masters cannot afford to ignore the public reception of ideas, nor can they be expected to. Accordingly, it is likely that those accountable to the public for their custodianship of the public purse will in major or minor ways seek to constrain inquiry in line with what is and is not acceptable to society at large. From this it follows, as it seems, that financial independence is an important precondition of intellectual autonomy. This observation is not a piece of cynicism.

Those who pay the piper will, almost invariably, call the tune, and state patronage in bygone eras and in contemporary dictatorships provides plenty of evidence in confirmation of this claim. But more importantly, in a democracy this is precisely what public paymasters *ought* to do; the governments of democratic countries are *properly* expected to reflect the interests of the public and to be responsible to the taxpayer, in the things they promote and spend money on. At the same time, political theorists have long alerted us to the possibility of a 'tyranny of the majority' and it is essential to see that a truly democratic society can *jeopardise* the rights and freedoms of individuals and hence the social goods that derive from these, a truth that the contemporary adulation of democracy very easily obscures. It is because of this possibility that the power to levy fees, and in every possible way generate income independently of political authority, is something to be welcomed by those who wish to preserve and promote institutions of untrammelled inquiry.

The last section argued that direct levying of fees is not contrary to social justice. Properly deployed (which is to say, not in the form of a flat fee centrally fixed and universally applied) fees have the potential to be a useful device by which the conduct of universities may reflect something of the interests and desires of those who study, and at the same time an effective way in which universities may compete for the expenditure of individual incomes. The argument of this section adds to these considerations a further, internal, reason for universities to endorse a system in which at least some significant part of university income comes directly in the form of fees that those who wish to study are willing to pay, namely that in this way universities can secure a measure of autonomy from public paymasters who must, inevitably, be concerned with the tides of public, and hence fashionable, opinion.

But fees are only one relatively independent source of income. The ancient universities were recipients of gifts and donations over many centuries, both in money and in kind. Without this we would not enjoy the inheritance we do. For almost the whole of their history US colleges and universities have looked to philanthropy to support and enhance their intellectual and pedagogical activities. In Europe, the socialist experiment that followed World War II led to a mentality in which only public finance was approved of and sought. The true price of such dependence is now more evident, and it is only by beginning the enormous task of breaking away from this mentality that the institutions we know as universities can regain something of their autonomy.

The idea of the university as first and foremost a haven within which the free pursuit of rational inquiry, wherever it may lead, is made secure, is a reasonably ancient one. But it needs to be stressed that it is not the only sort of institution using the name 'university' that can lay claim to worthy credentials. Some educational institutions reasonably restrict themselves to the task of training skilled personnel in practical skills. Others may add to this task the development of useful technology of an advanced kind. Since language will go where it will, both kinds of institution, if they provide chiefly for those past school age, may go by the name of university. But there is the further possibility, that there are other institutions, among which the oldest universities are to be counted, that are marked by two rather different aims — a broad based interest in intellectual study for its own sake and a commitment to provide the resources and context in which this may most fruitfully be pursued.

There is nothing wrong with any of these educational aims. The polytechnic, narrowly understood, has much that is admirable about it. Nor is there any reason why these different purposes cannot be combined in a single institution. Moreover, where they are embodied in distinct institutions, the mere fact that all are called 'universities' need not create special difficulties. Trouble only arises when there is confusion between the aims, and where the structure and purposes suitable to one are forced upon another. Such confusion, however, is precisely what is bedevilling the condition of most British universities at present. Recovering a proper understanding of what a university is for does not necessarily mean reserving the label for just one sort of institution. It means formulating clearly a certain educational ideal and the tradition in which this is embodied. Stewart Sutherland's lecture, with which this section began, correctly recognizes the changed world of university education and research. By calling for a re-conceptualization of the idea of a university to accommodate such changes, however, it runs the risk of inducing increased confusion over different educational aims and purposes, a confusion which has, in my view, sapped the confidence of traditional universities in the face of pressures from a largely utilitarian world, and an almost exclusively, and narrowly, utilitarian public purse.

The aim of this essay has been to set out the distinctive character of university education and university research as these have been emerged over several centuries, to explain their value and importance, and to display their credentials as genuine modes of social and personal enrichment. The academic in this sense, does not need to justify itself in terms of an indirect (and distorted) 'usefulness' to society. Once this is perceived clearly, the relation of the (traditional) universities to the individuals who study within them, and their role as distinctive institutions within society at large can indeed be reconsidered. But its reconsideration should lead to a reassertion of a role and value that is in danger of being lost, rather than a capitulation to an alien conception of a role and value to be imposed from without. It will also lead to firmer conceptual and critical ground from which such innovations as course evaluation, teaching quality assessment, research assessment, and executive management can be assessed in a clearer and hence more confident way by those who are subject to them.

No one can seriously doubt that universities and those within them must change and adapt their ideas and practices to meet the altered conditions of the world in which they operate. At the same time, if change takes place entirely at the bidding of those voices and forces that demand it, universities become straws which simply bend in the wind. For institutions whose purpose is in large part the inculcation of critical thought and solid learning, this cannot be a satisfactory outcome. It can be prevented, in my view, only in so far as intellectuals undertake serious reflection designed to formulate a solid self-understanding of their purposes. And this means recovering the essential idea of a university.

Human Nature and the Study of the Humanities[1]

In 1726 Bishop Joseph Butler delivered his famous *Sermons* in the Rolls Chapel in London, now part of the Library of King's College. By modern day standards they hardly count as sermons, since their spiritual content is minimal, and they are now widely regarded as possibly the finest work of moral philosophy in English.

The first three of these sermons are devoted to the subject of human nature. A large part of their purpose, to quote his Preface to the published edition, is to combat 'a strange affection in many people of explaining away all particular affections, and representing the whole of life as nothing but one continued exercise of self-love' (Butler 1983: 19). In other words, Butler aims to counter the mono-minded egoism of the agents who populate the state of nature in Hobbes's *Leviathan*, or provide the material for Mandeville's *Fable of the Bees*. Butler's *Sermons* were immensely influential in their day partly because their subtlety contrasts so sharply with the egoist's crude account of human motivation, a crudeness that still persists to the present, and now as then results, as he observes in a footnote, in 'absurdities which even men of capacity run into when they belie their nature' (Butler 1983: 27).

---

[1]   Originally given as the inaugural Butler Lecture at King's College London, October 2002.

Their content is not the only interesting feature of these *Sermons*, however. So too is their method, because it is a perennially important question as to how, if at all, human nature is to be discerned and studied. Butler is quite explicit on what he conceives to be the appropriate method for the study of human nature.

> [L]et it be observed that whether man be thus or otherwise constituted, what is the inward frame in this particular, is a mere matter of fact or natural history, not provable immediately by reason. It is therefore to be judged of and determined in the same way other facts or matters of natural history are: by appealing to the external senses or inward perceptions respectively, as the matter under consideration is cognizable by one or the other; by arguing from acknowledged facts and actions; for a great number of actions prove, to a certainty, what principles they do not, and, to the greatest probability, what principles they do proceed from; and lastly, by the testimony of mankind. (Butler 1983: 27–8)

The sentence construction here is a little tortuous, especially for a sermon, but its meaning is clear enough. In effect, Butler is commending a blend of social anthropology and psychological introspection as the best method by which to study human nature. In so doing, he is of course taking issue with Hobbes's approach, which did indeed aim to be 'provable immediately by reason'. Hobbes represents his political masterpiece *Leviathan* as an exercise in deductive reasoning comparable to the geometry of Euclid by which he was so impressed. Now while it is difficult not to admire the intellectual ambition and scope of *Leviathan*, no one other than Hobbes, probably, has ever been persuaded that his defence of absolute sovereignty does indeed proceed by pure deduction. And if Butler is right, it could not do so, or at least could not do so to any good purpose. The study of human nature is essentially empirical; it has to do with contingent facts, and there is no scope for the purely a priori.

Though novel in its day, such a view might seem incontestable now. Yet there are two serious doubts to be raised against Butler's advertized method, doubts that many contemporary thinkers share. The first is the more radical and it is this: is there such a thing as human nature? The eighteenth century would have answered this question with an unqualified 'Yes', but doubt arose precisely because in the century that followed Butler's, something like the anthropological inquiry he thinks essential was undertaken very seriously. The careful fieldwork of Frazer and Tylor, and then of Malinowski, Levy-Strauss, Evans-Prichard and so on, brought anthropologists to question whether there is anything that could be called a *universal* human nature. The cultural differences their researches uncovered were very great. More importantly, they appeared to show that culture has a deeply formative role in the understanding, attitudes, patterns of behaviour and even emotions of human beings. The result was that the idea of an underlying, *universal* nature, shared by all human beings *qua* human beings, came to be suspect, made even more suspect by the fact that it seemed itself to be a culturally relative conception.

There was a time, not so long ago, when this general doubt about the very idea of a human nature discoverable across space and time held sway almost without demur. It both fed into, and was in turn reinforced by the movement of ideas known as postmodernism. Postmodernism is not one thing, in my view, but in so far as all that falls under this label can be said to have a common theme, it lies in the belief that the so-called 'Enlightenment project' of the eighteenth century, with its confidence in the unlimited power of a transcendent reason, is now known to have failed. The outcome was this; that in place of the false hope of a universal conceptual language of rational discourse, an ineliminable variety of voices must be acknowledged, united if at all, in a purely contingent *conversation*, a conception given its most articulate philosophical expression in Richard Rorty's book, *Philosophy and the Mirror of Nature* (1979).

But academic opinion moves on. Postmodernism is now in retreat, and with its declining influence these anthropological strictures on the possibility of a discernible human nature have lost a good deal of their force, and have been further weakened by the ever increasing authority of evolutionary biology. Indeed the concept of human nature has explicitly returned, not in the writings of anthropologists or cultural theorists, but of sociobiologists. Most notable amongst these is E.O. Wilson. Wilson, whose short book entitled *On Human Nature* was first published in 1978, is the inventor of the term 'sociobiology', and sociobiology has found a congenial companion in evolutionary psychology, where writers such as Stephen Pinker can confidently speak in the abstract of *How the Mind Works* (1993), the title of one of his most successful books.

The cogency of both sociobiology and evolutionary psychology has been doubted, but their intellectual adequacy (or lack of it) is not the salient issue here. The point, rather, is that the concept of human nature is respectable once more in virtue of its employment in a scientific rather than a humanistic context. It is because people are in general persuaded of the great explanatory power of Darwinian biology, especially when it is amplified and strengthened by the science of genetics, that they give considerable credence to any concept of human nature arising from it (or at any rate seeming to do so). At the same time, this new conception of human nature easily gives rise to the second of the two doubts mentioned earlier. That doubt is this: Can a scientifically based conception of human nature have the right kind of *normative* character? Can it sustain a meaningful distinction between the normal and the abnormal in human behaviour?

Butler himself raises this issue with respect to the psychological egoism against which he was arguing.

> If by following nature were meant only acting as we please ... the very mention of deviating from nature would be absurd ... [T]he ancients speak of deviating from nature as vice, and of following nature [as] the perfection of virtue ... [s]o that language itself should teach people another sense of the words 'following nature' than barely acting as we please. Let it however be observed that though the words 'human nature' are to be explained, yet the real discourse is not concerning the meaning of words [but the need to] make out and explain the assertion that every man is naturally a law to himself, that everyone may find within himself the rule of right, and obligations to follow it. (Butler 1983: 36)

The concept of human nature that Butler here wants to focus on may be too normative for modern tastes, and bring with it some of the unwelcome connotations that the expression 'unnatural practices' can have (though set against this is the rhetorical power that the word 'natural' has acquired once again, in such expressions as 'natural remedies', 'natural diet', and 'natural childbirth'). But even if we hesitate to think of human nature as an internal rule of right with obligations, it is difficult not to draw a distinction between an external and internal aspect to the concept, the former relating simply to the observed behaviour of human beings as animals and the latter to the felt experience of human beings as *agents*.

This distinction and its importance in this context is not new of course. The Scottish Enlightenment, and the eighteenth century more broadly, is noted for its project of the 'science of man'. Indeed, the fact that the term 'moral sciences' (an expression that now seems antiquated) became current at that time is a clear reflection of the pre-eminence of this project. All major philosophers of the period subscribed to the ambition Hume expressly endorses in the preface to his *Treatise of Human Nature* (1739/40), to turn upon moral subjects the methods that

Bacon and Newton had used so successfully in the physical sciences — hence the term 'moral science'.

Butler was in the vanguard of this movement, which explains why Hume admired his *Sermons* though he had no use for his religion. And yet, the idea of a 'moral science' seems to have an ambiguity built into it. In so far as such an inquiry is truly moral — which is to say concerned with the basis of value and meaning — it cannot secure the kind of abstraction and detachment that its being a science would imply. The difference might be said to be that between participant and observer.

In the hands of some of their exponents, contemporary exercises in sociobiology, evolutionary psychology and the naturalization of mind amount to a new attempt to put moral subjects on a scientific basis. This is evident in a writer like E.O. Wilson. Accordingly it is instructive to see why the project of the moral sciences or the science of man faded in the course of nineteenth century, since this may have something to tell us about contemporary academic ambitions. One major factor was a growing awareness of the importance of the participant/observer distinction. The practitioners of the science of man called upon empirical evidence after the manner of Bacon, but they also made extensive use of psychological introspection as a method, something Butler alludes to in the passage I quoted at the start. The difficulty of so doing, however, is not merely that it brings with it a serious risk of subjective bias and generalizing too much from the particular. Introspection, rather, supposes a point of view that must forever escape the assembling of evidence, however careful or extensive that assembly is. This is the point of view of the mind that introspects. There is thus a dimension of mind that any science of mind cannot fail to omit, the inquiring mind itself. This is a criticism brought against the Scottish school of Reid and Hume by one of its successors, the now little known nineteenth-century philosopher J.F. Ferrier. Ferrier writes:

> There is a science called the 'science of the human mind', the object of which is to collect and systematise the phenomena of man's moral and intellectual nature. If this science accomplishes the end proposed, its method must be the very one we ought to make use of. But if it should appear that this science carries in its very conception such a radical defect that all the true and distinctive phenomena of man necessarily elude its grasp, and that it is forever doomed to fall short of the end it designs to compass, then our adoption of its method could only lead us to the poorest and most unsatisfactory results. That such is its real character will … become apparent. (Ferrier 1883: 16)

This passage appears in Chapter Three of Ferrier's *Introduction to the Philosophy of Consciousness* and in the chapters that follow he explains (at inordinate length perhaps) what this radical defect is and how it arises. Exponents of the modern version of the science of mind — empirical psychology and the social sciences — are unlikely to be persuaded (were they ever to read him) that Ferrier has proven all such study radically defective, and in this they may be right. At any rate, it is no part of my purpose here to advance or endorse wholesale scepticism about the prospects for the empirical study of psychology or sociology. But there is one aspect of Ferrier's analysis that is of special interest here. 'Man' he says 'is a "living soul"; but science has been trained among the *dead*. Man is a free agent; but science has taken her lessons from dependent things, the inheritors and transmitters of an activity, gigantic indeed, but which is not their own' (Ferrier 1883: 17). It is human beings in their character as free beings that elude any science of mind based upon strictly empirical observation. Science, says Ferrier, 'may introduce the causal nexus into thought, and call the result "association". But the man himself is not to be found in this "calculating machine"' (Ferrier 1883: 18). The same point can be made about all attempts to construe the mind as a kind of computer that might be replicated in software or information technology. *All* such models, if Ferrier is right, will inevitably leave out *what it is like to be* human. In short, while the physical or biological scientist studies *mere* objects that have no point of view of their own, the moral scientist must deal with subjects that do have their own point of view, and if that point of view is not the only one on human behaviour, it is nevertheless an ineliminable one.

> Leave the mind to its own natural workings, as manifested in the imagination of the poet, the fire and rapid combinations of the orator, the memory of the mathematician, the gigantic activities and never-failing resources of the warrior and statesman, or even the manifold powers put forth in everyday life by the most ordinary of men; and what can be more wonderful and precious than its productions? Cut into it metaphysically, with a view of … ascertaining the process by which all these bright results are elaborated … and every trace of 'what has been' vanishes … the breathing realities are dead, and lifeless abstractions are in their place … Look at thought, and feeling, and passion, as they glow on the pages of Shakespeare … Look at the same as they stagnate on the dissecting-table of Dr Brown, and marvel at the change. (Ferrier 1883: 17)

This reference to Shakespeare, and the contrast with the associationist psychology of Thomas Brown is especially germane to my present concerns, for it is on this point that an explanation and defence of the study of the humanities is to be erected. The human and social *sciences*, however interesting and invaluable their results may be, study human beings as *objects*. This inevitably excludes the point of view of the human being as *subject* — what it means to be a human being. The importance of the humanities, by contrast, resides precisely in their power to illuminate this meaning.

Anything that is properly called an education must, at a minimum, broaden the mental horizons of the person being educated. The purpose of education is to take us beyond the confines of our own experience. Education should be an antidote to personal bias, and that is why a science properly so called is concerned with abstract universals — the world as it is and not the world as individuals happen to find it. The simplest form of teaching and learning is the provision of information and the acquisition of knowledge. The result of both is to enrich the individual from sources other than his or her own experience. But of course the higher forms of education go far beyond this, and supply the inquiring mind not merely with additional facts, but new ways of apprehending those facts, and new ways of conceptualizing the elements of experience. In other words, education is not merely in subjects or topics, but in disciplines and methods.

These points apply equally to the distinction I drew between internal and external perspectives on human nature. We can be parochial and narrow minded with respect to knowledge of the objective facts about human beings, refusing for instance to go beyond received ideas of health and hygiene, delinquency and order, wealth creation and the alleviation of poverty, and it is the business of the medical and social sciences to challenge received ideas and to provide fresh approaches to the medical, social and economic problems that human beings perpetually encounter. But equally, it is possible to be parochial and narrow-minded about what it means to be a human being. The principal cause of this deficiency, in my view, is lack of imagination properly so called — the inability, left to our own devices, to enter imaginatively into the experience of others and thus to see in it both resonances and dissonances with our own. And it is here that the study of the humanities acts as a counter to confinement in the world of the subject, in just the way that the empirical human sciences act as a corrective to limited and distorted beliefs about the world of objects.

This study can be empirical — as it is in history or classics; it can be artistic — as it is in literature, fine art and music; it can be conceptual — as it is in philosophy and some branches of linguistics. But all of these are properly called humanistic studies to the degree that they enhance, expand and interpret subjective experience — the meaning of, rather than the facts about, human existence. We might summarize their concern as that of uncovering and exploring the dialectic between human nature and the human condition. I can think of no better description, in fact, for the work of the Latin poets, for Shakespeare's greatest plays, the historical investigations of Hume, Gibbon, Huizinga or Tawney, the philosophy of Plato, Kant or Hegel. Each of these, in their different ways, compels the person who seeks to understand them to enter into an engagement with apprehensions of experience that are enlarging, and because enlarging, enriching. What we find in them, in my view, is the element that Butler means to point to when he refers to the 'testimony' of mankind, for testimony is essentially first person, to be supplied by those who have seen or heard for themselves, and not those who have merely collected 'the facts' in a detached and impartial way.

Universities do many things, yet it is a constant temptation for those who work within them to discriminate between subjects by bestowing or withholding the accolade of academic respectability. In times past, it has been those subjects less easily described as 'sciences' that have come under pressure, and this may explain why there have been regular attempts to construe the humanities as 'moral sciences'. This pressure seems less today than previously, but it has been replaced by another — the need to demonstrate utilitarian credentials — usefulness. If anything, this is a more damaging pressure. It comes largely from outside the academy, but the understandable acquiescence of those within easily becomes a kind of collusion with the narrow consumerist climate of the times. This is a topic dealt with at length in the previous essay. Here it is enough to repeat that there is an important distinction to be drawn between the useful and the valuable. While the role of some subjects of study is to help us to live longer, healthier and more prosperous lives, the role of others is to make those longer, healthier lives worth living. The study of art, literature, music, philosophy and history are best advised, in my view, to lay claim to the second role not the first.

Such a distinction is easily misunderstood. There has been a tendency for academics in the humanities, especially in Britain, to look back with nostalgia on a misremembered past of classical education, and on the basis of these false memories to sniff and sneer at utilitarian subjects such as animal husbandry and hotel management. It is an attitude that has done much to erode the public's support and sympathy for universities in general, and the humanities in particular. So it is worth stating the obvious: utilitarian subjects are *useful*, a fact that rightly commends them. At the same time, human life is not to be confined to bread and circuses, or even vastly more sophisticated forms of nutrition and entertainment. It has meaning and value other than these, and it is the function of nearly everything that falls under the label 'arts and humanities' to explore, amplify and enhance this meaning. Both sides in this dispute need to remember that while 'man cannot live by bread alone', he cannot live without it either.

This is at best a broad brush explanation and defence of the place of the humanities in the curriculum of schools and colleges. The argument needs to be spelt out at much greater length (as I have tried to do for the arts in *Philosophy of the Arts* [London, Routledge 3rd edition 2005], Chapter 4). But even when this is done there is a residual topic of some interest. Is there a place for divinity as well as humanity among the subjects of the modern university? This question arises not simply because the effect of increasing secularization has been to bring the role and general relevance of theology into question, but because in the reorganization many universities have recently undergone, theology or divinity is regularly to be found located in the School of Humanities. This fact reflects, and also strengthens, an increasing tendency for Theology to become indistinguishable from Religious Studies. The difference is of course crucial — the subject of theology is *God*; the subject of religious studies is *belief about* God. Religious beliefs are the religious beliefs of human beings, and though there has been a powerful movement to construe religious studies as one of the human sciences, we may suppose that there is also room for its humanistic study. But a humanist study of *God* sounds like an absurdity. Where then can theology fit in?

Here I have only the briefest of remarks to make. Earlier I suggested that one way of locating the place of the humanities in the advancement of human understanding is to think of their comprising a dialogue between human nature and the human condition and thereby uncovering and exploring the value and meaning of our humanity. This is why they are to be called humanistic subjects. We ought not, however, to confuse this with *humanism*, which takes human value to be both the source and the summation of *all* that is valuable. This is what the American theologian R.R. Reno has named 'we-matter-most' humanism, and it is a view that modern Western Europe finds it almost impossible not to adopt. We-matter-most humanism is seductive to a largely secular world, but it is also potentially dangerous as environmentalists and others like to remind us. The doctrine is not new of course. Indeed it is nothing more than the modern reassertion of the ancient Protagorean thesis that 'man is the measure of all things, of those that are, that they are, and of those that are not, that they are not'. A genuinely inquiring mind, of the sort we aim to inculcate in schools and universities, will want to ask not only about its potential dangers, but about its truth and falsehood. *Is* man the measure of all things? And the only way this question can be asked and answered is by going beyond the internal dialogue between human nature and the human condition and inquiring into the alternative realities that might set it round. This means, in effect, theology. If beyond the human there is anything, it is the divine. Divinity thus provides a context and a foil against which the scope of explorations in the humanities are to be assessed and their limits, if any, to be established. In my view it is to be wished that the potential role of theology in this regard were proclaimed more confidently by those whose subject it is, and accepted more open-mindedly by the humanities with which they are now so often allied.

For a final word on this theme we can return to Butler. In my first paragraph I quoted him as saying that psychological egoism is one of the 'absurdities which even men of capacity run into when they have occasion to belie their nature'. The reason, he goes on to say, is that such a view of human nature 'will perversely disclaim that image of God which was originally stamped upon it, the traces of which, however feint, are plainly discernible upon the mind of man' (Butler 1983: 27).

Interdisciplinary versus Multidisciplinary Study[1]

Here is a familiar story that academics and policy makers in higher education often tell.

> The history of intellectual inquiry since the eighteenth century is one in which the human and natural sciences developed distinctive boundaries. Within these boundaries they pursued their own concerns and developed their own methods. For the most part, such specialization worked to the benefit of knowledge and understanding in general since it allowed and encouraged a highly productive intellectual division of labour. However, with the explosion of knowledge that marked the first half of the twentieth century, these traditional divisions became less relevant, and in some cases positively obstructive to intellectual advance. And while it is understandable that those brought up in the traditions of one discipline should have special loyalties to that discipline, the cause of knowledge as such is better served by transcending residual loyalties and working across disciplines.

This is the story that has prompted the widespread move to interdisciplinary study. More importantly, it has acted as a justifying narrative for those who want to press the case for academic and institutional changes that would dissolve the autonomy of traditional disciplines. It is a story that is easy to illustrate. The old division between zoology and botany, for example, is to a considerable extent irrelevant in a world that has discovered (at a micro

---

[1]   Originally delivered as a lecture to the Royal Irish Academy, June 2002

level) the fundamental importance of molecular and cell biology and come to appreciate (at a macro level) the new perspective of ecology. At either level the practice of studying animals or plants exclusively seems to have been rendered outdated. Consequently, any determination to continue in these old ways can only appear perverse, because intellectual seriousness requires us to relinquish inherited loyalties for the sake of new insights. The refusal to do so signals a preference for the familiar over the true, a preference that obviously cannot take precedence in an institution seriously committed to research that pushes at the edges of intellectual inquiry.

This particular illustration of the desirability of ignoring old divisions and abandoning established intellectual boundaries is drawn from the life sciences, but it provides us with a very compelling example of the need for academic adaptation to newly prevailing conditions, perhaps the most compelling of any of the examples that could be cited. Genetics and ecology are genuinely new areas of inquiry that have indeed called into question the wisdom of continuing to hold zoology and botany at arms length from each other.

The compellingness of this particular example, however, may be misleading, and even in this case there are complexities that make the familiar story I have just outlined a less than perfect fit. But I am not going to go into these. My contention is that, even if the story can be told accurately in this context, the *general* version is often sustained by a tacit assumption that what is true of the life sciences is true of intellectual inquiry as a whole. At a minimum, this assumption needs to be made explicit and its plausibility examined. In the absence of such examination, an important influence on contemporary thinking rests upon the fallacy of generalizing from a particular instance. Moreover, it is a fallacy that avoids exposure largely because of a constant and widespread tendency to confuse *inter*-disciplinarity with *multi*-disciplinarity. These are quite different things. So different are they in fact that an enthusiasm for multi-disciplinarity is quite compatible with deep scepticism about the potential value of *inter*-disciplinarity. It is the main purpose of this essay to explain why this is so.

Disciplines and subjects

The term 'discipline' is not always used with great precision. For the most part this does not matter, but in considering carefully the issues we are concerned with here, it is valuable to draw a distinction between a discipline and a subject. As I shall draw this distinction, 'Politics' is a subject, not a discipline. What I mean is this. Within the study of Politics, political philosophy, political history, political sociology and the science of comparative politics have equal claims to recognition. But philosophy, history and science are separate *disciplines*. The *subjects* that customarily fall under these labels have their own conventional topics no doubt — social obligation is one of political philosophy's traditional topics, the rise and fall of empires a topic of political history — but it is their distinctive methods that mark them off from each other as forms of inquiry.

A simple account of these distinctions is this. Philosophy is concerned with conceptual possibilities and normative conceptions, not with empirical facts. By contrast, science is concerned with empirical facts, but of a general, atemporal kind. History, on the other hand, while its shares with science an interest in empirical fact, fixes upon the particular and the historically located. Science generates falsifiable theories, while history and philosophy generate explanations whose merits are sometimes comprehensiveness rather than truth. And so on.

There is nothing novel to be claimed for this list of differences between philosophy, science and history. Yet its lack of contentiousness is in fact a strength in the present context. Stating the obvious has the notable advantage of appealing to things known to be true. The point of doing so, however, is to provide a solid basis for the more contentious inferences one wishes to draw. And the inferences I want to draw are these. First, the example of Politics shows that the idea of a subject whose study regularly and necessarily draws upon different disciplines is neither dramatically innovative, or in any way unfamiliar. Nor is Politics unusual in this regard. Take Classics or French. Both of these can properly include philosophical, historical, literary and linguistic inquiries. Second, the proper description of such studies, if we make Politics or French or Classics our guide, is *multi*disciplinary — i.e. involving more than one discipline — not *inter*disciplinary — i.e. involving the intersection of disciplines. One thing that this means is that over a wide range of cases, the different branches of these studies can happily proceed in relative separation from each other. There *may* be some reason to think that the investigations of historians into the politics of the Glorious Revolution of 1688 could illuminate the work of the political philosophers studying Locke's *Second Treatise of Civil Government*. However, this gives us no reason whatever to think that those who want to investigate the Roman corn trade will be better able to do so if they know something about the Stoicism of Marcus Aurelius. The former example is plausible, if in the end unpersuasive; the latter example does not even have an initial plausibility.

Examples such as these can be multiplied indefinitely. Knowledge of the architecture of St Mark's in Venice might illuminate the music of Giovanni Gabrieli to some extent. But between Gabrieli's music and the impact of tourism on property values in Tuscany there no connection whatever, other than the fact that both might accurately fall under the label 'Italian Studies'.

Synergy

Now whilst it might be thought that these remarks are of limited interest, in fact they bear directly and importantly on two voguish concepts — 'synergy' and 'critical mass' — concepts that I want to consider in turn. An important part of the concept of synergy (frequently invoked in the somewhat meaningless plural 'synergies'), at least in this context, is the implication that the whole is more than the sum of its parts. That is to say, the invocation of the concept normally implies that there are academic contexts and intellectual topics where, were the practitioners of two hitherto independent disciplines to combine their knowledge and methods, this would result in greater intellectual understanding than could be expected were they to continue to pursue their inquiries apart. In this respect, synergy is a concept that applies to *inter*disciplinarity, because where what is at issue is *multi*disciplinarity, the whole is *not* more than the sum of its parts. Italian Studies simply comprises Italian language *plus* Italian art *plus* Italian history, and so on.

This is not to say that that the sum is of no greater value than its parts. On the contrary, it is important to stress that from the point of view of multidisciplinarity, the sum is very likely to have more value than either of its parts alone. Students of French are better off for knowing about *both* French history *and* French poetry. The difference is that the benefit is greater quantitatively, not qualitatively. They know more about more things that fall under the label 'French', but they do not have a better understanding of French history *because* they also understand French poetry. By contrast, the believers in synergy, who are therefore proponents of interdisciplinarity, think that to engage in the investigation of a subject adequately, we need to engage with different disciplines. They hold, in other words, that the insights of one discipline will illuminate the subject matter of another better than it could expect to do relying only on its own methods. This is an important claim. Is it true *in general* that the investigations of a distinctive discipline are intellectually poorer for not being conducted alongside or in the company of other disciplines?

In assessing this claim, the first point to be made is that there is no scope for the a priori, no place for arguments of the form 'it's bound to be the case'. If the benefits of interdisciplinarity — synergy — are indeed real, this has to be a matter of experience and hence of evidence available to support the contention. Beyond certain restricted contexts, however, this does *not* appear to be the case. Some support for this claim can be derived from the fact that the cause of interdisciplinarity generally needs to be pressed upon a relatively reluctant academy. Academic planners and funding councils would not need the constant round of 'initiatives' they use to motivate interdisciplinary programmes of research if the practitioners of different disciplines regularly found, as a matter of personal experience, that the subjects in which they were interested were powerfully illuminated by the investigations of other disciplines. The point is similar to one that has often been made about co-operative enterprise. If co-operative enterprise has all the merits its advocates say, co-operative enterprises would long ago have displaced competitive ones. But they have not, and where co-operation has been imposed the results have varied from counterproductive to disastrous. In this respect, the example of the life sciences is again misleading; the subsumption of botany and zoology within genetics and ecology, which has been embraced with considerable enthusiasm in most quarters, is atypical.

There are, of course, other examples besides this, but the life sciences example may be unique by being relatively uncontentious. This brings us to the second point about interdisciplinarity. In most cases its intellectual profitability is itself a matter of genuine academic debate. Consider a different example. Empirical psychology, neurological studies of the brain, artificial intelligence and the philosophy of mind have generally conducted their investigations apart from each other. The aim of 'cognitive science' is to bring them together in a grand synthesis so that the insights of each may illuminate the others. To this end, especially in the US, huge amounts of research money have been devoted to building research teams in cognitive science. But of late, enthusiasm for this project has faded in some quarters (though by no means all) because its actual intellectual benefits are much less impressive than was hoped or expected. Cognitive science has not had anything like the success of genetics, for example, and though a great many research projects in cognitive science continue to be undertaken and to be funded, it is now a matter of some dispute as to whether such a synthesis is indeed the best way of advancing the study of mind. This is a context in which it is worth remembering that academic fashions change. An important contributor to the foundations of modern empirical psychology was the philosopher Alexander Bain, who in his day argued convincingly that mental phenomena would be better understood if empirical psychology and the philosophy of mind were *separated*. Unlike the case of genetics, the putative advantages of an interdisciplinary cognitive science are themselves a matter of intellectual contention.

Third, the degree of debate and contention can go very deep, much deeper than the debate between doubters and enthusiasts in cognitive science. For example, over a considerable period a movement within biblical scholarship has developed around the idea of treating the Bible as literature and thus applying the established methods of literary analysis to biblical texts. Research grants have been obtained, PhDs awarded, and new journals established under the auspices of this interdisciplinary initiative. To treat the Bible as literature, however, is to take a stand on its theological value. It implicitly denies the significance of the Bible as sacred history or revelation. While it casts it more easily into subject matter appropriate for the anthropological study of religion, by the very same token it cuts it off from Biblical theology. Now it is not my intention to take sides on this important issue, merely to point out that people who advocate the application of literary methods to Biblical study on the grounds of interdisciplinarity cannot be construed as simply urging a broader and more fruitful perspective than the one biblical scholars have traditionally employed. They are also advocating a highly contentious position within biblical exegesis, and in so far as they are interpreted as advocating a less traditional and more open methodology, the contentiousness of their position is disguised.

In summary, the relation between botany, zoology, genetics and ecology is an impressive example for the advocate of interdisciplinarity to invoke because it is one in which new perspectives that transcend traditional boundaries appear to have significantly advanced our understanding. In this respect, however, the life sciences are atypical. They differ from several other prominent attempts where there seem to be fewer intellectual benefits, and where the beneficial nature of those that there are can itself be legitimately questioned.

Critical mass

Potential synergy is not the only string to interdisciplinarity's bow. The other is 'critical mass'. The idea here is a very simple one, namely that some of the intellectual tasks confronting contemporary inquiry cannot effectively be tackled by small numbers of people working in separate locations. This is an obstacle compounded by current academic conditions, notably the limited amount of financial support available for expensive subjects. In the light of both considerations, the effective prosecution of the subjects in question requires an amalgamation of effort in which investigators are brought together in numbers sufficient to form a 'critical mass'.

The first point to be made about this argument is that it applies to some disciplines only. Although the critical mass story is frequently used to throw doubts on the viability of every small academic unit, it is evident that it does not apply universally, or even very widely. Many subjects are cheap, and no more expensive to engage in (relatively speaking) than they have ever been. Modern nuclear physics and molecular biology need large amounts of expensive equipment and substantial teams of investigators, and it is unreasonable to expect these to be replicated in institution after institution. This is undeniable. What is equally undeniable, however, is that the same cannot be said for history or literature or philosophy, and it can be said of law and the social sciences only in limited and special cases.

Sometimes, an attempt is made to extend the critical mass argument to these other subjects not by way of their cost but by way of intellectual stimulus. Though there will always be solitary scholars of genius, the argument goes, the more run-of-the-mill scholar or social scientist needs the stimulus of colleagues working in the same field. This seems to me true, but its implications are questionable. In the first place, the 'critical mass' that such an argument sustains may be very small — just three or four people perhaps. In the second place, intellectuals are never truly isolated from stimulating trends as long as they have books and periodicals, and this way of combating intellectual isolation has had a huge new aid put at its disposal in the form of email and the Internet. In so far as the 'critical mass' argument could formerly be applied to cheap as well as expensive subjects, its force has been seriously diminished by the advent of new information technology. Academics now have instant access from their desks to an enormous number of archived and current research periodicals as well as digitized books, prints, manuscripts, scores and historic documents. Moreover, thanks to the Internet and consortium library subscriptions, this is true of academics in small and minor institutions of whom it was not true before.

A third, but equally important point to be made is this. To the degree that there is substance to the critical mass argument, it can be advanced quite independently of any claims on behalf of interdisciplinarity. The concept of critical mass is more naturally taken to apply to the number of people doing the *same* thing, rather than numbers of people doing *different* things. In this respect, indeed, it might even be held that the need for critical mass tells *against* interdisciplinary programmes of investigation, since inevitably these will dilute the concentration of specialists in one area. Academic managers should be cautious about advocating the two together, and even more cautious about institutional reforms that aim to realize both, since these are likely to contain within themselves the seeds of their own failure.

Information Systems and the Concept of a Library[1]

In a good many academic institutions the library and the computing service have been merged into a single service, often renamed the 'directorate of information services', or something similar. Mergers of this kind have come about largely because of the vastly extended use of computers in the last 25 years. These computers, the software programmes they employ and the networks that link them are almost always lumped together under the general label 'information technology' or IT for short. Now while for most purposes there is nothing wrong with this label, it can obscure certain important issues that are crucial to assessing the wisdom and desirability of the changes that the appeal to 'information technology' usually ushers in. Moreover, since 'information technology' has a modern and progressive ring to it, it not infrequently happens that the questions the use of the expression obscures, cannot be raised and explored in a wholly open and critical fashion, because such criticism is so easily branded 'Luddite'. The effect of branding it in this way is to place it in the same category as (say) a preference for the quill pen over the word processor, a preference that almost willfully fails to acknowledge the inevitable march of technological devel-

---

[1] Originally delivered in the Humanities Lecture Series 2003-4, King's College London, November 2003

opment and advancement, an attitude that most people would find it impossible to defend.

Still, while Luddism is certainly a cast of mind to be avoided, it is wrong to silence criticism by innuendo, since the uncritical endorsement of all technological change in the name of progress is scarcely any less objectionable. Modern technology does not always secure advances. It is said, for instance, that (at least until recently) journey times in central London had returned to those of the mid nineteenth century, despite the evident technological superiority of the motor car to the horse and cart.

Sometimes, even, the latest technology can be more cumbersome and costly than that which it has replaced, and in some instances this cost takes the form of the hidden displacement of valuable resources. To cite an example familiar to many: the introduction of computer controlled finance systems generally renders redundant the extensive knowledge and expertise currently possessed by those operating the existing system, and where comparable expertise in the new system does not fall speedily into place, the loss, even if it is medium rather than long term, is very considerable. The position is somewhat similar to that of workers going on strike; even when their action is successful, the resulting pay increase can take several years to compensate effectively for earnings lost during the strike.

In this essay my aim is to look critically at some contemporary assumptions about libraries as information systems. I want to explore the contrast between a conception of information technology as the means by which the traditional library is to be transformed, and the more limited conception of IT as the library's most powerful new servant. The key element in this exploration is a careful examination of the key concepts of information and knowledge.

The power of IT

Let us begin with this question: is a library an information retrieval system? There is certainly a familiar conceptual picture, widely accepted, that construes it in this way. According to this picture, books and journal articles are the products of information gathering, and these products are then stored in the library. The task of the librarian is to organize the store in such a way that the information it contains can be accessed quickly and easily by users (or 'readers' to use an older expression). Accordingly, the skill of the librarian lies chiefly in what is now called 'information management', which is to say the classification, preservation, storage and distribution of the information that the library possesses.

In the light of this picture it is easy to see why it is thought that information technology is a natural ally of the librarian. Computer hardware and software are highly efficient media for information storage and retrieval. As is well known, the equivalent of huge numbers of books and periodicals can be stored digitally in a very small physical compass, and computer searchable databases can sort, find and deliver information by request and from a vast pool at incredible speeds, speeds that no alternative means could possibly match. In addition to these advantages, there are those relating to access. In the mediaeval library one treasured copy of each book was chained to a table for the use of one reader at a time. In the era of the Internet, libraries can become spatially and temporally dispersed, their contents available to anyone at any time anywhere in the world. The removal of time and space constraints has the potential of massively increasing the number of users of any given item and thus massively reducing the cost per use. In the light of all this, IT is easily construed as more than the ally of the library; it is the means by which libraries are to be transformed (or 'aufgehoben' to use the more accurate Hegelian term), their previous limitations being overcome in a new historical/technological era. How could it *not* be the case that digital technology provides us with the opportunity to do what libraries have always sought to do, but with levels of efficiency and effectiveness that were hitherto inconceivable?

It is in on the strength of this point about extending the pool of users that a great deal of time and money has recently been put into programmes of digitization whereby existing library holdings are scanned electronically in order for them to be accessed and searched online. Digitization makes perfect sense, if what we are witnessing truly is the transformation of the traditional library, because in that case there will come a day when material that is *not* available digitally will be inaccessible to the vast majority of a library's users. Furthermore, because of new patterns of teaching and learning, any material that is not available in electronic form is likely to be neglected or ignored by the relatively small number to whom it remains physically accessible. This is, I believe, the driving motivation behind most (possibly all) digitizing projects, but of course a similar line of thought has lain behind the huge investment that there has been in computer hardware and software in general.

Information, storage and retrieval

Now, while this conceptual picture, together with the practical and financial recommendations that it appears to imply, has been found persuasive by a great many people, it seems to me that there are three important doubts about its cogency. The first arises from a crucial ambiguity in the term 'information'. In everyday use, 'information' is a normative term with a positive implication. Information is something valuable, and to be contrasted with its detrimental counterpart '*mis*information'. But in its specialist use within the world of computing, 'information' has no corresponding negative term. Digital 'information' consists in electronic impulses that cannot be right or wrong, they simply are. In this sense of the term, a well functioning 'information' storage and retrieval system can store and retrieve misinformation (in the normal sense). In other words, although properly described as storing and distributing digital information with all the power and efficiency of the very best computer systems, it nonetheless seriously misleads those who access it. And does so to a greater degree, perhaps, just because the power of the technology lends the 'information' it produces an important air of authority.

It is a point that hardly needs emphasizing for those who have discovered how easily students can be misinformed by material they find on the web, and how detrimental this can be to their understanding. Every one who marks essays knows that the undiscriminating student is much more impressed, and hence more easily misled, by specious web sites than by the poor quality printed material that amateur philosophers, historians and scientists were able to produce hitherto. Quality of content and quality of style can diverge far more radically on the Internet than they ever could in older media. This is an issue to be returned to.

The second defect in the picture of the library transformed into a modern 'information system' in this; it conflates a library and an archive, and many libraries are not archives. The two are not the same, and for the purposes of the present analysis it is essential to distinguish them carefully. However, it has to be admitted that the terms 'archive' and 'library' are not always used with the precision I am giving them, so that the difference I have in mind needs to be explained.

By 'archive' I mean a simple collection of recorded data, whether this be large or small. In this sense, the following are all examples of archives: the data collected in a census or run of censuses, a manufacturer's online catalogue, the student records of a university or other educational institution, an industrial company's data base of customers and suppliers, both actual and potential, the repository of Acts of Parliament housed in Westminster. Such archives are usually paper based (though until very recently Acts of Parliament were inscribed on vellum, i.e. goatskin). They generate problems of storage, preservation (the reason for vellum), organization and retrieval and it is these problems that constitute the subject matter of their management.

The traditional user of an archive is someone who seeks a specific item of information — the price of a good, the address of a supplier, the birth date of an ancestor. Accordingly, the task of the archivist is to ensure first and foremost that each item is stored and preserved in a way sufficient to ensure long term access to it, and to further ensure that the whole archive is organized in a way that makes finding and retrieving items of information as easy as possible. With the increased study of social history (and the other social sciences), large scale marketing campaigns by business and industry, government policy studies, and similar generalizing uses of data, an important limitation of the traditional archive has become apparent. To study census data, say, with an eye to general trends rather than particular facts, is very costly in terms of research time and effort. This is where computer technology truly comes into its own. In the compilation and manipulation of data sets, it is unrivalled. When this overwhelming advantage is combined with more cost efficient storage and less susceptibility to physical decay (possibly), it seems incontestable that a computerized archive is greatly superior to the traditional one. By implication, anyone who clings to the latter because of, say, a preference for vellum over liquid crystal display screens, is indeed guilty of a kind of Luddism, which can be characterized as the attitude that lies behind the physical destruction of new technologies just because they are new.

That information technology brings huge advantages to the maintenance and use of archives, then, is clear. Yet it would be illicit to argue from this to a much more general conclusion, namely that the age of IT also heralds the transformation of libraries. This is because not all libraries are archives. By 'library' I shall mean a collection of cultural artefacts, generally but not necessarily of a linguistic nature. Many libraries have holdings of music, prints and engravings, technical drawings, maps, photographs and so on, as well as books, periodicals, newspapers and other written or printed items. Now it is simply not the case that all these sorts of things can accurately be described as kinds of information. A music score is not in any obvious sense a piece of information; indeed philosophers have often explored the difficulties involved in saying just what it is. So too with many prints and engravings. Nor is this a difference between the visual image and the printed word. Maps may be said to contain or comprise a great deal of information in graphic rather than literal form, while countless numbers of books and periodicals cannot properly be described as information at all — novels and poetry magazines being among the most obvious instances.

If this is correct, if libraries, in contrast to archives, contain large numbers of cultural artefacts that are not significant or interesting for their information value, it follows, contrary to the proposition with which we began, that a library is not an information storage and retrieval system. And from this it follows in turn, that there is no reason to expect a library to be replaced or transformed by a technology whose great advantage lies in the storage and retrieval of information. Any supposition to the contrary is thus, at best distorting, and will lead in all likelihood to the sort of costly errors that arise from setting off firmly down the wrong path.

Since quite a few institutions appear to have set off along this path it is worth speculating perhaps, on why this is. One factor, in my estimation, is that the IT cast of mind is powerfully inclined to conflate first and second order uses of library holdings, and to regard second order use as primary. What I mean is this. I can read the poetry of John Donne (say) for the sake of reading poetry. This is a first order use. But I can also read it as a way of gathering historical information about the period in which he wrote. This is a second order use, and this second order use does convert the poetry of John Donne into a source of information about the early seveteenth century. A similar point might be made about Hogarth's celebrated series of engravings *The Rake's Progress* and *The Harlot's Progress*, which may indeed be more frequently viewed for the historical information they reveal than for the moral and social messages they were meant to convey, or even the aesthetic character they continue to have.

In both cases the *primary* significance of the poetry or the prints is not the historical information that can be derived from them, however useful that information may prove to be. Yet this confusion of primary and secondary value is a mistake often and easily made by those who have a prior commitment to, and a preconception about the relation of IT to the library. Thus, by a sort of conceptual sleight-of-hand, the erroneous conception of the library as an archive of information is maintained, while the true nature of the library is obscured.

Knowledge

Even were such confusion dispelled, however, there is a third flaw in the conceptual picture I have been examining. This lies not in its concept of information so much as its conception of knowledge. Here, the picture at work is an old one, one that has long been powerfully influential in philosophy, especially in the empiricist tradition, and more recently in the investigations of cognitive science and artificial intelligence. This models the mind on a receptacle in which items of information are placed, and the knowing mind is thus one that, almost literally, *contains* a great deal of information. One immediate problem for such a conception lies in the fact that the possession of knowledge does not seem to be exclusive in quite the way the model suggests. My owning a car excludes your owning it (special arrangements aside), but my knowing something does not exclude your knowing it as well. This is a problem that can be got round without too much difficulty, perhaps, as it is in Locke's picture of the mind as (roughly) a soft surfaced tablet upon which experience impresses items of information which together comprise a person's knowledge .

But whichever analogy we use — the container or the tablet — knowing is being construed as something passive; we know something if, and after, we have been acted upon by the external world. The only scope for activity, on this account, is that of collecting and gathering, or, on the Lockean picture, putting ourselves in the right position to receive an 'impression'.

This is not the place to engage in an extended discussion of what is a major topic in the history of philosophy, but it is pertinent to remark that there is much to be said for thinking of knowing, not as a state of *being*, but a kind of *doing*. To know the Greek alphabet, for example, is not to have its characters stored in one's head, but to be able to recite its constituent letters in order. To know where London is in relation to Aberdeen is not (*pace* some geographers) to be possessed of an internal 'mental' map, but to be able to pick out the two places on a real map, or give someone general instructions about getting from one to the other ('Go about 500 miles in a south-southeasterly direction'). That knowing is in this sense active rather than passive is born out by our commonly saying that we 'grasp' the facts about this or that. We never say that we 'encounter' them in the way that we encounter loud noises and bright lights.

The relevance of all this to the subject in hand — information technology and the library — is this. The conception of the library as an information retrieval system gains much of its plausibility from the mistaken idea that the business of teaching and learning is a matter of filling empty minds. Yet every university teacher knows the phenomenon of the essay or examination script in which the student simply regurgitates material from books and lectures, and also knows just how far this falls short of the idea of educational accomplishment. But if knowing were indeed as the 'information storage and retrieval' conception suggests, the regurgitating student would be a fine example of its success.

If, on the contrary, knowing is active, what the student or other library user requires is coaching and instruction in the skills of acquiring and reproducing genuine knowledge. We might put it this way: the task of the teacher is to inculcate a knowing mind, not to pass on information. The question then arises as to how this fact bears upon our conception of the library and upon its use of information technology.

Searching, surfing and browsing

One of the unquestionable advantages of computing technology is the search facility. Vast amounts of material can be searched in periods of time impossible to believe if it were not that they are happening all the time. Google, the most successful Internet search engine, currently (late 2004) reviews over 8 billion web pages, in as little as 1.2 seconds. It is not so good for browsing, however. The difference is that the searcher knows what he or she wants to find, while the browser is someone who wants to discover what is worth finding.

To make the point I want to make clearly, we should perhaps distinguish between 'surfing' and browsing'. Surfing the Internet is a diverting and sometimes profitable activity but there is a random element to it that marks it off from browsing, at least compared with browsing in a good library, bookshop or gallery. This difference arises from two factors — quality and organization. One important feature of the Internet is that there are no quality controls screening what appears there. I am not here thinking about pornography, for which general 'blocking' methods have been devised and are available. I am thinking rather of something referred to earlier — the amateurish investigations and invalid assertions about every subject under the sun that can be found in abundance on the Internet.

One consequence of this fact is that the use of the Internet for the purposes of learning and inquiry requires critical judgement on the part of the inquirer. Sometimes education policy makers, and occasionally educationalists, forget or ignore this. Enraptured by the prospects of e-learning, they launch expensive programmes aimed at giving every classroom access to the web, without appreciating that such access is not itself an educational experience. Its value depends upon those who use it being already educated, and thus able to discriminate between the interesting and the trivial, the bogus and the authentic. Here, too it seems to me, the Lockean picture is at work, for it is supposed that the mind of the child (or the student) can be filled with useful information simply by encountering the vast amounts of material that the Internet comprises.

Contrast this with the traditional library, where relatively stringent quality controls do exist, both direct and indirect. Librarians decide what will go on the shelves, and select from sources — publishers and the like — that are themselves controllers of quality. About 110,000 new titles are now published in Britain every year, and there are many more typescripts that never find a publisher. Of those that are published a large majority never make it to library shelves. Both publishers and librarians can make mistakes, obviously, but this is powerful evidence that a very high level of quality control is being exercised in the medium of print that has no counterpart on the Internet.

Accordingly, surfing the Internet is not like browsing in a library because while the first — surfing — ranges over material assembled without regard to worth or quality, the second — browsing — moves around material that has been selected in accordance with certain principles. And there is this further difference — organization. The systems of library organization that have evolved over the years — Dewey classification, Library of Congress and so on — are not geared simply to locating specific items in large collections, but to grouping items cognately so that the browser's attention is drawn to hitherto unknown material relevant to his or her interests. This is a crucial feature of the organization of libraries and another element that sets them apart from mere stores of information available for retrieval.

Of course, something similar can be done with online materials. Online bookshops, for instance, regularly draw the customer's attention to items related in some way to those that they have just purchased or inspected. So too with library resources online, and we may suppose that new and more imaginative ways of doing this will develop over time. This possibility, however, does nothing to undermine the point I have been making. On the contrary, it speaks powerfully in favour of the second of the two conceptions with which I began — the conception of information technology as the librarian's most powerful new tool.

The merger of libraries and computing systems has sometimes given hegemony to the information technologist over the librarian. This is often for no better reason than that the technologist seems more representative of the new regime, while the librarian seems more to be left over from the old. There is a danger in such circumstances, however, that the technologists begin to re-invent the wheel, because, having discarded or at least discounted the tried and tested methods of the librarian, they have to create new systems of organization which, inevitably, will have faults and failings that might have been avoided if a more instrumental conception of technology as primarily the librarian's assistant had been in place.

But there is often a more important idea at work too, and that is a belief in what we might call the neutrality of information. Neutrality in this sense is most easily illustrated by transport, an analogy often invoked by talk of the electronic 'superhighway' and so on. Consider a road system or a rail network. Those who have the responsibility of designing, creating and maintaining these are strictly neutral with respect to the purposes to which they are put. It is the concern of road and rail engineers to enable me to travel safely and efficiently from A to B. It is no concern of theirs whether I do so for a serious or a trivial purpose, whether I am a surgeon on my way to perform a life saving operation, or someone merely staving off boredom with a trip to the shops. Now information technologists sometimes suppose that they too should assume a position of neutrality in this sense, and make available the best computer networks irrespective of the purposes to which they are put. This seems plausible when the 'information' in mind is accounts and records as much as books and periodicals. It is not the business of the information service to favour one over the other. However, this idea of IT's essential neutrality is not a view that is easily sustained when espoused in a different context; should the information technologist be neutral as between pornographic materials and medical records, for example?

Strictly, though, important as it is, this is not an issue for us here. In this context it is enough to observe that were we to take a neutralist view of IT, this would further undermine the idea that IT is the means by which the traditional library is to be transformed. On the contrary, it would emphasize IT's *subservience* to the traditional purposes of the library in so far as these are educational in the broadest sense. That is because, as I have been arguing, quality control and selective organization i.e. *non*-neutrality are what make a library a genuinely educational resource as opposed to a mere information store.

To summarize: the widely held belief that information technology heralds the transformation of the library and its incorporation into a much more general 'information delivery system' rests upon some important confusions. There is first the mistaken idea that the word 'information' means the same in the context of computing as it does in the wider world. Second, there is the tendency to confuse archives, or data stores, with libraries properly so called, whose content is not data but cultural artefacts. Third, there is a mistaken idea that knowledge is a matter of the passive acquisition of items of information, an erroneous conception whose error is compounded by a specious aspiration to neutrality of a mere 'information highway' and the questionable inferences that are often drawn from this. The conclusion to be drawn is that libraries should no more allow their purposes to be subsumed within a new world of 'information technology' than government departments should give way to the office of statistics once it has gone digital.

Such a conclusion, is quite consistent with a recognition that the development of modern information technology and its extensive employment has presented libraries with an immense range of new possibilities that will greatly enhance their scope and service. It is also consistent with the belief that in the era of IT, there is much fresh thinking to be done about how libraries are organized and used. The important point, however, and one that it has been the principal purpose of this essay to make, is that such re-thinking will be better undertaken if some of the conceptual confusions that commonly infect the debates are cleared away.

The Prospects For E-Learning[1]

Technology and its reception

In the history of technology we tend to remember the 'big' winners — the wheel, the printing press, the gun, the mechanical loom, the telephone, the aeroplane and so on — but of course it is also a history filled with failures — devices and inventions that have been long since forgotten. More interesting than mere flops, however, are those inventions and developments that in their day were initially regarded as the heralds of a major revolution, but which, for one reason or another, have in the end proved not to be so.

One such example is nuclear power, plausibly and reasonably hailed as the means by which human beings would cease to be dependent on fossil fuel, an outcome to be welcomed with enthusiasm and relief, given the polluting nature of coal, gas and oil, and the finite quantity of resources that would ultimately be exhausted. By contrast, nuclear power promised to be atmospherically clean and effectively limitless. And so indeed it is. Yet despite this, a variety of factors, some having to do with political opinion and attitudes to risk, and some the result of purely contingent events like those at Three Mile Island and Chernobyl, have brought it about that the nuclear revolution in power

[1]   Originally delivered as a lecture to a Scottish Enterprise conference in Edinburgh, February 2004

has not happened and is unlikely to do so in the foreseeable future.

This example should make us cautious about predicting the impact of new technologies even when we have a clear and informed understanding of their distinctive properties and special merits. All that was said by the proponents of nuclear power is true. Its safety record far excels that of coal, gas or oil, and being cleaner than all these other forms of power generation, it contributes nothing to the greenhouse effect which many people believe to lie at the heart of global warming. This second point is especially important for those who share the view that global warming is the most serious contemporary threat that human beings face. But the key to nuclear power's failure lay in its reception, not in its nature. Curiously to my mind, people have romantically lamented the demise of coal, despite the large number of mining disasters that have taken indefinitely many lives, while at the same time entertaining the darkest fears about nuclear energy, in the production of which not a single death has been officially recorded. Likewise, environmentalists who are loudest in their warning of climate change, are equally loud in their rejection of a technology that might do something to deduce the effects they fear. But whether such attitudes are contradictory or not, they are influential, and the result has been the near demise of nuclear power.

What this shows is that we should be cautiously sceptical when it is predicted that some new technology will have a revolutionary impact on the way we live, because, as in the case of nuclear power, this crucially turns not just on the nature of the technology itself but on the attitudes of those who are to use it. Technological determinism – the doctrine that ways of life are determined by the technology that underlies them – is a recurrent theme in social theory, but whatever truth there is in it, it has to accommodate those incontestable instances in which a powerful new technology has by and large been rejected.

There is also this further possibility. The impact of new technologies may be limited because the truly innovative capacities they have are largely unemployed. It is well known that most computer users exploit only a small proportion of the technology available to them, and that immensely powerful machines are often used as little more than hi-tech typewriters and calculators. In this way, what we might call the conservative adaptability of human beings, can convert something that has the potential for revolutionary impact into something rather more mundane. Arguably, this is what has happened with television. Now that computers, home video and rising levels of prosperity have eroded much of television's former pre-eminence, there is an argument to be made for the view that this putative 'revolution' in communication has in the end amounted to little more than an alternative medium for entertainment and the dissemination of news.

Prediction and assessment

For anyone concerned with the prospects for e-learning, these are important *caveats*. Time and again, enthusiasts for this or that dash ahead of the pack with schemes based upon little more than their own enthusiasm. The result, very often, is expensive upheaval that is, if anything, counterproductive. At the same time, to retreat to the comfortable belief that there is nothing new under the sun, and that consequently innovators can be ignored, is also a mistake. It simply is impossible to deny that there have been technological innovations, developed and promoted by individuals whose enthusiasm has sometimes approached obsession, that have had huge, lasting and beneficial effects. The examples with which we began — the printing press, the loom, electric light, the telephone, the motorcar and the aeroplane — are all of this kind. No doubt they have had their downsides, but unquestionably human experience and modes of existence have been fundamentally changed by them and in ways that have been hugely beneficial to enormous numbers of people on a social as well as an economic level.

Of course, this is a judgement made in hindsight, and judgement in hindsight is easy. The more intriguing problem is to make such judgements in advance, to spot the developments that are worth investing thought, time and money in. Given the example of nuclear power and similar instances, how is this to be done with confidence? In fact, can it be done?

The answer is twofold, a sort of no and yes. The negative part of the answer arises from the fact that human beings are bad at prediction, especially when it comes to social prediction. This is a truth that cannot be repeated too often because planners and others are so inclined to forget it. Even the most well-informed and astute economists failed to predict the Wall Street crash of 1929, and a whole army of Kremlinologists failed to predict the collapse of the Soviet Union. Technological prediction fares no better. Asked in 1898 to speculate on the invention most likely to have a major impact in the twentieth century, no one at the Chicago World Fair mentioned the motor car.

On the other hand, since we live in a world of invention and innovation and simply do not have the option of standing still, it seems that we must make *some* attempt to assess the wisdom of future courses of action. This includes the assessment of proposals relating to technological change and social re-organization. What is needed is a framework within which to think of such things.

The key elements in this framework will seek answers to the following five questions.

1. What is the anticipated benefit of the innovation and will it be a genuinely *additional* benefit?

2. Is the chance of its being implemented successfully much higher than the chance of its failure?

3. What is the cost of its introduction in terms of disruption to existing systems that are known, tried and reliable?

4. How stable is the circumstance in which the proposed innovation is to be made?

5. Are there recurrent patterns of behaviour that would give some pointers to its likely reception?

Even if it is accepted that future-gazing is futile, all these, it seems to me, are questions that admit of more and less plausible answers. More importantly, they are the questions that bear most directly on the lives of the people for whom the innovation is intended and by whom it must be implemented. It is only positive answers to these questions honestly arrived at that can make the proposed innovation a rational one, and it is the same questions upon which the fairness with which producers treat purchasers and managers treat employees is to be assessed.

There are many instances in which the introduction of computer technology has been undertaken without these questions having received satisfactory answers, or even being asked at all. One that has been documented fully is the introduction of a new company wide IT system (ERP) by the Canadian telephone company BCTel in 1998. It was brought to the attention of the management of this company that there were within it a number of incompatible computer systems. The claim was made that if all the different sectors — finance, marketing, operations, and so on — were able to 'talk' to each other on a company wide basis, the outcome would be a better service to customers provided by a smaller workforce, thereby reducing costs.

On this basis a software system was purchased and introduced at very considerable expense. The result was near
disaster. Almost nothing worked, and under conditions of
great strain and stress the employees used their ingenuity
and commitment to devise 'work round' solutions until,
after a year, some measure of stability was arrived at. But
by then, in the changing landscape of telecommunications,
BCTel was involved in negotiating a merger with another
company SAP. One of the reasons given for the suitability
of the merger was the fact that SAP had also installed ERP.
Unfortunately, their version was slightly but significantly
different, and when the merger finally went ahead it was
this other SAP's IT that was selected for use across the
newly merged entity. So BCTel's replacement system was
abandoned, together with all the 'work round' solutions in
which its employees had invested energy, imagination
and commitment. In short, in the name of technological
improvement a huge cost in terms of personnel as well as
money had been incurred quite pointlessly.

BCTel's experience is not unique, at least in outline.
Nevertheless it is a single instance from which we cannot
validly infer very much. But the point of referring to it is
not to begin a process of generalization, so much as to
illustrate the pertinence of the key questions I have identified. First, it is plausible to hold in this case that the anticipated benefits of the new system were marginal rather
than substantial, especially since the suggestion did not
arise from customer complaint and regular failure of the
existing system. Second, when it comes to the introduction
of large scale software, we have quite a lot of experience to
go on, and we know that the chance of trouble free introduction is small. Third, given that what was proposed was
a total, all at once, systemic change in a large company,
very high ancillary costs in terms of burdens on staff could
be expected. Fourth, the instability of the telecommunications industry in the wake of mobile phones was well

known. The fifth question — about patterns of behaviour — is not strictly relevant here, though it has some bearing on the question of marginal versus substantial benefits. But as we will see it is relevant to the main subject in hand, and to which we now turn, e-learning.

Technology, cost and benefit

It is best to begin by attempting to characterise what might be meant by 'e-learning'. I shall mean the extensive deployment of email and the internet to serve the personal, vocational and professional education of individuals. Now the impulse to move in the direction of e-learning can come from the supply side or the demand side, from teachers (and educational institutions) or from learners. There is a general assumption, I think, that the interests of both sides will coincide, but it is not entirely clear that this is the case. What is nowadays referred to as the 'delivery' of courses may be cheaper and more efficient from the point of view of the providing institutions (in which we should include governments) while being less effective or satisfactory from the point of view of the student. Conversely, methods of learning that are cheap and convenient for students may place new and costly burdens on teachers and/or the organizations for which they work. However, though this is a matter to be returned to briefly, for the moment we will assume that the desirability of the widespread introduction of e-learning can be assessed from a single point of view that incorporates the interests of both teachers and learners.

Let us return to the key questions and ask first of all, What are the anticipated benefits of e-learning and are they genuinely additional benefits? It is evident, I think, that the anticipated benefits lie primarily in greater accessibility with respect to both time and space. The educational experience e-learning can provide is not restricted to any geographical or even spatial location, and depending on how facilities for inquiry and discussion are designed, there need be no temporal restriction either. This spatio-temporal flexibility, obviously, means hugely enhanced accessibility — *in principle*, we need to add, for there are qualifications to be entered. Electronic communication is not infallible, and it may be prone to forms of interruption, corruption and destruction that do not plague other media. There is also a measure of confinement that does not affect other media. Although unrestricted to any particular space, there is spatial restriction in this sense; the learner must be at a computer or other interface. As has been remarked frequently, the book has an advantage that the computer, even the laptop, generally lacks. It can be slipped in a pocket or a handbag and read on the bus, train or plane. Hand held computers the size of a mobile phone exist and their use is likely to become more widespread than it is, but the limited popularity of hand held televisions suggests that they are unlikely to be as reader-friendly as the book. We should conclude from this that the extent to which e-learning makes educational materials more widely accessible, is a matter of degree. The book is a marvellous invention from this point of view, and consequently we need to be confident that the *added* benefit of e-learning media is sufficiently great to outweigh the additional cost of implementation.

But surely, it will be said, the cost of e-learning is inevitably lower than traditional methods of education precisely because of the vastly higher levels of participation. It is worth remarking that nothing is *inevitably* the case here. Everything turns on an empirical calculation about contingent outcomes. The problem is that such calculations are extremely hard to make, and it is doubtful if they can ever be made with quantitative precision. This leaves them as a matter of judgement, and equally well informed and competent judges can differ. However, bearing the following considerations in mind, rational judges will avoid all claims of the form 'it's bound to be the case'. This is because we know that in addition to incurred costs, there are hidden, displaced and opportunity costs to be taken into account.

It is well known that when IT systems are in use, large amounts of staff time, sometimes at a high level, go into informal problem solving sessions. When efforts have been made to calculate these in terms of hourly payment, even conservative estimates turn out to be astonishingly high. If the head of a reasonably large section spends the equivalent of a morning a week helping employees solve their (low level) computing problems, in the course of the year this comes to a very considerable sum. Multiplied across a large organization with many sections, the total annual expenditure will constitute a major hidden cost attaching to the IT system.

This is a possibility that e-learning systems must also take into account, and here the hidden cost may also be a displaced one. The home based student, having problems with the technology, gets the help and advice of a relative, friend or neighbour. The resulting time spent cannot easily be assigned monetary value, but it is a cost nonetheless, and one not merely hidden but displaced — from the educational provider to the educational recipient. This is just one instance of a displaced cost, and others may be more easily quantifiable in monetary terms. IT purchase and maintenance, for example, may easily pass from institutional provider to individual learner, as does the cost of lighting, heating and maintaining the room in which the learning is undertaken. This is one point at which the interests of teachers and learners may pull apart. This much is true, certainly, we will not have properly assessed the cost of a shift to e-learning if we simply compute the costs to educational institutions of designing software, preparing materials and providing them on-line.

There is also opportunity cost. This applies to every kind of activity of course, and there is no reason to think that it presents e-learning with a special difficulty. However, notoriously, the creation of software and the preparation of materials almost always takes longer than anticipated, and their life-time (i.e. before revision and amendment is required) is almost always shorter than expected. There are few instances, in my experience, in which the amount of concentrated time given to web page and similar construction is devoted to classroom instruction or the writing of text books, precisely because the former is thought of as innovative. If there were, if old and new were treated alike, the normal calculation in favour of web based material would not look so obvious.

These remarks are simply reminders and should not be taken to imply that e-learning is less efficient, and has fewer additional benefits. I do not think that such a sweeping generalization can be sustained. The calculation of benefits has to be made time and again for specific proposals and particular systems. The purpose of distinguishing hidden, displaced and opportunity costs in addition to the direct costs of acquisition and installation, is to underline the complexity of estimating benefit over cost and the various dimensions that have to be taken into account if it is to be made honestly.

The second key issue is that of realization. How likely is it that any proposed move from traditional education to e-learning will be brought to fruition? Here again there are complexities. Time scale is one. There have been several expensive modern weapon systems whose introduction took far longer than anticipated. Ignoring the additional financial cost associated with delay, are these to count as successful changes? A solution to a problem postponed long enough is no solution. However, in the case of e-learning, I am inclined to think that the most interesting and important issue surrounding realization relates to the fifth of the key questions I raised — its relation to existing patterns of behaviour — and consequently, I will defer any extended examination of the question until that point.

Before that there remain the other two key questions — systematic disruption and contextual stability. The first is in some ways the most important factor to be considered in any system change. Existing systems of organization, including both their underlying technology and the people who run them, are not merely systems extraneous to the knowledge or expertise that goes into their construction. They are also embodiments of expertise, and to scrap or replace them is to discard that expertise. The cost of this can be very high because the form of its embodiment is diffuse and often imperceptible. It will include acquired familiarity that often makes for maximum efficiency. An illuminating parallel will be found in driving a car or operating a mobile phone. Most people are so practised at these that they need give virtually no attention to the direct operation itself and can concentrate all their attention on the purposes for which these skills have been acquired. So it is with the running of organizations. Accordingly, to replace them is like having everyone change from a car to a motorbike. Leaving other considerations aside, we would expect journey times to be longer, stress levels to be higher, and the number of accidents to be greater because the knowledge base is lower. This is exactly what happens in most organizational changes of any magnitude. Of course over time, skillful use of the new system will be acquired, and this will eventually be embodied in the people and the technology that comprise it. But we need to know that the advantages of the new system sufficiently outweigh the cost of the disruption to warrant the change.

They do not always do so. In an educational institution known to me, the timetabling system by which classes were assigned to rooms was done on an historic adjustment basis. A review of the system revealed that this did not take account of maximising room space use, and a software programme which promised to integrate multiple factors — class size, room size, student choice and staff availability — was purchased at considerable expense. The trouble was that it was wholly new and could draw on none of the knowledge derived from experience that was embodied in the old system. The result was that the start of the academic year approached more rapidly than familiarity with the new system which had to be abandoned at the last minute. The institution fell back on the old system, but without the same preparatory time (or staff confidence) and the result was that timetabling became more inflexible and inefficient than it had ever been.

Systematic disruption of this kind is hugely costly in terms of both skills and morale. Old systems that can appear inefficient from, so to speak, the point of view of the drawing board can have embodied skill and knowledge that is in fact very hard to replace. So it could be with e-learning. The embodied skills that teachers and learners have with respect to more traditional educational methods may contribute far more to the educational process than is evident and we therefore need good and substantial grounds to abandon them.

The issue of stability is a little different, and not to be spelt out in terms of costs and benefits, but in terms of the lifetime of an innovation. In the case of BCTel, the instability that rendered the new system redundant in a very short space of time, lay in the commercial conditions prevailing. This does not really apply in the e-learning case. But what does apply is potential instability in educational fashions and in the technology itself. The second point is an easy one to make. In general the pace of change in information technology is very rapid. For example, anyone who invested heavily in digital imaging technology at an early stage of its development speedily found themselves left with expensive equipment that was technically much inferior to the far cheaper systems that succeeded it. Commercial survival depended upon passing this loss onto customers, but though this proved possible in many cases, it does not detract from the fact that someone somewhere was paying the price of the mistake.

However, more interesting than instability in the technology itself, is instability in the educational culture that e-learning is intended to serve. Here I shall simply sketch one illustrative possibility. In the course of the second half of the twentieth century there was a shift in Britain that took technical learning out of the workplace and into the classroom. Apprenticeship was replaced by a combination of work experience and day release. This removal to the classroom had advantages and disadvantages, but that is not the point here. Let us suppose that e-learning as it develops is primarily derivative of and adapted from classroom teaching. Should it be the case that against this background, the earlier trend is reversed and technical education returns to the workplace, there is serious danger that a great many of the techniques, devices and materials that comprise e-learning are rendered redundant. I should stress that I am not contending that this is or will be the case, only that for proponents of e-learning, the possibility of contextual instability is as much an issue as it is in others cases.

Education and e-learning

It is time now to turn to the fifth key issue — the relation between e-learning and the patterns of behaviour that comprise the world of education. This is the most interesting from a philosophical point of view because it involves reflection on one of the concepts that play a structuring role in securing a valuable and meaningful existence, namely education.

What is the purpose of education? In answering this question all education can be classified in one of two ways. Either its purpose is to serve some further end or it is undertaken for its own sake. People learn to use a computer in order to do other things — write essays, email their friends, buy travel tickets online — but they learn to play bridge for no other reason than playing bridge. Similarly, and at different level, people study medicine in order to make sick people well, whereas they study history or philosophy for its own sake.

Of course these two purposes, though distinguishable, are not necessarily exclusive. Many people find the study of medicine intrinsically interesting, and some people hold that philosophical and historical studies generate transferable intellectual skills. But the ultimate explanation of medicine's value lies its use, not its interest, while the ultimate explanation of the value of history lies in its interest not its use.

This distinction between use and interest is closely related to the distinction between use and value that was explored at length in Essay I and in the context of university education. But it can be applied across the whole spectrum of education. The difficulty of doing so arises not from the unclarity of the distinction itself, or from the fact that it is not exclusive, but from a powerful tendency (also discussed earlier) for contemporary culture to regard the useful as the only mark of value. It is an assumption (as we saw in Essay IV) that often gets embodied in the word 'information' especially in the expression 'information technology'. There is a widespread assumption that information technology simply stores and transmits information to be put to whatever purpose the end-user chooses. The information itself is purpose neutral.

To repeat an earlier point, this idea is importantly reinforced by the fact that electronic impulses are usually referred to as digital 'information', and this is of course meaning neutral. A set of digital impulses can as easily transmit *mis*information as it can transmit information properly so called, and the confusion between the digital information and information more generally has led to the mistaken assumption that the latter as well as the former is neutral. But it is not. As every teacher knows, the internet is a ready source of misinformation and fabrication for the unwary student, some of it placed there maliciously with the intent to deceive, but most of it arising from ignorance and error.

One essential point to be made is this. It is a central purpose of education to give those who undergo it the knowledge and critical abilities to assess and to judge the authenticity, relevance and value of the putative 'information' with which they are presented, its usefulness and its interest. In other words, the mind that confronts the computer screen is not a passive recipient of something called 'information'. Rather the mind must actively scrutinise and question the material presented if it is to assimilate and learn from it.

This point applies of course to all sorts of information and not just that encountered on-line. But it important to note that traditionally these critical skills have been acquired in the context of a community of teachers and learners — the classroom, the lecture hall, the lecture, the seminar. The question thus arises as to whether these pre-requisites can be replicated in e-learning. There are chat rooms, notice boards and the like, certainly, and it may indeed be the case that the essential context of learning, that both precedes and goes beyond the mere 'delivery' of 'information' (for which information technology is eminently suited) can indeed be realized in e-learning. But this needs to be shown rather than pre-supposed before we can proceed to introduce large scale e-learning systems with confidence.

However, there is a larger issue of a similar nature yet to be addressed. I noted earlier that some education is 'for its own sake' rather than for some utilitarian purpose. Such education is meant to be enriching rather than useful. The person who takes up local history, or wants a better understanding and appreciation of the world of art, say, does so not to enhance career prospects or increase income, but as an intrinsic, non-material enrichment of the life they lead. Now what this suggests is that they do not simply require useful information, but a composite educational experience, and it may be that this is not something that digital technology can supply because such experience crucially involves learning with others. An analogy might be this. No amount of reading plays will substitute adequately for the experience of going to the theatre. To have read the plays is better than being entirely ignorant of them. In this way it is a valuable substitute, but not an entirely satisfactory one. So too, perhaps, with distance learning that employs the very best in multi-media digital technology. To attend a virtual school or college is certainly better than attending no school or college at all, but it may still fall considerably far short of the educational experience that people have generally sought and valued enough to favour over other rival activities.

In short, there is a question as to whether e-learning, whose advantages are many and perhaps sufficiently great to outweigh the earlier concerns of relative cost and benefit, and whose usefulness is not open to dispute, can fully replicate the nature of educational experience for its own sake. If it can, then the prospects for e-learning are bright. Whether it can or not is a matter that will be decided not by policy, but by the dialectic between the imaginations of supply side educationalists and technologists on the one hand, and the desires, beliefs and aspirations of potential learners on the other. This is a dialectic in which, as in the BCTel case, managers and technicians have not always been able or willing to engage in, a theme to be returned to in Essay VIII . Perhaps those charged with promoting the future of e-learning will respond differently. In my view, the success and value of the ingenuity, time and resources devoted to it will crucially depend upon their doing so.

Intellectual Integrity and the Realities of Funding[1]

It is perhaps a recurrent concern that scientific research (and academic inquiry more generally) can be influenced improperly by the body that has funded it. But this concern is much greater in a world where the increase in the number of competitors exceeds the increase in the funds for which they are competing. Universities currently operate in just such a world. Furthermore, pressure to secure financial backing for research is intensified by the fact that academic prestige and even academic survival may depend upon success in doing so. The purpose of this essay is first to identify what exactly the problem of improper influence is supposed to be, and secondly to explore alternative responses to it.

The problem of improper influence

Consider these two cases.

1. A paper published in *The Lancet* in 1998 by Dr Andrew Wakefield attracted very widespread attention when it linked the MMR vaccine with autism in children, and led to a serious reduction in the uptake of the vaccines. Now, six years later, the GMC is considering a formal investigation into claims that Dr Wakefield's research was 'fatally flawed' by a conflict of interest. The current editor of *The Lancet* has said that he would not

[1]   Originally delivered to a meeting of the National Committee of University Professors in King's College London, May 2004.

have published the findings, had he known that Dr Wakefield was being paid for a study that sought to support legal action by parents who thought that the MMR vaccine had harmed their children. Several alternative bodies of evidence, including a Finnish study of 3 million vaccinations between of 1982 and 1996, seem to contradict Wakefield's findings.

2.   In February 2004 Dr David Carpenter published a study in *Science*, which caused consternation in the aquaculture industry. In it he suggested that no more than one portion of farmed Scottish salmon should be eaten every four months, to avoid an increased risk of cancer. Closer examination revealed that this research was funded by a body with a clear environmental agenda against the industry. Moreover, the methodology seemed to be flawed, since no comparison sample of wild Atlantic salmon was tested for toxins. Dr Carpenter subsequently withdrew from several speaking engagements, and legal action now seems imminent.

These are just two of the cases that have widely been thought to give cause for concern. But concern about what? Let us suppose that both of them are indeed good examples of defective scientific investigation. If this is the extent of the problem, unhappily it cannot be said to constitute anything new. As long as there is science there will be bad science. Indeed, as long as there is intellectual inquiry there will be defective instances of it, a contention that the history of universities and learned societies confirms. So if we are to be especially concerned with cases like these there must be more to them than merely bad science, because bad scientists, like the poor, will always be with us.

Could this extra element lie in the fact that the investigations in question were thought to have serious practical implications? This seems implausible, for two reasons. First, a lot of scientific investigation has practical implications, and while by extension this means that there will be quite of lot of poorly conducted scientific investigation of this kind, there is no reason to think that practically impor-

tant science *must* be defective. Secondly, and more importantly, the scope of these implications is a function not just
of the research itself, but of the media coverage it gets, and
the reaction of the public to it. Properly conducted science
can be irresponsibly reported by the media, and the public
can react irrationally to genuine research findings. Neither
Carpenter nor Wakefield can rightly be blamed for the
reception of their work by an irresponsible press or an irra-
tional public. Indeed, in my view both factors played a
large part in Wakefield's paper having the impact it did.

Some people will think that the key element in these
cases, the thing that makes them dubious, is obvious. It is
the fact that the research in question was financially
underwritten by sources that had a vested interest in its
results turning out one way rather than another. But this is
not obvious. Had Carpenter's or Wakefield's results been
the outcome of scientific research projects that were
demonstrably impeccable, then the fact that they were
paid to undertake their research by the groups that did pay
them, would not invalidate those results. How could it?
And any scientist who discounted impeccably conducted
research, not because of demonstrable intellectual failings,
but because of extraneous considerations about funding
sources, could rightly be accused of prejudice and ignoring the canons of scientific inquiry. The truth is the truth
regardless of who has paid for its production. Conversely,
falsehood is not any better because it has resulted from
inquiries conducted with funds from impeccable sources.
A similar point can be made about practical implications.
If Wakefield's research was properly conducted and
funded from a wholly independent source, it could not be
faulted for having attracted a high level of media attention, or even for having aroused widespread anxiety and,
as a result, a substantial reduction in the take up of the
MMR vaccine.

We can conclude, I think, that any adequate account of what should concern us about cases like these must involve all three (alleged) features. That is to say, neither bad science, nor funders with vested interests, nor practical impact, is a sufficient condition for special concern. Rather, if this is where the heart of the problem lies, these features must combine in some way or other. But in what way?

One answer would be this. If scientists are hard enough pressed for funds to support their work, they will be driven to seek finance from sources with a vested interest in the outcome of the research, and hence tempted to skew their findings in directions that the funder favours. This temptation is powerfully intensified if and when (as is not infrequently the case) a certain research outcome will greatly increase the chances of further funding from the same source. Thus stated of course, this analysis makes no special reference to practically oriented research, but it is plausible to think that it is only research with some practical implication that is likely to attract support from lobbyists and other vested interests. ('Practical' should be understood broadly here. It may refer to impact on public debate and culture as much as practical guidance. The immensely wealthy North American Templeton Foundation supports a wide variety of research into the abstract relation between science and religion. Some scientists, philosophers and theologians have been reluctant to accept finance from this source because they believe the Foundation has a preference for some outcomes of the inquiry over others. If there is anything that could be called a practical outcome to the question of whether, for example, Darwinian evolution is compatible with the Bible, it lies in the public perception of winners and losers in the debate between Christians and atheists, and not in medical or dietary advice.)

On this account, then, we can weave together the three elements that have been identified as striking features of the examples with which we began, and thus provide a reasonably illuminating analysis of what is worrying about contemporary funding of science. However, there is a further important observation to be made. My analysis implies that two crucial features connect the quality of science and the source of the funding. One is psychological, the other economic and, perhaps, political. The psychological factor is the temptation scientists may feel to distort the results of their work in order to please their funders. Of course, such temptation does not necessarily result in dubious outcomes, because temptation can be resisted. But economic and political conditions may make it much harder to resist if, as a matter of fact, independent sources of funding are in short supply. This perhaps, is the key to present concerns. There will always be rogue scientists who manufacture evidence, fail to observe proper research procedures and distort results, sometimes for personal advancement, sometimes in pursuit of fame and sometimes for financial inducement. But the vast majority of scientists are unlikely to act improperly from questionable motives, unless, that is, they are pressured into it by circumstances in which economic realities suggest that some relaxation of intellectual standards is a condition of securing funds on a regular basis.

Whether this truly is the contemporary economic situation in which scientific, and intellectual research work more generally has to be conducted is a factual question, but not one that will be considered here. For present purposes it is often said to be because, true or not, it is the perception that conditions something like this currently prevail that gives rise to the anxieties I have been analysing.

Perhaps pressure to secure research funding is not as bad as is often alleged, but let us suppose that it is. Where, if anywhere, does the solution lie? On this point there are two familiar suggestions. The first is that we need a code of conduct for scientists that will give clear guidance on the acceptance of financial support from interested parties. The second is that we need to guard against over dependence on such sources by ensuring sufficiently high levels of independent financial support, provided by the state but allocated through something like research councils. It is these two proposals that I now want to explore.

Codes of conduct

The formulation of professional codes of conduct is a widespread feature of contemporary culture over the last four decades or so. Just why this is, is an interesting topic. In my view, it has had two powerful stimulants — an increasing desire on the part of what formerly were trades or simply occupations to become professions, and a general tendency to replace trust with accountability. Yet I think it can be shown that the pursuit of such codes has in an important sense been futile. This is not to say that they cannot be formulated. They can, and have been in large numbers. The problem is that the process of their formulation virtually ensures that the principles expressed in them lack any 'cutting edge'. This is because the authority of such codes is derived from the consensus of the profession in question. Under conditions of moral disagreement, which generally prevail in the modern world, this consensus can only settle on what is the highest common factor, or as it is usually expressed (though inaccurately) the lowest common denominator. The outcome is a code consisting in prescriptions and proscriptions that no one is likely to disagree with, and its provisions usually take the form of principles too abstract to provide any actual guidance. The result is that such codes never require people to act in ways other than those they would have acted in anyway.

This phenomenon can be found illustrated again and again in the published codes of many professions. A particularly striking example is medicine. The Hippocratic Oath, long regarded as the professional code of the doctor, has a great deal of 'cutting edge' to it. It expressly rules out abortion for example, which, it says, doctors may never justifiably use their skills to bring about. Now the trouble is that, though in this respect the Oath is both clear and practically powerful, it conflicts with what many modern doctors believe — that it is justifiable to secure an abortion in the interests of a patient. Consequently, if there is to be a medical code that the profession can endorse, it has to exclude such express proscriptions as are to be found in the Hippocratic Oath. But then, what it ends up including is some combination of rules that do not need a special professional code (for example, that doctors ought not to steal from their patients) and/or principles too vague to give guidance — that doctors should act in the best interests of their patients' health. This second type of principle is easily endorsed, but only because it is silent on genuine differences. What does it imply when, for example, the doctor confronts the question of whether or not to tell a patient what the gloomiest prognostication is with respect to their condition. Doing so and not doing so, can *both* be made consistent with the principle that doctors should act in the best interests of their patients' health. But from this it follows that the principle cannot actually tell us what to do.

So too with any funding code for scientists we might try to formulate. Suppose such a code were to give unequivocal guidance like this: scientists must never accept research funding from sources that have any interest other than a purely intellectual one in the outcomes of the research. This is clear and practically powerful, but no one, or hardly anyone would accept it, and for good reason in many cases. High quality research can be done with resources provided by interested parties. It is the aim of all the cancer charities to find effective reliefs and cures for cancer, and absurd to think that they cannot legitimately support properly scientific investigation to this end.

Suppose on the other hand the code contains principles like this: scientists should never accept funds where a condition of grant is that any published outcome must favour the views of the funder irrespective of evidence. No one will disagree with this, but that is because no self respecting scientist needs to be told it. And how many grant applications would *not* be lodged in the light of this principle? That is to say, is it plausible to think that applications would be lodged which did not satisfy this principle if the principle did not appear in a professional code of conduct?

It might be thought that I am overstating the case here. Surely, it will be said, there are useful principles of conduct that fall somewhere between the extremes of the overly proscriptive and the uselessly bland. Perhaps there are some. But the general thrust of my analysis will be borne out by the examination of actual codes. These invariably state principles so uncontentious that they fail to give any concrete guidance. In any case there is this further consideration. The psychological element in my analysis of how scientific integrity and the realities of funding can conflict was that scientists are tempted to skew their results in directions favoured by their funders. To describe this as a temptation, however, is already to imply a recognition on their part that what they are doing is ethically questionable. In that case, what is missing is not knowledge of right and wrong, so much as the inability to resist temptation.

This brings us to the second factor — prevailing economic and political conditions. While we might attribute the inability to resist temptation to the will of the individual — what used to be called a lack of moral fibre — we have to acknowledge that, since scientists are no more saintly than any other profession, a more productive approach than preaching is to address the source of the temptation.

State funding

Pleas to increase the state's funding of scientific research can be based on a number of grounds. The most common, if not the most honest or accurate, pins its faith on practical, often economic benefit. Even research that on almost any interpretation could hardly be said to have practical value — cosmology for example — is described as 'blue skies' with the vague suggestion that practical value might result from it in the future, and an appeal to ignorance — who knows what may come of it? Another is international standing and prestige; the state should spend more on science so that it can hold its head up higher amongst the community of nations. Less common, but more pertinent to present purposes, is a case based upon the need for intellectual independence. State funding, this argument supposes, will come with fewer strings attached — none in the ideal case — and thus significantly lessen the dependency of scientists on sources with specific interests in research outcomes.

In order for this line of argument to be convincing, certain empirical conditions must actually pertain. For example, access to state funding must in general be easier than to non-state funding. If there is a lot of state money but it is very hard to get compared with non-state money, then the position will be different. However, these are contingent conditions about which we cannot generalize very much, and so the more profitable course for present purposes is to assume that no special factors of this sort come into play. Other things being equal, then, is it true that more state funding means fewer strings attached, and hence greater scientific and intellectual autonomy? There is no reason to think that this *is* true. In the first place, the state can have a vested interest in the outcomes of research of just the kind that non-state funders have, as the examples with which we started illustrate. Increasing reluctance on the part of the public to use the MMR vaccine created significant problems for public health policy and the government department charged with implementing it. As a result, British ministers and civil servants had a clear interest in Wakefield's research being shown to be flawed. So too with Carpenter's allegations about farmed salmon. These were profoundly unwelcome to the Scottish Executive, coming as they did at a time when the Scottish fishing industry was undergoing massive contraction and fish farming was being held out as an alternative with significant potential for growth.

But more importantly, there are ways in which strings can be attached other than by offering unspoken inducements to skew the results of research. One is what we might call agenda setting — the ability to determine not the results but the topics of research. On this score, state funding is actually far more likely to undermine scientific autonomy than is most non-state funding. This can happen in terms of very general categories — a preference for applied over pure science — at less general levels — a preference for interdisciplinary over single discipline research — and at quite specific levels — a preference for research into health over culture for example. All of these are thoroughly familiar research agendas that are set top down rather than bottom up, to use a familiar expression. Now while some very rich foundations — Leverhulme and the Wellcome Trust are plausible examples — can have quite a powerful influence on the setting of specific research agendas, only the state has resources on a scale that could plausibly undertake it at more general levels. States in combination, as in the European Union, are even more powerful in this regard, and it is in fact the case that almost all European research funding is tied to specific research agendas.

Of course, it is often supposed that the solution to this kind of distorting influence is the creation of peer populated buffers between the provider and the recipient of funding, between governments and working scientists. Research Councils and their assessment panels are usually thought of in this way. The theory is that while the government decides the total amount of funding, the allocation of that total to particular research projects lies in the hands of the academic community itself through its representatives on research councils. This is an account of the position that is both idealized and dated, however. Governments always, but especially of late, have a strong inclination to be interventionist wherever significant sums of money are involved. Perhaps they have a responsibility to be so in fact. In any case, faced with political intervention, research councils and the like have usually proved fairly supine, easily dragooned into implementing the research preferences of the government funder. This is not just a matter of weakness on the part of those who run such councils. The combination of a democratic culture which attributes to governments the authority of the general will, weakness and uncertainty on the part of professional bodies, and sheer financial muscle, makes it very difficult for those who allocate public funds for science, and intellectual activity in general, to resist the policy directives of their political masters.

What then is to be done? If neither a professional code nor increased state funding can be expected to provide an adequate means of protecting the integrity of academic research, what could? In the concluding section I shall simply outline a suggestion, but to do so in a reasonably convincing way, it is necessary to return to the examples with which we began.

Academic authority

Consider first the Carpenter case. Carpenter's work, we are told was flawed. I myself have no idea of the facts of the matter, but let us suppose that he did indeed skew the results of his research in a way intended to favour the pre-conceptions of the lobbyists who were paying him. This is not the crucial point. Carpenter's case would have attracted less attention and had far less credence, had it not been published in *Science*. Similarly, Wakefield's research would not have carried the weight it did had it not been published in *The Lancet*. There are two important observations to be made on this. First, as far as public reception is concerned, it is the vehicle not the methodology of research that makes it authoritative. Members of the press and of the public had never heard of Wakefield or Carpenter; it was in *Science* and *The Lancet* that they placed their trust.

Combined with the fact (if it is a fact) that the actual research in both these cases was seriously flawed, this has an interesting implication. The scientific community has it within its power to deny rogue science public credibility if only it will ensure that the most rigorous standards are applied to publication in authoritative places. Funders may be able to offer inducements to skew the results of research work, but they cannot use their resources to manipulate the academic and intellectual authority of publishing journals.

The second important observation on this score is that the application of the canons of research is sufficient. The editor of *The Lancet* is reported as saying he would not have published Wakefield's work had he known the source of his funding. But this is a profound mistake in my judgement. Wakefield's research *ought* to have been published if it met the most rigorous standards of refereeing and review, regardless of who paid for it. Indeed, journals like *The Lancet* ought to be kept in ignorance of the funding source of research submissions, as they often are of the identity of the author, since this is a consideration quite extraneous to the only one that matters — the intellectual quality of the work.

To this conclusion we can add a more contentious suggestion. If part of the problem arises from shortage of research funds, one solution would be for scientists to become entirely open to what is often called 'tainted' money. Some time ago, Nottingham University came in for severe criticism because of its willingness to accept research funding from the tobacco industry, criticism so severe that the money had in the end to be rejected. Let us agree for the sake of the argument that this was conscience money born of the fact that it consisted in profits made from selling lethal substances whose use has resulted in the deaths of millions. This fact does nothing in and of itself to invalidate the scientific worth of the research that might have been undertaken with the help of tainted money. While it is understandable that an institution should be concerned about its public image, in the end it must take whatever steps it needs to protect and promote its essential purposes. For a university research laboratory, rigorous investigation of intellectually significant theories and hypotheses is an essential purpose, which is to say, one of the purposes for which it exists. If this can be carried out more extensively by accepting offers of 'conscience' money this is of no consequence to that essential purpose.

This much is true. Whatever responsibilities university public relations departments may have, the responsibility of scientists within universities seems clear. First, in the research they undertake, they should be indifferent to the intellectual results that will speak to the interest of those who provide financial support for their work. Second, in their conduct of the process of refereeing, they should be scientifically rigorous enough to exclude any distortion that might arise in the work of scientists who fail to maintain their indifference to funders' interests. These two principles lie at the heart of the analysis of what went wrong in the Wakefield and Carpenter cases. But they have implications in more than one direction. Both scientists *qua* scientists, and those who have the responsibility of reviewing the scientific adequacy of their work, should be equally indifferent when funds from unpopular or unfashionable sources pay for work that is impeccably conducted. This is especially so when its publication would genuinely illuminate the intellectual problems it is the special business of science and the academy to address.

Spiritual Values and the Knowledge Economy[1]

What place, if any, do spiritual values have in the knowledge economy? I raise this question in this form because there are two striking facts about contemporary higher education in Britain (and elsewhere) that are rarely, if ever, considered together. The first is that those who are now its political masters expect the universities of Britain to be major contributors to something called 'the knowledge economy'. It is in the light of this expectation that most budgetary decisions about expenditure through the agency of the Funding Councils are made, and in the name of this contribution that the university sector generally makes its case for increased financial support. My second observation, and on the surface at any rate, one wholly unconnected with the first, is the fact that amongst our universities, the oldest, and some of the most prestigious still — Oxford, Cambridge, St Andrews, Edinburgh, King's College London — are religious foundations. This is a matter of recorded history and thus no less a reality than contemporary educational policy is. But is it a reality that matters? Can the two be connected in any way? Does religious foundation have anything to do with modern relevance and social importance? Or is it to be forgotten and ignored?

---

[1]   This is a substantially revised version of a lecture given to the Scottish Ecumenical Assembly, Edinburgh, Sept 2001.

The knowledge economy

What is a 'knowledge economy' exactly? I cannot say that I have come across of any clear account of its meaning; public pronouncements on the issue are generally clouded in jargon. At the same time, it is not hard to guess what people who use the phrase have in mind. There is a widespread belief that the state of the modern world is one in which familiarity with innovative technologies is essential to economic prosperity. 'Fitting the nation for the twenty-first century' is another commonly used expression that encapsulates the same idea. Now this much is true; many jobs require a knowledge of the new media — such things as computers, the Internet, e-mail and electronic marketing techniques. There is also bio-technology. Food processing and supply, the development of medications and the production of new materials are clearly a feature of the world in which we live that cannot be ignored. At the same time, there has been a recorded shift from manufacturing to service industries. The finance sector, insurance, and government bureaucracy for that matter, are major employers. Call centres employ far more people than heavy industries. Perhaps it is true that it is not possible to hold down a job in one of these areas without being computer literate and familiar with all the apparatus of electronic communication. We have to say 'perhaps' because it seems equally obvious that much of the service sector — the supermarkets, pub chains, coffee shops and leisure complexes that are so prominent a feature of contemporary commerce — requires a relatively elementary knowledge of these new technologies on the part of most of their staff. They need to operate the machines, certainly, but they need know virtually nothing of the technology that went into their manufacture.

Two important facts have brought this about. First, the whole tendency in modern technology, especially information technology, has been in the direction of 'user-friendliness'. That is to say, it has proved in the interests of manufacturers to make information technology require *less* knowledge of the science that underlies it rather than more. When the use of computers first began to grow, the amount of special instruction required to use them effectively was quite high. A knowledge of computer languages was needed if they were to be used for complex tasks, for example, and accordingly training courses often lasted several weeks. But in the course of their development, and especially with the introduction of the Personal Computer (by IBM in 1981), far greater use was made of existing knowledge and general intuition. Software was reconceived so that what seems obvious and natural turns out to be what works. Apple computers set the standard in this regard, and PCs have followed. The development of both has meant that the use of computers requires very little special training. Institutions run special courses, still, but often these last no more than a morning, and in many cases there is a genuine question as to how far they are really needed. Certainly there is a lot of specialist software that needs people to be trained in it, but far more that does not. The profitability of selling huge numbers of computers to ordinary people has been a powerful commercial impetus to ensuring that in general even the most sophisticated software can be used by people who know nothing about its inner working. Computer games are like this, but Word, Excel and Internet Explorer are equally obvious instances.

A particularly striking example is the modern till. The technology behind it is immensely sophisticated, but all the checkout operator has to do is pass a barcode in front of a reading device. Likewise, the technology of the ATM — the cash machine — is a technology that almost everyone has rapidly managed to master and requires no special training. This is an example worth dwelling on. Use of the ATM is a skill that is virtually indispensable now, and a product of the hi-tech age in which we live. These machines have played a large part in the expansion of contemporary commerce. Could anyone seriously suggest that their operation needs special education, still less at university level? The truth, on the contrary, is that quite deliberately ATMs have been made accessible to and operable by the least technologically minded, and it is in virtue of this fact that they have become so important to the retail sector. Precisely the same point can be made about the technology of the Internet. The ATM and the Internet are vital to a modern economy. They could not have come into existence without very high levels of scientific knowledge and technical expertise. But to infer from this that we need a system of education that will distribute such levels of knowledge widely across the population is evidently a mistake. We need lots of people employed in call centres, but only a very small proportion need to know how they work or how to fix them when things go wrong. It is only a blind adherence to the dogma of 'the knowledge economy' that could incline anyone to think the success of a hi-tech economy requires widespread education in technology.

Second, there is this important fact. Even when there has not been a special push to 'user friendly' operation, it seems that children can find out how to work many types of hi-tech machinery without lessons. It is standardly remarked that when VCRs first appeared in classrooms, the pupils were more likely to show the teacher how it worked than vice versa. What should we conclude from this? It should alert us to the real possibility that time and resources invested in formal sessions of technical training may well be wasted. Experience shows that technology, unlike mathematics or spelling, is something that children learn rapidly and easily when left to their own devices. They do so because they quickly see the advantages of doing so, and as result they want to master them. If this is true then at least at this level, 'the knowledge economy' can take care of itself, and needs no state funded formal provision.

Where then does the need for *special* provision lie? One answer that is often given to this question appeals to the concept of flexibility. According to a familiar contention, formerly people were trained in a specific skill that they and their employers expected to last them a lifetime. Nowadays, the pace of change has quickened so dramatically, educational programmes must prepare people to adapt to rapidly changing circumstances.

The expression 'the pace of change' raises important metaphysical questions, and there is a doubt as to whether this sharp contrast between past and present is not simply an instance of the tendency of every age to think itself unique; similar claims were made in the Victorian era. But these are not issues to be explored here. It is enough to observe that the preceding remarks about user friendliness and the motivation to learn useful skills imply that, even the constant need to adapt may not require much special training. Machinery, there is every reason to think, will become even more user friendly, and natural curiosity, assisted by practical benefit, will lead most people to master it so that over a wide range of cases, people themselves will adapt pretty readily.

Even where there is a proven need for special training, this may not imply much about the curriculum of schools and universities. Arguably, no technological development has ever had so great an impact on the way human beings live than the motor car. For a great many people today, the ability to drive a car is essential. Yet driving, which *does* need special lessons, has played no part in the formal curriculum of our educational institutions. It has not needed to. The evident desirability of being able to drive, and the general desire to do so, have been stimuli enough to make it happen. And, it might be added, neither the requirement to pay for such instruction nor the introduction of government oversight of its provision and assessment, has pushed it into those institutions. Debates about educa-

tional policy and provision and arguments over the introduction of fees would benefit greatly, in my view, from
closer attention to this humble but hugely important form
of mass education.

Taken together, these reflections suggest that there has
been a serious overestimation of the need for our educational system to accommodate the novelty and rapid
spread of modern technology. Nowhere to my knowledge
has it been shown, or even made plausible, that formal
education in new technologies is a *sine qua none* of employment in a modern economy. Consequently, in many
circumstances government resources devoted to this purpose could be diverted to other better uses. 'The knowledge
economy' may be more mythical than real.

The managerial state

Possibly, it is as much ideological as mythical. By 'mythical' I mean here a concept or idea that has widespread currency and influence in public debate but will not actually
stand up to critical scrutiny in the light of reality. (This is
not always how the term 'mythical' is understood, of
course.) By 'ideological' I mean a conception which may or
may not be mythical, but whose currency and influence is
to be explained by its consonance with the cultural and
ethical presuppositions of its time. This characterization of
the ideological clearly owes something to Marxist theory,
but a crucial difference is that ideology in this sense need
not be driven by underlying economic factors or serve the
interests of any identifiable class.

The concept of 'the knowledge economy' is ideological
to this extent. It invokes and justifies a programme of political initiatives and public expenditure that is powerfully in
tune with a widespread belief in multiculturalism and the
need for a neutral State. We live, it is almost universally
assumed, in a society that comprises many different cul-
tures, religions and moral codes. In times past, the story

runs, society was largely monocultural. It had fundamental beliefs and values that were shared by nearly all its members. As a result, the laws of the land and government policies could be based upon that common base. But conditions have changed dramatically, and modern society is multicultural. It members include people of widely differing backgrounds and loyalties, whose deepest ideals and values cannot be assumed to be the same and may even be in conflict. In such circumstances, it is essential that the State and the laws of the country, which everyone is expected to obey, should be able to command the support of citizens from a wide moral and cultural spectrum. This is only possible if the State itself is neutral with respect to these cultural differences and is seen to serve the interests of all, regardless of ethnicity, religion, or ethical belief.

The political neutrality of the State is of course a central strand in the most recent version of the political philosophy of liberalism. Its leading exponent, John Rawls, is best known precisely for his advocacy of the view that in a pluralist society only a State that eschews any one substantial conception of the good life can be justified. Its task is to provide its citizens with certain primary goods such as basic health care, rudimentary education, a minimum income. These are the things that make it possible for individuals to choose different life styles for themselves.

The Rawlsian project has dominated contemporary political philosophy and generated a literature far too vast to be considered here. For present purposes it is enough to highlight the conception of political activity it seems to sustain — the conception of politics as a form of management. This conceives of politicians on the model of the company executive. It speaks of 'targets' and 'objectives' with respect to 'services', and both promises and assesses political success in terms of their 'delivery'.

At the heart of this idea is neutrality. Its best model is a postal service or a transportation network. The mail says nothing, and asks nothing, of the meaning or worth of the letters it carries; be they 'junk' mail or letters of condolence, the task of the 'service' is just to carry them with as great a degree of efficiency as possible. The same is true of the railways or the road network. From the point of view of their being well run, the surgeon's drive to a life saving operation is on a par with a shopping trip in search of unnecessary trinkets. The role of the transport engineer is simply to get the traveller to his or her chosen destination efficiently, and to do so in a style and at a cost that the travelling public finds acceptable.

Now the managerial conception thinks of politics along the same lines. The role of the politician is to 'deliver' public services effectively and efficiently and the test of their doing so is that the voters express 'customer satisfaction' through the polls at election time. When a government is returned, this is evidence that its running of the country has met with the approval of the voters in just the way that the management of a company might meet with the approval of its shareholders at the AGM, an image that governments have occasionally expressly invoked.

The promotion of 'the knowledge economy' is very well suited to this conception of the managerial State, and it can be described as an ideological conception to the extent that its currency and influence is to explained by this suitability. In a multicultural society, everyone, *whatever* their ethical orientation, can agree on the value of economic prosperity and the need to secure this prosperity in an increasingly competitive global economy. The conditions prevailing in this economy give the edge to the technically advanced, from which it seems to follow that a policy of technological education for all is one that all sectors in a multicultural society can reasonably be expected (in both senses) to subscribe to.

This is a very familiar story. And yet the objections to it are legion. In this context, however, the principal objection is that the illusion of managerial neutrality hides the inescapability of real choices between competing values, most evidently in the case of education. The State cannot provide an education without determining the content of what is taught, and to teach one subject, given time constraints, is not to teach another. There can be the semblance of neutrality, of course. Education can be represented as essentially the inculcation of 'skills', the basic equipment that citizens need to lead a successful and fulfilling life of their own choosing. But education in science (to take just one example) does not fit this picture. A proper scientific education cannot avoid the question of truth, and truth may be precisely what is at issue between certain social groups. There is only one reason why creationism should not be taught in schools on an equal footing with evolutionary biology, for example, and that is because it is *false*. Every other reason that might be given by those determined to uphold the ideal of the neutral State — the need for children to cope with a scientifically driven world for example — is simply skirting the main issue.

Precisely the same point could be made about subjects that lie at the heart of multiculturalism. Sex education is a particularly striking example. It is not possible to teach sex education in a way that is neutral between Catholic, Muslim and progressive secularist views of sexuality. The alternative is to eliminate sex education from the curriculum altogether, but this is avoidance rather neutrality.

Education is only one example of the activity of the managerial state that falsely claims the legitimacy of neutrality. Economic prosperity is another. There are in fact value choices at work, and it could not be otherwise. The goal of economic growth tacitly discounts some sources. Its pursuit is quite compatible with the wholesale destruction of profitable trade when this is disapproved of for some other reason. The production and sale of heroin and cocaine in South America or Afghanistan is a good example. Billions of State dollars have been used to destroy the most promising export crop that poor peasant farmers have come upon in a lifetime of labour. There are reasons for this, of course, but they are not the supposedly neutral ones of promoting economic development.

Enrichment

The concept of 'the knowledge economy', then, is flawed. So too is the assumption within it, that education for the purposes of economic prosperity is a suitably neutral goal for the government of a multicultural society to pursue. Nevertheless, it is certainly the case that economic prosperity is a valuable social goal. Poverty is a great scourge. It remains so in very many parts of the contemporary world and to work for its elimination is not to acquiesce in a purely materialistic set of values. At the same time, it is a mistake to conflate the concept of economic prosperity or wealth creation with the concept of enrichment. In so far as wealth creation means simply increased purchasing power, it does not of itself constitute enrichment. To be enriched in the fullest sense, we need an increase in value and not merely in wealth. That is to say, an increase in purchasing power does not enrich us unless there is more for us to purchase. The miser who accumulates money but refuses to spend it is richer only in the most attenuated sense. Furthermore, simple quantitative increase is not enough. Since too much of the one thing palls, past a certain point more of the same is no enrichment.

Enrichment properly so called is not an increase in purchasing power, or an increase in the quantity of goods already available, but the creation of new goods. A particularly powerful example is music. Before there was music the world was a far poorer place. With its advent a new good came into existence, but at the point of its emergence (about which we know nothing of course), the potential value of this new good could not have been anticipated.

Retrospectively, we know that something of incalculable value came into existence. Material wealth can be used to access this good by buying instruments, CDs, concert tickets, but not to buy the good itself. Singing in a group is free, but no amount of money will enable the tone deaf to engage in it. Purchasing power is a means to the valuable, but not something valuable in itself. Consequently, economic or educational policies devoted to increasing it, should not be confused with policies for social or cultural enrichment.

The same thing can be said about another value that has huge influence on government policy and is also regarded as neutral as between different values and life styles — health. Politicians frequently campaign on the ground of improved medical provision and states spend immense sums on it. Now while health increases both the vitality and the length of life of the individual, in itself, though, it is curiously empty. What is that increased vitality and longevity to be spent doing? A long and healthy life spent in isolation and boredom, or worse degradation and humiliation, is a curse, not a benefit. It is precisely this sort of condition in which people are driven to the thought 'I wish I had never been born'. Better health in other words, is a neutral improvement in the human condition. Its value depends on other improvements. Of course, contemporary culture in Western Europe has a ready answer. Increased vitality and longevity are to be valued in so far as people can expect to lead pleasurable and enjoyable lives. Here however, there looms a daunting, and in the literal sense I think, dispiriting prospect — that the ultimate purpose of human existence is that of 'amusing ourselves to death' (as a phrase of Neil Postman's has it). What might the alternatives be? An answer does not seem far to seek. As well as enjoyment, a healthy and a long life is enriched by opportunities for intellectual engagement, aesthetic enlargement, communal participation, family life and moral endeavour. These are the principal alternatives to 'amusing ourselves to death'. They raise this further question. If such things are not necessarily made available by the purchasing power, what does make them available?

The answer is threefold — the existence of longstanding traditions, well established practices and social institutions. Amongst the traditions are such things as historical consciousness (a part of which is what people call 'national identity'), a shared sense of the value of learning and the exercise of civic responsibility. Among the practices are science, literature, law, music and the other arts, parliamentary democracy, agriculture, trade and industry. Among the institutions are museums, art galleries, churches, hospitals, orchestras, the courts, the press, schools, radio and television, trade associations, libraries and most significant for present purposes, universities.

The role of universities in cultural enrichment

The ancient universities of Europe had it as a large part of their purpose to promote reflective engagement with the culture, religion and professions of the society in which they were situated. They were also custodians of cultural artifacts, most obviously of the books in their libraries, but of other artifacts also. Though the British Museum (which advertises itself as the oldest in the world) was created by Act of Parliament, Oxford University's Ashmolean Museum pre-dates it by some seventy years. Universities were important contributors to cultural production as well cultural conservation. It was principally academic presses like those of Oxford and Cambridge that made the technology of the book into the great organ of the diffusion of letters it has become. Universities cannot claim a monopoly on cultural accretion. The history of painting and sculpture, music and poetry, even science, medicine and philosophy shows Church, State, voluntary associations and private individuals to have played a large part in their development. Nonetheless, though the full story is complex, it is unquestionably the case that universities across Europe, and later in the United States of America, were crucial in sustaining, reflecting upon and advancing the traditions, practices and institutions that go to make up the sources of our enrichment. Historical study does not merely stock the museums; it interprets the meaning of their stock, in much the same way that the study of art is related to its creation. Science and medical faculties do not merely advance science and medicine; they also take stock of those advances. Law Faculties seek to relate the work of the Courts to wider conceptions of justice. In short, when they are working well and in accordance with their proper purpose, universities are places that enrich the society to which they belong. But if so, the principal form of the enrichment we can look to universities to provide is *not* the simple generation of increased earning power through the inculcation of economically marketable skills. This is the laudable aim of schools and training colleges (though not the sole aim of these either). But universities have had, and can continue to have the far more fundamental role of stimulating, assimilating and assessing the range and nature of the valuable commodities upon which any increase in our earnings is to be spent.

The mistake of thinking otherwise is twofold. To confine or even focus the role of university education and research in the way that the concept of 'the knowledge economy' usually does, not only obscures their real role in enrichment, it quite falsely attributes to them special aptitude as places in which increased earning potential is fostered in both teaching and research. Some may be. It is unquestionably true that there are aspects of university research and education, especially in the newer universities, that are directly connected with increased economic prosperity. No one interested in defending the traditional university need deny this, and can indeed welcome it. What is at issue is whether this is to be the chief claim that universities have upon public approval and support. If it were, a great deal of what goes on in some of its best and most prestigious departments would have nothing to commend it. To take just one example. The ancient Scottish universities played an essential role in the promotion of philosophical inquiry. As a result, and somewhat surprisingly for such a small nation, Scottish philosophy can more than hold its own in the full sweep of intellectual history — Hume, Reid and Smith have relatively few rivals in the intellectual firmament. But they make a poor showing in the narrowly economic stakes if we take Carnegie, Rockefeller, Ford, or Gates as our standard. Adam Smith's contribution to the development of economics was enormous, but it was of quite a different kind to that of his near contemporaries who founded the Bank of Scotland, the first ever joint stock bank.

In the second place, despite common assumptions about transferable skills, there is not much evidence that students who master the challenging subjects of genetics, metaphysics, Hebrew, plate techtonics or pure mathematics, are better at enterprise and innovation than those who never study these things. In a utilitarian climate it is in the interests of university managers to claim that university education equips the nation with its entrepreneurial talent but empirically speaking this is a most implausible claim. The error in thinking that the value of higher education in itself (there are obvious exceptions) lies in its contribution to earning potential is disguised by the fact that talented people are indeed likely to succeed in *both* universities *and* in business. Real talent is relatively rarely confined to just one type of activity. But to pretend that its success in business is *a result of* its success in universities is, in my view, to connive in a deception.

A similar point may be made about commercialization. In very many universities 'research and commercialization' are bracketed together for both administrative and promotional purposes, but the truth is that hardly any university research has potential commercialization, and even where there is this potential, universities have proved poor at capitalizing upon it. The record of 'spin out' companies is not very impressive.

If this is so, if university study is in large part economically *useless*, what then is to be said for universities? In answering this question it ought to be emphasized once more that increased earning potential is not the same as enrichment. To be wealthier is not in and of itself to be richer; I am no better off, however great my income, if I have nothing better to buy. This is the point at which to return to the original foundation of the most venerable institutions and to the topic of spiritual values. Let us assume (contrary to some points in the foregoing analysis), that 'the knowledge economy' is an essential precondition of prosperity in the twenty-first century. There is still this question: What is the increased income the knowledge economy generates to be spent on? It could of course be spent on personal gratification — more holidays, more visits to pubs and restaurants, more fashionable clothes, computer games, gossip magazines, DVDs, television quiz programmes and so on. But is there nothing more significant that we might purchase with it? The answer is that there *is* something else, provided there are healthy traditions, practices and institutions in place to supply it.

Collectively, these form a society's cultural infrastructure. This infrastructure sustains the individual's sense of identity and civic responsibility, and the communal projects of science, law, the arts, religion and politics. Since the cultural infrastructure needs financial support whether public, private or corporative, economic prosperity is to be valued. But 'resourcing' is not the key to its vibrancy, which lies rather in its ability constantly to renew the inspiration that comes from the enlargement of human horizons. In short, an increasingly wealthy society benefits most from its increasing wealth if it has a cultural infrastructure that holds out ambitions greater than those of immediate gratification and passing entertainment. Without this, there is a serious risk that the opportunity for enrichment a great increase in wealth presents, be lost. Such a cultural infrastructure can be 'invested' in, but in a rather special sense. The sense in which, for instance, Paul Getty 'invested' in art through his massive benefaction to the Getty Museum is quite different to the sense in which he invested in the oil industry by means of which he made his great wealth.

Older universities are unquestionably part of this cultural infrastructure, and newer ones may come to be so. It is a role that ought expressly to be acknowledged, and contrasted with that of training colleges and business schools in which investment in the more straightforward sense is appropriate. To represent financial support for the cultural infrastructure as though it were economic investment is both a distortion and a mistake. At the same time, the cultural role of universities ought not to be stressed to the denigration of training colleges or business schools. Nor should it be suggested that universities are unique in this respect. The cultural infrastructure stretches far beyond the universities. But one of their most important roles is not that of increasing income generation so much as supplying and sustaining the ultimate goods on which increased income is to be spent.

Does this invoke the idea of *spiritual* values, the subject we began with? The rejection of the supernatural is almost a defining characteristic of contemporary Western Europe. This does not necessarily imply a rejection of 'the spiritual' since this expression does not have to be interpreted as pointing to some transcendent realm. The familiar phrase 'triumph of the human spirit' draws our attention to phenomena that may be both spiritual and natural. As the modern world speaks of it, the human spirit is to be encountered in many of the things previously alluded to — scientific theorizing, musical composition, artistic vision, political leadership, the pursuit of justice — and if we confine ourselves to it and invoke no other spirits, divine or angelic, it seems we have a spiritual counter to the materialistic inclinations of our time without any super-naturalistic overtones. If this is true, then we need only return to the founding principles of our ancient universities in part; something like the non-utilitarian explanation of the value of universities and other cultural institutions can be defended with a conception of spiritual value that requires no appeal to Christian or other religious values.

Meaning and materialism

The greatest challenge to contemporary Christianity (as indeed to other religions) is not the onslaught of materialism so much as an alternative account of spiritual values. In the United States it seems that a very powerful materialism can co-exist with high levels of religiosity. But in Europe, Canada and Australia (and some parts of the US) there is something else in prospect — a new humanism that will triumph over an outmoded religion by providing a more adequate outlet for the spiritual yearnings that make human beings dissatisfied with materialism. What, if anything, does the Christian have to say in reply to this humanist alternative? And how does it relate to universities?

The answer, if there is one, begins with this thought: humanism depends upon the Protagorean doctrine that 'man is the measure of all things'. The normal expansion of this familiar saying (not an historically accurate one, it may be) runs: 'of that which is, that it is, and of that which is not, that it is not'. Protagoras was an ancient Greek philosopher, but the doctrine with which his name is associated is fashionable again in the realms of postmodernism. But can we really believe this? Could it be true that it is human beings that are the measure of what exists and what does not? Interestingly it is religion's most widely perceived opponent — natural science — that generates deep doubts about Protagoras's claim, and natural science is the sphere in which postmodernism has made least impact. This is because Protagorean relativism flies in the face of the spectacular, and progressive, advances that have been made in physics, chemistry and biology. However plausible the allegations of the Protagoreans and postmodernists may be with respect to the humanities and social sciences, they lose all their plausibility when it comes to natural science.

Not many people are inclined to deny this, but it has an implication that is especially relevant here. Suppose it is true that the worlds studied by physics and biology exist independently of the human mind. There is still this question: what is the point and the value of studying them? If the answer to *this* question is a matter entirely relative to human purposes and values, what is it? If the *value* of science (in contrast to technology) is not to be explained in terms of usefulness, and if the world of values is none the less bounded by the interests of human beings, then the only explanation we can give of the value of pure science lies in human curiosity and the desire to know.

Now about this we might make the following observation. Human curiosity is a very varied thing. Human beings can be curious about the most trivial affairs. If human interest is the ultimate explanation of the value of science, it is a very poor one. Gossip magazines satisfy human curiosity at least as well, if not better, than anything universities have to offer. In short, the satisfaction of human curiosity is a value indifferent to the huge gap between gossip and science, and trivializes the magisterial understanding that the latter has to offer.

Much more would need to be said in explication of this point for it to become wholly persuasive. Yet it does direct attention to an important thought. If the value of natural science, and all the other non-utilitarian branches of learning, cannot be explained adequately by the appeal to human curiosity, the explanation must lie elsewhere, in something rather larger and of greater import than the human spirit humanly conceived. This is precisely what the religious founders of our ancient universities thought — that in the life of the mind and the explorations of the intellect, we reach beyond the human and begin to see and to appreciate, albeit dimly, the mind that *made* the world we occupy, a world which we certainly cannot fashion but which, mysteriously, we can hope to understand. Thus stated, this thought is not much more than suggestive, but in the conspicuous absence of any other explanation of the value of understanding, ancient universities should be hesitant to declare their religious foundation irrelevant. And they should be even more hesitant to pin their faith on the contribution they make to 'the knowledge economy' for fear of eliminating their distinctive purposes, and emptying their most fundamental activities of meaning.

Reforming Universities: How to Lose the Plot[1]

There is an old saying: 'If it isn't broken, don't fix it'. This seems so obviously true that it is often cited as a fundamental principle of common sense. On occasions it is elevated to the status of a political principle, and used in defense of a conservative attitude to social institutions and their reform. Yet even when it is recited with approval, it seems to carry little weight in practice. Why is this? The answer is that although the expression appears to have the strength and authority of the obviously true, it has two important weaknesses. First, there is the difficulty of knowing when it is applicable. Secondly, it says nothing about improvement.

Even if we stick to the relatively simple sphere of instruments and machines, these weaknesses are easily made apparent. A tap that gives no water, or flows all the time is plainly broken. But what about a tap that leaks just a little and only from time to time? Is a computer broken whose central functions work perfectly but a few of whose peripheral functions do not? When we turn from these simple examples to the complex cases of social and political institutions, the scope for uncertainty and hence dispute about what counts as 'working' broadens immeasurably.

---

[1]   Originally delivered as a lecture to Trinity College Dublin, April 2004, and in a revised form to the University of Coimbra in Portugal, May 2004.

The second problem with the 'don't fix what isn't broken' principle is more important. Why should we rest content with the machine we happen to have? Why not seek improved models? The latest computers do far more and do it better than the earliest ones, even when those early ones worked exactly as they were supposed (and designed) to do. The same can be said of social and political institutions. Almost any contemporary hospital is better than the hospitals that existed before, say, the reforms inspired by Florence Nightingale. We cannot assume, it is true, that later always means better; social institutions, like some bits of technology, can get worse as they get older. But in general, the 'don't fix what isn't broken' principle, when it is used against proposals for improvement, does turn into an expression of what we might call brute conservatism — we like what we have and we don't want to change what we like.

There are aspects of brute conservatism which can make it a valuable attitude. It creates stability, and it puts an onus on the merely dissatisfied to ground their dissatisfaction in reason and evidence. On the other hand, it often stands in the way of sensible and beneficial reform. Moreover, an attitude of brute conservatism may serve to disguise special pleading on the part of vested interests. It is easier to like and want to preserve a setup that suits you well, than to support reforms from which other people and other interests are more likely to benefit. Conservatism of this sort is to be opposed, not just by rational progressivism, but by equity and fairness as well.

These general reflections can be applied to universities as much as to any other human institution. Over the period of the last twenty years British universities have undergone almost continuous changes of one sort or another. The 'don't fix what isn't broken' principle has been invoked by those resisting many of these changes, but to little effect. This is partly because what has been at issue is

not so much 'fixing' as 'reform'. But perhaps more importantly, the principle has been interpreted by the protagonists of reform as little better than the expression of a
vested interest. A prominent and influential view holds
that for a long time university lecturers had a comfortable
and untroubled existence at the expense of taxpayers,
many of whom never benefited directly from what goes on
in universities. From this point of view it is both reasonable and right that they be required to give an account of
their activities in a way that will justify this expense to the
public. Confronted with this requirement, however, a certain type of conservatism kicks in, and under the banner of
academic freedom, or traditional intellectual values, or
university autonomy, reforms that would be genuinely
beneficial beyond the confines of the senior common room
are resisted. If and when this is the case, those who have
ultimate charge of the public purse and responsibility for
the general interests of society, can rightly appeal to a
combination of political responsibility and rational public
policy making in their efforts to press reforms upon recal-
citrant institutions and the people who run them.

At the same time, it needs to be observed — emphasized
indeed — that precisely the same considerations — political responsibility and rational public policy making —
require such reforms to be carried out effectively. The person who takes apart a television set to improve what is
unquestionably a poor picture, may, if they do the job
incorrectly, end up with an even worse picture, or possibly, no picture at all. Correctly identifying a need for
change and obstacles that stand in the way of it is not a
sufficient condition for the rational justification of any particular policy of improvement. It also has to be shown that
the policy proposed will actually be effective with respect
to the change that is needed.

A similar phenomenon is both possible and recordable
in the case of universities. It is certainly true that a

self-interested fondness for 'the good old days' (which never existed) has sometimes stood in the way of genuine improvement in standards of university teaching and research. But it is also true that on occasions misguided attempts at reform (inspired sometimes by a 'brave new world' which does not exist either) have left things worse than they were. How is this to be avoided? How are we to act responsibly with respect to the social institutions of which we have charge by developing rational policies for their reform, while at the same time avoiding both brute conservatism and the mistakes that arise from an ill considered reformist zeal? The answer lies in identifying the sorts of errors that existing programmes of reform have revealed to be real dangers.

There are four important mistakes that the experience of reforming British universities over the last two decades has uncovered. The purpose of this essay is to explore them in some detail. Since the immediate topic is university reform, illustrations will be drawn from this particular context, but the issues under discussion are relevant to the managerial reform of social institutions in general.

Mistaking change for improvement

The first general error to be pinpointed is that of mistaking change for improvement. This is a mistake that is so evident when it is pointed out, it may seem surprising that it is ever made. However, while the mistake is evident in the abstract, it is easy for it to become much less evident in practice. In fact, it is an error so easy to fall into, that it is avoidable only if we are constantly on our guard against it.

The problem arises partly because of a common, but misleadingly inexact pattern of reasoning that often prompts the instigation of reform. The opening premises are these.

- Things are not working well (or at least not as well as they might be)

- They will not improve until there is a change in the way that things are done.

To the extent that such claims are true in any particular circumstance, we can only say 'so far so good'. However, their being true is a *necessary*, but not a *sufficient* condition of licensing change. It does not in itself imply that *any* changes we might think of will secure the desired improvement. Only *some* will. The trouble is, that it is never, or hardly ever, obvious just what changes it is that would do the trick. This leads to a further inference.

- The process of reform has to begin with an attempt to discover which of a variety of possible changes would be truly effective.

Usually, this is taken to imply that reform has to start by putting people in a position to effect change, without quite knowing what the changes to be effected are. In turn this implies that the first step in the direction we want to travel must be a change in management structures. So, from the initial perception that all is not well, the following conclusion is drawn.

- We will only be in a position to run the system better if first we change the way in which it is managed.

'Managing change' or 'managing the challenge of change' has been a frequent topic for high level corporate seminars and conferences in the last decade or more. But 'change' is an abstract notion. In one sense, there is no such thing; the real subject matter about which there is need to confer must be specific changes in some particular aspect of organization. Managing change as such is like using space as such; the number of things that can be said at a general level is very limited, and most of them are scarcely worth saying. Space is different from time, and should be used efficiently rather than inefficiently are examples. Both propositions are true, but neither tell us how to arrange any particular office or factory to maximum effect. So too with 'change'. *General* truths about change itself are so limited that they are hardly worth knowing — change means new and different ways of doing things; it means re-training in these different methods and procedures; it means a period of uncertainty and a measure of experimentation; etc, etc.

These remarks border on a large and important topic in contemporary culture. Is management a transferable skill, as is so often assumed? Is it possible to manage health or education (say) effectively, when knowing little about either, but a lot about 'management' in the abstract? The now common practice of recruiting and employing managers across quite different kinds of business, assumes a positive answer to this question, and yet there are many doubts to be raised on this score. It is an issue that applies equally well to contemporary universities. It is usual now for professional 'headhunters' to be used in the appointment of Vice-chancellors and Principals, and not unusual for them to identify people who have never held an academic post as suitable candidates.

However, important though it is to examine the assumptions behind this practice critically, for present purposes the central question is a related but different one. If we begin the process of reforming an institution with a change in management structures, it is easy to think of this initial change as part of the improvement we seek. But it isn't. The crucial issue is whether the changes in management structure that are instituted are beneficial or not. This is not a matter of the nature of the changes themselves, but their later effects in other parts of the institution. Yet it is easy to confuse the two and to think that changes whose purpose is improvement are themselves improvements.

This conflation arises because the effort and upheaval, and the resources (of energy as well as finance) that need to be put into changing management structures can deflect us from the end in view. It is not hard to find examples of large institutions where almost all senior and experienced personnel have spent upwards to a year wholly occupied with meetings, briefings and consultations whose purpose is impending organizational change. To accompany these activities, and as a consequence, a large proportion of the administrative support system has been devoted to bringing about changes in management structure. One frequent consequence is that throughout this period the purposes from which, ultimately, these management changes take their rationale, have been largely 'on hold'. This is a consequence of crucial importance to the purposes of the institution, because 'on hold' is actually a euphemism for 'neglected'.

When this happens, the result is that at the end of the period of management change, these proper purposes struggle to recover their previous centrality. What ought to be the principal focus of activity, is no longer the principal focus. Part of the explanation lies in the fact that a kind of collective exhaustion has set in, and part of it in the fact that people have lost sight of what all the change was initially about. A further important factor is to be found in the vested interests of the people charged with 'managing change'. It simply is a mistake to suppose that the interests of managers automatically coincide with the interests of the 'core business' of the organization. They may do, but not necessarily so. When the two pull apart in a commercial enterprise subject to the market place (as sometimes happens) the enterprise in question goes out of business. When the same thing happens in a publicly funded institution such as a school, university, hospital, or national broadcasting network such as the BBC, the institution often simply carries on, protected as it is from the real force of supply and demand. But it does so in worse shape than it was when the whole process began. Managerial change initiated for the sake of improvement has declined into managerial change pure and simple, to the detriment of the things that were to be improved.

How is such an outcome to be avoided? One answer that is frequently given to this question appeals to the concept of 'performance targets'. We can avoid costly and ineffective change, and secure real improvement, (this line of argument goes) if we make regular checks on what the purpose of changing management structures is. This requires us to identify clearly the real goals of the institution or organization in question. If we do this, we are far less likely to be deflected from our ultimate target, because it is precisely that target which we have constantly in view. Stated in this general form, the proposition can hardly be disputed. But the particular can so easily depart from the general. This brings me to the second error I want to discuss.

Employing inappropriate analogies

Changes in the use of language are often instructive. At one time, people would normally have distinguished between industry, agriculture and commerce, and used these words exclusively, but in recent decades the first of them — industry — has moved to a position of dominance. Agriculture is now regularly referred to as an industry, and expressions such as 'the finance industry' or 'the tourist industry' are common. Even the expression 'the university industry' is not unknown. Do such linguistic changes signify, or do they matter only to the grammarian and the pedant? The answer is that they signify to the extent that they reflect new and different ways of thinking. Consider the expression 'the arts industry'. This is now a familiar but relatively recent usage. Why is it odd to imagine

Michelangelo, Mozart, Shakespeare, or Tolstoy describing themselves as working in 'the arts industry'? The oddness lies in the inappropriate inferences that such language inclines us to make. The revenue generated by producing and selling copies of Shakespeare's plays over four centuries is probably enormous, and may well exceed the value generated by some sorts of industrial production that have had a limited life span; the gas mantle might be an example. But to think that the value of Shakespeare, or the contribution his plays have made to the sum of human welfare should, or even could, be measured in these terms is absurd.

This does not mean that *no* assessment of their value can be made. It means that the assessment is not to be made in the same way that the value of industrial production is. Perhaps in this instance, no one feels inclined to do so, but if they do, it is likely to be because of their desire for a *quantifiable* measure of value. The aesthetic value of Shakespeare's plays or Mozart's music cannot be quantified, but in principle at any rate, their commercial value can be. To some minds, this makes their commercial value a more significant dimension on which to assess them, just as to some minds the real worth of a painting by a great master lies in its value as an investment. To others, the quantifiable assessment is not more significant, but simply more useful for comparative purposes. Both of these attitudes embody important mistakes. In the case of estimating the importance of Shakespeare or Michelangelo the mistake is evident. In other contexts, however, the same kind of mistake is just as important, but much less evident. Universities is one such context.

It is difficult to determine when exactly people, including university academics, began to talk in terms of delivering (and even packaging) educational courses, to describe books and articles as 'research outputs', and to speak of students as 'units of resource'. It is a change of some consequence, however, and has been prompted by three factors. There is first the need for the sort of performance targets already described, second a preference for quantification, and thirdly the deployment of a model of cost/benefit analysis drawn from manufacture. The motivation of each of the three is easily identified. First, performance targets seem to offer a counter to the possibility of change without improvement that was discussed in the previous section. Second, government departments and policy makers have a natural preference for quantifiable performance targets since they must ultimately be set against things that are inescapably quantifiable, namely tax revenues, government borrowing and public expenditure. Third, the manufacturing model of cost/benefit analysis offers an attractively simple conception of efficiency expressed in terms of reduced input resulting in greater output.

But though the motivation for thinking in this way is understandable, if our concern truly is with genuine reform and improvement, it is a profound mistake to apply inappropriate analogies. Doing so is comparable to estimating the respective merits of different television sets in terms of the number of place settings that can be laid out on top of them. Of course, a television can indeed be used as a table; but this is not what it is for.

Now something of the same mistake, but with more far-reaching consequences can be made with respect to universities, and it is a mistake seriously exacerbated by the deployment of whole sets of inappropriate analogies. The overarching analogy between universities and industry, which sustains the language of delivery and output, generates several sub-analogies that are no less influential — the student as customer is one, and with it the teacher as supplier. These sub-analogies can be highly misleading; there are essential aspects to the teacher/student relationship that are quite different to the supplier/customer relationship, for example, a topic discussed at some length in

Essay I. But the aim in this essay is to point to the possibility that by the use of inappropriate analogies, genuine attempts to assess performance and efficiency can be led to set their sights on the wrong aims. In the case of the universities of Britain (and other parts of Europe) these alternative aims have gradually emerged as two — economic prosperity and social inclusion.

Universities are educational institutions. This sentence may be thought to be stating the obvious, but the remark is worth making because it enables us to raise a doubt about government policy with respect to them. Economic prosperity and social inclusion are important social goals. But why should we think — indeed should we think — that an institution of higher education is a specially good instrument to secure them? Consider a parallel. The purpose of the legal system is the administration of justice. As a by-product of this, the institutions that comprise the system — law courts, police, prisons and so on — generate employment, and broadly speaking there is indeed a relation between their employing a larger number of people on the one hand, and their being able to administer justice effectively on the other. But sometimes the two can pull drastically apart. Suppose we find that the legal system is employing more and more people. High employment is a good thing, so is this not a point in its favour? We can hardly think so if the explanation of its employing more people is a steadily rising level of criminality and an increasing inability on the part of the legal system to deal with it. In this circumstance, focussing upon numbers employed as a measure of its success, will point us in quite the wrong direction.

A similar point can be made with respect to universities. It is part of their proper role to admit students for the purposes of higher education. As a by-product of this, students from quite different social backgrounds may end up in better paid forms of employment than they would otherwise have done. We can easily imagine circumstances, however, in which (say) educational standards are seriously *lowered* in order to admit more students from a wider socio-economic background, just as we can imagine circumstances where it is factors other than educational attainment that lead to an improvement in their employment prospects. When these conditions prevail, universities are actually performing badly *as educational institutions*. Yet, a focus on them as instruments of social and economic engineering will falsely imply that they are doing well.

A more important possibility is the reverse of this, the circumstance in which a university gives a first class intellectual and educational experience to its students, but makes little difference to their earning potential. They could, let us say, have reached similar salary levels by age 30, if they had gone straight from school to the job market. In this case, the university is succeeding, but it is not doing so according to the measure of earnings potential. Something of this sort happened dramatically in the Californian university system during the explosion of computer technology that created Silicon Valley. While the college courses on offer in mathematics and computing were designed to give students a good education in the subject, what they actually needed to know in order to secure highly paid jobs in the sector fell far short of this. The result was that students at (for example) San José State University were dropping out of degree courses at an early stage because those courses were doing little or nothing to advance their earning prospects. The professors teaching these courses came under pressure to change the curriculum, but their only option was to take a stand on the fact that they were first and foremost educators, and not employment agencies.

Of course, a university's paymasters may decide to apply the measure of economic relevance to its performance, and require that changes be put in place to improve it with that end in view. But their doing so makes as much sense as insisting that a bakery which successfully makes cakes should start making violins instead, on the grounds that only in this way will it make a significant contribution to the musical life of the community. The general point is that institutions and organizations should be judged by the criteria appropriate to them and not by standards generated elsewhere, even where there is a contingent connection between the two. Music can calm the troubled breast, but a good musician should be judged as such, and not urged to take up psycho-therapy if this should prove to calm the troubled breast more effectively. Similarly as a teacher of philosophy my expertise lies in teaching the subject well. Since philosophy involves a greater element of discussion than many other subjects, it may be the case a philosophical education assists sociability. It may also teach a level of clear thinking that is useful in business. But *qua* philosopher my expertise lies in neither social integration nor business management. It is rational and only reasonable for my performance to be judged in accordance with my professed and acknowledged expertise, not in accordance with the extraneous and unconnected goals, however worthy and desirable these may be.

However, clarity on this point does not dispense with the crucial matter of assessment. Even when it is accepted that universities should be judged in accordance with criteria relevant to the kind of institution they are, and not the kind of institution their political paymasters would like them to be, it still seems right to set in place performance targets and ways in which the achievement or non-achievement of these targets can be measured. Philosophers are not to be judged as though they were employment agencies or social workers, but this does not mean that they are not to be judged at all. This brings us to another potential error that has bedevilled programmes of reform.

Replacing trust with accountability

There is something manifestly inappropriate about any attempt to evaluate Shakespeare or Mozart in terms of their contribution to the economy. The absurdity of the attempt is not because they cannot be said to have made major contributions to economic activity over several centuries, contributions, moreover, that in principle can be assessed in monetary values. Shakespeare's plays have generated a great deal of business for the printing and paper making industries. Mozart's music has generated a lot of employment in orchestras, concert halls and recording studios. But in both examples (as in countless others) these are spin-offs. It is *aesthetic* accomplishment that is central to estimating the worth and value of a Shakespeare or a Mozart, and this cannot be assessed in monetary terms, *even in principle*. How then *is* it to be assessed?

The answer is — by the exercise of judgement. Many people believe, of course, that music and poetry are ultimately matters of subjective taste and preference and not objective judgement. This is not the place in which to debate the matter[2]. The point that needs to be made here is that there are contexts in which assessment is a matter for judgement, and that judgement cannot be replaced by quantitative measures. Since there is not space to argue the case, I shall simply assert here that education and the life of the mind is one such context. Whether a lecture has had substance and been well delivered, whether an academic paper or book is a genuine contribution to its discipline, are matters for judgment not measurement. In the absence of measurement, we have to trust to those qualified and competent to judge.

In her Reith Lectures 2002 (subsequently published under the title *A Question of Trust*) Onora O'Neill drew

---

[2]   I discuss the issue at length in *Philosophy of the Arts* 3rd edition (Routledge, 2005) Chp 11.

attention to a striking feature of contemporary public life that is of particular relevance here. The theme of her lectures was the widespread inclination to replace trust with systems of accountability. This tendency has probably arisen in part because trust has been abused. In times past, professors, doctors, teachers, priests, lawyers and so on, were widely trusted to uphold and advance the values of their respective professions, and to observe high standards of professional conduct. For whatever reason, this trust was abused sufficiently often to undermine the public's confidence, and to do so to a degree sufficient to call forth political scrutiny. The scandals implicating Catholic priests in child sex abuse, and the spectacular degree to which the notorious Dr Harold Shipman exploited the trust placed in him by elderly patients are especially notable examples.

Once such scrutiny becomes a regular feature of public life, the faith of public and politicians shifts and is placed in systems of accountability. These seem less reliant on trust and so less vulnerable to its abuse. Yet, however understandable recent history may have made this shift, for a number of reasons the attempt to replace trust with accountability is ultimately futile. This is because judgment is ineliminable so that even the most transparent and rigorous systems of accountability must rely on trust at some point. The effect of replacing the language of trust with that of accountability is not that trust is rendered redundant, but that its role may be both less perspicuous and less reliable.

An illuminating illustration of this point is to be found in the Research Assessment Exercises to which British universities are subject. Since these exercises were discussed at length in Essay I, it will be sufficient to point to just one feature specially salient to the topic of this essay. These exercises attempt to assess the value of the research work going on in British universities in a way that allows for meaningful comparison across both disciplines and universities with the ultimate objective of determining whether the public money that is spent on such research is well spent and thus introducing accountability for such expenditure by ensuring that a poor result in the exercise leads to a reduction in financial support. The assessments are to a degree quantitative. They aim to capture aspects of an institution's research activity to which numbers can be assigned; the number of staff returned as 'research active', the number of publications, the number of years under review. More importantly, the expression of the results of the final assessment is numerical — hitherto 1 to 5*, in future 0 to 4*. At the same time, in arriving at this final assessment the use of peer review of publications is a key feature. This seems unavoidable. Who else but a suitably qualified expert could be in a position to assess the value of a research publication? Such peer review is not new. It has long gone on in referees' reports on manuscripts submitted to journals and publishers, and it can only take the form of professional *judgement*. It follows that the truly new element in the RAE is its quantitative aspect.

So what does this additional quantification accomplish? One thing it allows is the construction of a formula for the allocation of resources. While formulae have their uses, this merely punctuates, and does not replace, the business of entrusting resources to institutions and those who run them. When the numerical results of the exercise are known and published, public money still has to be allocated for periods into the future, and it can only be allocated on the basis of judgement with the hope that it is used wisely and well. The employment of numbers gives a misleadingly formulaic expression to what is actually a matter of judgment. To this degree it disguises the fact that the system still has to operate on the basis of trust.

A proponent of such assessment exercises might reply in this vein. Yes, trust and judgement must remain at the heart of the system, but why not add this element of quantitative assessment and public transparency? Surely a measure of accountability is no bad thing. This brings us back to the question of reform. If there is any truth and substance to the 'don't fix what isn't broken' principle, it lies in the observation that being 'no bad thing' is not enough. Reforms must be positively good or they simply do not count as improvements. Systems of assessment such as the RAE do not come for free. They cost money, and they also cost immense amounts of time and effort. The question is whether the added benefit is worth the extra effort. This is a difficult matter to assess, but, it is certainly arguable that the cost of these vast paper generating exercises has significantly outweighed their benefits.

Establishing the truth in this case, as in many other systems of accountability, requires empirical investigation. Strangely, this is hardly ever undertaken with real thoroughness. This is partly because of a further danger attendant upon reforming institutions, and that is the tendency on the part of reformers to confuse criticism with resistance.

Criticism and resistance

One reason why there has been little empirical investigation into the efficacy of systems of accountability like the RAE is that there are commitments on both sides that might conflict with its discoveries. It is an attractive thought that universities are places committed to the rule of reason, and that as a result their special character is both to encourage and to rely on informed rationality in decision making, rather than, say, merely to follow educational fashion or seek compromises between competing interests. Unhappily this is not so. Curiously indeed, universities are often very defensive in this regard. While many of them actively promote and support research into the efficacy of a wide range of public policies and economic initiatives, serious investigation of the real effectiveness of reforms and initiatives that come from within is almost nonexistent. In short, when it comes to debates and disagreements about their own affairs, universities are as prone to self-protecting flights of unreason as are any other institutions.

One explanation for this, an explanation that holds more generally, is vested interest. This works on both sides. People tend to like what they know and cling to what they like. As noted previously, this natural conservatism makes for stability. Yet stability is only one organizational value. On occasions it has to be traded off against improvement. Faced with such trades-offs, some people persist in their conservatism, but they usually feel constrained to construct arguments in its defence. More often than not, such arguments are quite specious, and serve only to disguise the real motives at work. It is in this way that unreasoning resistance can masquerade as rational criticism.

Alongside this important truth, however, it is no less important to observe that reformers too can have vested interests and deploy specious arguments to defend them. People invest time and money in institutional reorganization. Understandably they are then reluctant to admit that their investment has been largely wasted. They also stake their reputations on its success, and the preservation of such reputations can be of vital importance to both the maintenance of self-esteem and personal career advancement. Because of this, it is unsurprising if the motives of reformers as well as conservatives are questioned. On the one side, what purports to be a rational defence of constructive reform is decried as dogmatic zeal for passing fashion. On the other side, criticism of reform is construed as gut resistance to change. Of course, dogmatic zeal and unthinking resistance are recurrent features of human experience. Yet both interpretations *can* be mistaken. There is such a thing as rationally motivated desire for change, and there is such a thing as rationally based criticism of change.

It is overlooking the second possibility that has proved most damaging in the reform of British universities. For a variety of reasons, genuine, and valuable criticism of what should be innovative reform has been discounted by being mistaken for simple resistance. One of the most elementary educational and research strategies is trial and error. It is, however, a strategy that can only be employed to good effect if we are open to the possibility of error, and more importantly perhaps, to the necessity of being alerted to error by those who are, so to say, on the front line. Generally speaking, whether in health, education or the law, reforms generated at management level change the activities of those institutions, whether to good or to bad effect, primarily at levels other than those of overall management. It follows that senior managers who have a serious commitment to adopting beneficial changes and avoiding detrimental ones will *want* to know of failure as well as success. They will thus welcome an information feed back system that lends special significance to front line workers. But once a mentality is adopted (or encouraged) in which criticism is interpreted as resistance, the possibility of learning from error in this way recedes rapidly.

It is a mentality that is often reinforced by the culture of 'line management' but more subtly by the invocation of 'best practice'. This is a phrase that now has a wide currency. But though fashionable, it can be used as cover for some important errors, chief amongst which is that 'best practice' aids top down dogmatism. We are once more bordering on an important and interesting question in the theory of management that cannot be explored in detail here. The principal argument in the present context can be set out in the following propositions.

- Institutions need genuine feed back systems if reform is to be effective.

- Efficacy to the right end is the indispensable mark of rational activity.

- It is the special role of universities to advocate the rule of reason in practice as well as theory.

- Genuine feedback is possible only if criticism is taken seriously.

Therefore

- Universities should shun those dismissive attitudes of mind which tend to re-interpret criticism in ways that make discounting it easy.

This last point connects with the topic of the previous section, and with the general theme of this book. Within universities there has been a loss of trust that has been damaging, and it has been two-way. Academics who have taken up the reins of management have generally seen themselves as 'realists', people prepared to adapt pragmatically to the reality of prevailing political and financial circumstances. Such people are, in their own eyes and very often in those of their political paymasters, to be contrasted with 'idealists' who cling nostalgically to an unsustainable past that was not so very good in any case. When this is the self-image of management, criticism is easily discounted as simple resistance. On the other side, critics of the new style of management easily represent it as having sold the pass, and view themselves as being a sort of 'saving remnant', which, if it holds out long enough, will survive and triumph in the end. As with other saving remnants, innovation is systematically reinterpreted as betrayal. The result is that neither side has much trust in or respect for the other.

Yet, of course, rationality requires us to be on our guard against deluding and distorting self-images whichever side of a debate we happen to be on. Nothing is accomplished by depriving ourselves of critical voices or the fruits of real experience. This point crucially applies beyond universities as well as within them. Politicians have a duty to ensure that public resources are properly spent on both projects and institutions that can be shown to have an important part to play in the public good. However, precisely because of this, they and the civil servants who assist them have reason to open their minds, and to avoid the dogmatic *a priorism* that magically bestows knowledge in advance of experience and dismisses criticism as a form of special pleading.

In the case of universities three implications of this analysis are worth underlining. First, in order to improve our universities we must first have a clear idea of what they are for, and what they can and cannot do. There is no doubt that often they could do what they should do better, but charging them with the wrong tasks runs a risk of destroying the good thing that we have. It is similar to, but less easy to see than, the mistaken project of reforming supermarkets as though they were hospitals, on the grounds that hospitals are a good thing, and since supermarkets already carry a limited number of medications, they ought to be offering much more in the way of health care. Second, it should always be remembered how easy it is, and how disastrous, to lose sight of the fact that changing management structures is never a valuable end in itself. Its value lies entirely in the extent to which something other than management is improved thereby. Thirdly, this is a judgement that can be made rationally only if it is constantly open to criticism from, so to speak, the end user. In some ways, this last point is the most important. In the chaos of change that has beset British universities over the last two decades, few things have done more damage than the blinkered attitude to debate that says 'they would say that wouldn't they'. Whichever side says this, it expresses an abandonment of trust in the judgement and good faith of others that is in fact indispensable in the effective functioning of any aspect of communal life.

References

Aristotle, *Nicomachean Ethics* ed Broadie and Rowe, Oxford University Press, 2002

Barnett, Ronald, *The Idea of Higher Education*, Milton Keynes, Open University Press, 1990

Butler, Joseph, *Five Sermons* edited Stephen L Darwell Hackett Publishing, Indianapolis, 1983

Ferrier, J F, *Philosophical Works* Volume 3 (1883) Reprinted Thoemmes Press, Bristol, 2001

Graham, Gordon, *Philosophy of the Arts* 3rd edition, Routledge, London, 2005

Graham, Gordon, *The Internet: a philosophical inquiry*, Routledge, London, 1999

Hobbes, Thomas, *Leviathan* ed. Michael Oakeshott, Blackwell, Oxford, 1960

Hume, David, *A Treatise of Human Nature* ed. Selby-Bigge, Oxford University Press, 1967

Kolakowski, Leszek, *Modernity on Endless Trial*, Chicago University Press, 1990

Maskell, Duke and Ian Robinson, *The New Idea of a University*, Exeter, Imprint Academic, 2002

Newman, J H, *The Idea of a University* ed. M J Svaglic, Notre Dame, University of Notre Dame Press. (1982)

Oakeshott, Michael, *The Voice of Liberal Learning*, New Haven, Yale University Press, 1989

O'Neill, Onora, *A Question of Trust*, Cambridge University Press, 2002

Pinker, Stephen, *How the Mind Works*, Penguin, Harmondsworth, 1999

Rawls, John, *A Theory of Justice*, Oxford, Clarendon Press, 1972

Rorty, Richard, *Philosophy and the Mirror of Nature*, Princeton University Press, 1980

Sutherland, S, *Universities: Crisis of Confidence or Identity*, University of Melbourne, 1996

Weber, Max, 'Science as a Vocation' in *From Max Weber: essays in sociology* ed. Gerth and Wright Mills, London, Routledge, 1948
Wilson, E O, *On Human Nature*, London, Penguin, 1995

Index